PRAISE
LOST IN SUMMERLAND

"Swanson . . . serves as a candid and empathetic narrator, guiding us with restrained cynicism and enticing prose as he interrogates the stories we tell ourselves to paper over truths we'd rather not face . . . Swanson finds more questions than answers in his quest, but he reaches a meaningful starting point for treating the ills of our age: elevating the virtue of love above the idea of conquest . . . His essays reveal a thinker willing to wrestle with the realization that there is more beyond his sight."

— ALBERT SAMAHA, *The New York Times Book Review*

"With potent lucidity and fierce intelligence, Barrett Swanson pierces the superficial arguments that make so much of our moment strange and alienating. The range of these essays is astonishing, but more electrifying still is the agility with which Swanson probes the deep mysteries of masculinity, ecological threat, capitalism, and race to reveal thrilling if terrifying connections. Barrett Swanson is a tremendous writer, and this collection provides one of the truest, most haunting portraits of our time I've ever read."

— BRANDON TAYLOR, author of *The Late Americans*

"As the narrative of American exceptionalism collapses swiftly and spectacularly all around us, I'm grateful for Barrett Swanson's brilliance and clarity, his affectionate skepticism of our most violent games and lies, his earnest and anxious interrogations of twenty-first-century masculinity. *Lost in Summerland* is an essay collection of the very highest order: a book that poses more questions than it seeks to answer, a book that has wrestled my empathy for the fucked-up citizens of our tragicomic era and country into new, uncomfortable, gorgeously fruitful places."

— LAUREN GROFF, author of *Florida*

"More than most writers, Barrett Swanson is a first-rate cultural anthropologist. Perceptive, amusing, searching, he scans and gazes past the variety of scrims the world has set out to cloud our vision. His brilliant essays bring so much back into focus, while also noting the American surrealism of the American dream. There is not a weak link in this collection. Every piece is a gem." —LORRIE MOORE

"The brilliance of these essays is their ability to illuminate the personal through the critical, the political, and the unflinching specifics of place while shining a light into that seemingly distant ideal—the universal." —CHRISTOPHER NOTARNICOLA, *The Paris Review*

"Swanson's essays are big, embracing, singing works of literary art. You get the sense that he writes each piece as though it might be his last and best. His writing, especially the diction, manages to be genuinely earnest, often somber, while also being unarguably funny—a precision so consistent that his pen can often feel like a scalpel . . . A distinctly spiritual, deeply humane collection of essays." —GEOFF MARTIN, *The New Quarterly*

"*Lost in Summerland* collects a singular sensibility: fourteen essays of searing intelligence throbbing with uncommon sensitivity and executed with incomparable style. Barrett Swanson is his generation's Joan Didion, running down the centrifugal flingings where the center once held, exorcising the pain and folly of living in a nation fervently in denial of and devoted to its own decline. An absolutely essential read." —CLAIRE VAYE WATKINS, author of *I Love You But I've Chosen Darkness*

"Barrett Swanson is our eloquent guide on this tour through the toxic masculinity industrial complex, disaster capitalism, and other exhibits of a lonely, lost America. In essays that are moving and candid, personal and sweeping,

Lost in Summerland seeks alternatives to national myths and tries to name the 'unnamable turbulence' we're living through, to rescue the ineffable from invisibility." —ELISA GABBERT, author of *The Unreality of Memory*

"Casting a net of electric prose, these essays—miraculously—catch midair the hot shrapnel of an exploding moment. In Swanson's humane and gifted hands, the glowing fragments light a path through our national dreamlife, illuminating America's new paradoxes and precarities."
—WELLS TOWER, author of *Everything Ravaged, Everything Burned*

"Barrett Swanson achieves a sublime density of intellect and soul in *Lost in Summerland*, a vivid, immersive, fiercely openhearted survey of the American landscape and spirit. In handsome lyrical prose, with the sensitivity of a cultural seismologist, Swanson finds humor and insight erupting everywhere. His unstinting honesty is that of the best memoirists, who remind us that it is reasonable and perverse and exalted just to be a person, awake, alive, listening for the quiet essence in things. Reality is so palpable in these essays that I found myself nostalgic for moments I had never lived."
—GREG JACKSON, author of *Prodigals*

LOST IN SUMMERLAND

SUMMER
LAND

LOST IN

Essays

BARRETT SWANSON

COUNTERPOINT
Berkeley, California

Lost in Summerland

Grateful acknowledgment is made to the following for permission to publish reprinted material under different titles or in somewhat altered form: *New England Review* and *Best American Travel Writing 2018*, edited by Cheryl Strayed ("Notes from a Last Man"); *Harper's Magazine* ("Consciousness Razing" and "Disaster City"); *Ninth Letter* ("Okay Forever"); *Orion* ("The Soldier and the Soil"); *The Believer* ("Midwestern Gothic"); *Pacific Standard* ("Prophet of the Swamp"); *Mississippi Review* ("Calling Audibles"); *The Point* ("Starving"); *Guernica* ("Letter from a Target-Rich Environment"); *The Paris Review* ("Political Fictions" and "Flood Myths"); *The Atavist* and *The Best American Travel Writing 2020*, edited by Robert Macfarlane ("Lost in Summerland"); and *Salmagundi* ("Church Not Made with Hands").

The Library of Congress has cataloged the hardcover edition as follows:
Names: Swanson, Barrett, author.
Title: Lost in summerland : essays Barrett Swanson.
Description: First hardcover edition. | Berkeley, California : Counterpoint Press, 2021.
Identifiers: LCCN 2020021819 | ISBN 9781640094185 (hardcover) | ISBN 9781640094192 (ebook)
Subjects: LCSH: United States—Social conditions—21st century. | Consumption (Economics)—United States—History—21st century. | Social ecology—United States. | Social psychology—United States.
Classification: LCC HN59.4 .S84 2021 | DDC 306.0973—dc23
LC record available at https://lccn.loc.gov/2020021819
Paperback ISBN: 978-1-64009-532-8

Cover design by Alison Forner
Cover photographs: sky © Tetra Images / Getty; crack © Shutterstock / Moolkum
Book design by Jordan Koluch

COUNTERPOINT
2560 Ninth Street, Suite 318
Berkeley, CA 94710
www.counterpointpress.com

Printed in the United States of America
10 9 8 7 6 5 4 3 2 1

For Luke

Contents

Notes from a Last Man   3

Consciousness Razing   25

Okay Forever   52

The Soldier and the Soil   78

Midwestern Gothic   105

Prophet of the Swamp   121

Calling Audibles   145

Flood Myths   170

Letter from a Target-Rich Environment   179

Starving   192

Political Fictions   201

Lost in Summerland   212

Disaster City   240

Church Not Made with Hands   267

Acknowledgments   287

LOST IN SUMMERLAND

NOTES FROM
A LAST MAN

It was a belated wedding present. Early last January my wife and I were offered the chance to spend three months in Fort Lauderdale, a touristic city on Florida's southeastern edge, one that in the 1950s served as the nativity scene for the American Spring Break. Around that time, her grandfather bought an apartment four blocks from the ocean, and her family has been vacationing there ever since. The building is a squat midcentury complex with a stucco-white exterior, and in the shared courtyard out back, there is a kidney-shaped pool cordoned off from onlookers with a hem of clacking palm trees. Most of the amenities inside the apartment haven't been updated since the Kennedy administration. There are turquoise couches and sun-faded curtains, terrazzo floors and senile kitchen appliances.

My wife's grandfather would let us stay there in balmy reprieve from the bleak winter months of Wisconsin, where we'd been living for the past five years. Since both of us were teaching online that semester and thus had no fixed geographical commitments, we decided the trip might have a salutary effect and embarked on the cross-country trek at dawn on New Year's Day.

I suppose the date carried some symbolic importance, a version of that old chestnut: *a new year, a new you.* Perhaps the tropical climate would render us porous to sunny influences and slacken our sense of self. Over the next forty-eight hours, we watched the tundra of the Midwest gradually defrost into the profligate greenery of Kentucky, noting the steady accretion of drawl among gas station attendants anytime we stopped to fuel up. Doing our best to scrimp, we spent our nights in budget motels with glowing marquees that whirred electrically near the roadside, advertising their amenities with an oddly poetic phrase:

KING BEDS OPEN

VACANT HBO

After two days, we finally crossed the Florida state line, entering a corridor of sugarcane and everglades where we were made to endure an endless parade of weather-battered billboards, signs that spoke of surf shops and alligator wrestling, but the promises seemed dubious with their bubbled fluorescent fonts. Somewhere south of Gainesville, we came across a billboard that offered a mortal riddle. TEXTING WHILE DRIVING KILLS, it said. FOR MORE DRIVING TIPS, TEXT "SAFETY" TO 79171.

We reached the ocean by nightfall. The sky was rinsed with sherbet colors, the edges of distant clouds rimmed with a vulgar pink. I suppose I thought I'd feel relieved, that confronting the edge of the country might offer a bolt of fresh enlightenment, some timely mitigation of mood. But I was worried because we had just crossed the entire continent and I didn't feel a thing. We parked along the boardwalk and piled out of the car, with chip wrappers and empty soda cans spilling from the open doors, to which we pretended to give chase. The shoreline was dimpled and forlorn, and as we watched the silver mulch of crashing waves, the moment soon acquired the breathy impressionism of a Terrence Malick film. For a few minutes, I gazed distractedly at the horizon and felt my wife turn to me, her expression bright with anticipation. "How do you feel?" she said. "Good," I said. She raised an eyebrow, unconvinced. "Really good."

—

We needed a break from the Midwest. That was our public reason. Whenever friends or family members asked about our abrupt change of plans, we responded with stock answers, a litany of complaints—Wisconsin was too cold; we felt too isolated in our insular college town; plus, we hadn't taken a vacation in years. You have to understand that this kind of preemptive apology is necessary in the Midwest, where the dominant aesthetic is utilitarian, where suffering often takes on a grim inevitability. There, even the slightest indulgence will be interrogated if it's left unexplained.

But we were, in fact, due for a holiday. For the last five years I had been teaching English at a small Midwestern college, grading stacks of student papers riddled with bad logic and woeful syntax. On campus, I taught five sections of freshman composition, and while I was only an adjunct instructor, I let my students call me "professor," even though it was precisely this misnomer that obscured the gross pay differentials that existed between my colleagues and me. Still, by dint of coupons and self-restraint, my wife and I managed to evade the coercions of debt collectors, and my measly income made us eligible for food stamps and Medicaid. Our apartment was a thrifty university recommendation, in a complex of brick buildings with a scrubby garden and a windswept piazza, where in late summer grad students would smoke clove cigarettes while frowning at Camus novels. Each year, by October, there was snow on the ground, and the confected hills of our courtyard made the walk to the mailbox seem like a chore of Benny Hill pratfalls, a lethal prank. But for a few years there, I managed to keep up appearances to the best of my abilities. I woke at dawn to tinker with a novel. I held office hours. I wore tortoiseshell glasses and kept my beard at an urban length. Cigarettes were permitted on special occasions, and I eschewed one classic novel after another, spending my nights, instead, in front of the latest HBO series, which was better at depicting structural injustice anyway. As the months flickered past, I snuggled with my wife on a comfy IKEA couch, in a rent-to-own building, in the middle of the country, in one of the safest cities in the world. And this was enough, if only for a little while, to make me feel as though I had somehow managed to escape that unnamable turbulence of mind that seemed always to be nipping at my heels.

Apart from my online teaching, I was supposed to be finishing a novel, but for various reasons, I no longer had a mind for narrative, neither fictional nor memoiristic, and could not seem to plot the events of my life on some sturdy dramatic trajectory. Every Freytag Triangle seemed to swell into a circle where the climax was the beginning and the beginning was the denouement. Perhaps it could be attributed to living in the Midwest, yet through the scrim of our bunkered isolation, it was hard not to think that greater forces were at play, that the stitching had unraveled, that what had appeared to be the grand sweep of history was actually a patchwork job in which answers were furnished in loose, ad hoc fashion. Meaning was historical, I had been told, but we were said to be living at the end of history. A few years earlier, when I'd been in grad school, amid the sweetly fragranced wood of the lecture hall, I could dispassionately accept the way in which the Omega circled back toward the Alpha, which is why those acts of critical deconstruction had felt so rejuvenating and alive, why it was with no small amount of relish that I proceeded to unpack and dismantle every last story of consequence, armored with the theories of trendy midcentury thinkers, toting dog-eared copies of "Signature Event Context" and the work of Paul de Man. Nothing was sacred. No one was spared. One weekend, my wife and I were invited to a service at a local Unitarian church, which we attended with the heartless curiosity of anthropologists, and on the ride home, we mauled its à la carte theology for sport, lampooning the hand-holding of the parishioners as they swayed to effulgent major-chord hymns. Within the gates of the university, among likeminded colleagues, this had felt purposeful and important, as if we could peel back the hard rind of the apple to reveal its hollow core.

I could spout French names at you, could speak knowledgeably about Lyotard, Derrida, or even Gilles Deleuze. But a survey of postmodern thinking wouldn't go very far in expressing the sadness I felt during those years, that eerie twilight hour of history. That I bumbled through each day, attendant to its requirements, ever mindful of its issues, but that I did so passively, without an inkling as to its real meaning, was an agitation from which I could no longer find a viable distraction. To admit these feelings at dinner parties or departmental mixers was to be met with baffled incomprehension. It seemed never to have occurred to my colleagues that the hermeneutics of suspicion which they so reliably brought to bear on literary texts could be just as easily applied to the events of their own lives. Somehow they seemed able to maintain an impervious distance between ideas and affect, between ideology and state of mind. Theirs was a happy nihilism, and whatever spiritual desolation they felt could be readily assuaged with a menu of epicurean comforts. Of course, I too tried to laugh off the world's disappointments. I too devoted myself to "the myriad small needs of the body." I too wrote for the little magazines and invented droll theories about what Trump's ascendancy might mean for America. But such conjectures necessitated a belief in the old stories, an abiding faith in the system itself, and the truth was that I no longer had the heart to keep up the pretense, to keep the game going. When it came to the Mayberry fantasies of the Right or the technocratic utopia of the Left, I could no longer suspend my disbelief.

When you are trained in this manner of thinking, long periods of isolation are to be avoided. And yet in the fall of 2015, as these preoccupations seemed to gain new urgency, I began turning down invitations and failing to return calls. Everything seemed beside the point, untethered from telos or impact. There were no more faces in the clouds, no more symbols to chart and decode, no more sermons to be found in the debacle, as Joan Didion once put it. Occasionally, my wife and I would take weekends away, and we would traipse along the shoreline of Lake Michigan, watching ducks paddle through kelpy surf, but the water did not promise the absolution of Noah's flood nor evoke Hegel's grand historical flux. Educated to possess a literary worldview, to believe reality was endowed with meaning, I finally reached a point in my life where the skin of allusion had been peeled away from everything, where the world was nothing more than a brittle material husk. It was during those long autumnal months that the water was only the water and the world was always the case. As the days wore on, I grew quiet and abstracted. I was losing weight. And in the glacial blue twilight of those late November evenings, it became difficult to ignore the concern in my wife's face.

So it was in this spirit of recuperation that we headed south that New Year's Day. Maybe the coastal air would alleviate the lethargies of winter and offer us a galvanic dose of vitamin D. Perhaps we'd channel our best selves by lying sun-struck on the beach, basking alongside the college students with their beery pledges and the millionaires with their cut-loose, notional workdays. In some sense, we were partaking in that age-old American custom first started by the colonial elite. In the early nineteenth century, they would escape the brutal winters of the north and sojourn to mineral springs and watering holes for several months at a time. Of course, these aristocrats were merely imitating the gentry of the Old World, who'd been marinating in spas since the Middle Ages, even sipping from the briny pool in which they soaked as if to confirm their faith in that old Latin maxim, *Sanitas per aquam*—or "health through water." Still, it seemed strange to head to the sea when I was feeling rudderless and unmoored, but we decided that a few months in the tropics might lend us some perspective.

—

Four blocks from our apartment, along the strip of oceanfront hotels, there is a hollow building stretching twenty-four stories into the sky. The construction signage identifies the development as the Conrad Hotel, but it is more widely known by the unofficial designation the locals have given it: Trump Tower. In a disastrous licensing scheme a few years ago, Trump lent his brand to the venture, which motivated buyers to shell out a half million dollars per condo. But when wind of bad prospects eventually ruffled the elaborate comb-over of the real estate mogul, he quickly dropped his name from the project, and almost immediately the hotel tanked. Now, the Tower looms on the horizon like a totem, begging to be read as a portent of something, an emblem of the culture itself. Not only is the edifice wholly untenanted, it's also unfinished, its interior carpeted with the sawdust of renovation. We've only been here two days, but already my wife and I have taken turns coming up with inane interpretations.

"It's a symbol of ineffectual patriarchy—empty but erect," I say. "A symbol of the Viagra generation."

"No, no," my wife says. "It's aesthetics over essence. Name recognition trumps—ahem—everything."

As we meander down the boardwalk, we do our best to make each other laugh, but in truth I can't help but feel a needling unease every time we come upon the specter of the empty building. It is a terrain without substance. It could mean anything.

"But you're right," she says, "it really does look like an erection."

My wife has been coming here with her family since she was a girl and reinhabits this space seamlessly. When we return to the apartment, she changes into a flowing daisy-print muumuu and a pair of jelly sandals that are the color of vodka-cream sauce. Fleetwood Mac booms through the stereo, and she twirls around the kitchen, drinking diet root beers and seeming visibly unclenched from the doldrums of regular life. There is a strange "House of the Rising Sun" quality to her dancing—languid gestures, lots of swaying.

"Shall I throw a chiffon over the lamp?" I say.

"This is my homage to Stevie Nicks," she says.

She continues to boogie, unfazed.

I myself am having a harder go of it.

———

Our apartment complex is a corridor of gossip. Voices ricochet up the concrete patio steps, and owing to the tropical climate, the walls of the building are uninsulated, providing a barrier that is merely ornamental. Our neighbors' daily habits resound with alarming clarity, making us inadvertent eavesdroppers of their private dramas. Through the bubble-thin walls we discern belches and bowel movements, tiffs and endearments, confronting, in other words, alternative ways of life.

Next door is an octogenarian married couple from Kentucky, and all morning long we can hear their preferred daytime talk shows blaring in the living room—the pep-squad ebullience of Kathy Lee Gifford, the nasally homiletics of Dr. Phil. Our apartment has a view of the pool in the courtyard, and in the afternoon I sometimes watch the two of them lounging on deck chairs in distressing casket-ready postures. Most of the other residents here are retired senior citizens, affluent snowbirds from New York and southern Québec, many of whom congregate in the open-air atrium around 4:30 p.m. for group trips to Cracker Barrel. My wife and I are in our early thirties, and our relative youth makes us a magnet for their attention. One morning, after returning from a jog, I amble out to the courtyard for a brisk round of pushups, and when I flip over for crunches, bronzed and shellacked in sweat, I notice several gray-haired ladies watching me from their apartment windows, like a panopticon run by AARP. Without quite noticing it, we gradually become the apartment building's de facto form of tech support. Last week, I created a Facebook account for an unregenerate codger named Harold, whose profile picture I snapped by the swimming pool, for which he posed in a crimson leisure suit whose stench of mothballs was vainly undercut by a cloud of Brut cologne. My wife and I muse about a potential racket, a Geek Squad for geriatrics.

There's one younger permanent resident in the complex, a lanky English guy in his late forties who's rumored to be the scion of a London-based department store. He spends most of his days sunning by the pool and reading dog-eared paperbacks by Alain de Botton. Currently, he's ripping through *Religion for Atheists*. Though twice I've told him my name, he persists in calling me "chap," which feels somehow both credibly British and deliberately impersonal. Still, his charm seems battery-powered, and because he's the youngest permanent resident in the complex, he is the source of fervent gossip among the old ladies. Apparently, he spends the entire winter down here, summoning a revolving door of women from Canada, Europe, and other parts of the U.S., some of whom tote children who are, presumably, his. Whenever we hang around the pool, the old ladies report his dalliances in scandalized tones, grasping our forearms and confiding their theories. "My theory is that he's got a whole harem of these broads," one says. "My theory is that he's trying to make it work with the one from Bulgaria." One Sunday evening a few weeks ago, one of the residents found him "porking" a brunette in the laundry hutch, his trousers puddled around his ankles. "They even had the dryer going!" I suspect their intrigue stems from the fact that the man lives in a blatant state of flux, trading old lovers for new ones, eschewing the standard midlife trajectory of settling down.

But sooner or later the ladies chide themselves for talking out of school, for spreading unwholesome impressions. Gossip, they tell us, is not a Christian habit of mind. Almost every week one of them will invite us to their church, and though we smile and make idle promises, my wife and I have no intention of joining them. Wasteful, we think, to have a sermon fall on deaf ears. But sometimes in the morning I watch these women assemble near the pool for prayer and morning devotions, their leather-bound Bibles thrown open to Leviticus or Ephesians or John 3:16, and I'm struck by the rigor they bring to these studies, the neatly inscribed jottings they make in small

Mead notebooks. Much has been said about the erosion of literacy in this country, our customs of skim and glance, but one need only look at a Bible study conducted by Midwestern ladies to find a paragon of close-reading. Perhaps I shouldn't be shocked, exactly, especially when this particular act of interpretation can mean the difference between providence and perdition, when the arc of that story imbues every moment of their lives with the glimmer of cosmic meaning. Occasionally, when the wind isn't too rough and stray bits of their conversation float up to our apartment unimpeded, I am struck by the elegance of the scripture they recite, the lilt and rhythm of delivered praise. "In a moment, in the twinkling of an eye, at the last trumpet," they say, in doddering unison. "For the trumpet shall sound, and the dead will be raised incorruptible." I watch them from the window, a circle of tinsel-haired women sitting at a patio table made of frosted glass, their heads bowed in the auspicious Florida sun, the pool flickering chimerically beside them, a loop of blue and gold. Max Weber once called himself "religiously unmusical," and while I can appreciate the kernel of his sentiment, I fall into a different strain of unbeliever, for I can still hear the melody in the parable, can still feel my neck kindle at the timbre of grace, even though it's a song I cannot bring myself to sing. "In a moment," the ladies say. "In the twinkling of an eye. We shall be changed."

—

Our rebirth, however, is of a more intemperate sort. We fall prey to other stories and put our faith in different beliefs. During the first couple weeks of our stay, my wife and I eschew work and become dedicated practitioners of sloth, letting emails and texts go unanswered, watching as every day stretches out before us like a great open lawn, rambling with possibility. We buy cheap sunglasses with fluorescent rims and stroll aimlessly down the boardwalk, sipping beverages of deliquesced fruit from a calligraphy of neon straws. It's on mornings like this, with a boulevard of sunlight coruscating on the Atlantic, that it becomes difficult to summon those old political enthusiasms, to pretend that this climate hasn't loosened the stiff joint of your convictions.

Something inside of us is becoming unhinged. Or rather I feel as though the whole notion of selfhood is becoming unhinged. In the words of our Midwestern grandmothers, we start "acting out of character." At night, we skinny-dip in the courtyard pool, our voices echoey and resonant, the underwater halogens turning the water the rinsed blue of Barbicide. And even though we've been vegetarians for years, we soon find ourselves ordering quarter-pounders with cheese, our napkins blotted translucently with the grease of contradiction. Even our professions are open to reform. One night, we watch a documentary about heroin addicts, one of whom admits to her substance-abuse counselor that she's been turning tricks, allegedly earning three hundred dollars per john.

"That's what I should do," my wife says.

My eyebrows shoot up. "Go on dates?" I ask.

"Become an addiction counselor," she says.

One could argue we've been penned in for too long, that we're simply recuperating from a long cabin fever. But it becomes hard not to sense a certain questing spirit in our activities, as if the happiness we were chasing were an American rite of passage, a national pastime.

—

There's a television ad on heavy rotation. Since our arrival, scarcely a day has passed that it hasn't aired at least a dozen times. The commercial opens with a montage of tropical motifs—sweeping aerial shots of wan coastlines and schooners marring cobalt horizons. The screen flashes with a row of deck chairs occupied by blonde women in bikinis who toast one another with mimosas. The theme music is clubby and has a vaguely sexual backbeat, and after a short instrumental prelude, we are soon addressed by the lecherous voice of Pitbull—patron saint of Miami pop—who admonishes us in a series of gravel-toned blandishments: "Feel free / to do whatever you want / whenever you want / with whoever you want. Feel free / who cares what they say / just live your life / cause we don't live twice." As the song rollicks on, the images of lotus-eating come to us in torrents. Butter-glazed lobsters on silver trays. Rowdy men playing pickup basketball. A gang of half-nude twentysomethings jumping exuberantly from a seaside cliff. But halfway through the ad something strange happens: the vocals cut out, and short gnomic messages colonize the screen, which somehow gives the impression that the viewer is supposed to sing along, like a congregant during the praise chorus at church.

> Rules are for land
> Out here you're free
> Free to indulge
> Free to explore
> Free to laugh
> Free to love
> Free to feast
> Free to dance
> Free to relax
> Free to enjoy life's best moments.
> See a horizon.
> Change your view.

The captions here give prestige to an older American ethos, the freedom-lust of the frontier cowboy and the backwoods pioneer, both of whom roamed and rutted as they pleased. Like these national icons, the cruiser—it is an ad for Swedish Cruise Lines—should not feel beholden to any ideological commitments. Instead, unfettered from the strictures of the continent, he can change course at the slightest whim and set out for new horizons, all while engaging in a derby of carnal pursuits.

In light of the last couple weeks the commercial serves as a cruel looking glass for our behavior, and I throw a sheepish glance in my wife's direction only to find that she's fallen asleep, head tipped back in a fluty snore, which means I have no one to chide me for this halfhearted anthropology. Instead, I'm left alone to contemplate a Nietzsche reference.

> And this is a universal law: a living thing can be healthy, strong and fruitful only when bounded by a horizon; if it is incapable of drawing a horizon around itself, and at the same time too self-centered to enclose its own view within that of another, it will pine away slowly or hasten to its timely end.

Nietzsche was responding to a cast of mind that had become prevalent in Germany after the Franco–Prussian War, which suggested that history was nothing more than a welter of pointless battles waged over grim, untenable ideologies. That morality was relative to the tenor of a given historical moment. The result of such a worldview, Nietzsche believed, was that individuals would commit their lives to petty agendas: the crass gratification of bodily urges, the bloodless quest of idle pastimes. There'd be no more grand causes, no more systems of belief. "We [would] desire the happiness of animals," he wrote. "But not on their terms." Instead, we'd float through life with the mutability of grocery bags drifting insouciantly in the wind, seeking only lavish foods, luminous vistas, and titillating incidents. Nietzsche had several terms for these individuals. He called them "men without chests" or "beasts with red cheeks." He called them "last men."

I can't explain it, but the commercial makes me sad. It makes me sad in the way certain dusking hours on a Sunday afternoon often can—a despondency immune to consolation. I suppose you could say that over the past few years I'd been approaching the end of something, that I was running up against the frontier of a certain manner of thinking. For so long, I had fallen under the misapprehension that the point of life was to chase down a succession of exotic experiences, to accumulate anecdotes, to construct a lurid diary, to toggle indiscriminately between the apparel of possible selves. Rather like Nietzsche's gutless milquetoast, my chest had grown hollow, and I had come begrudgingly to believe that no cause was better than any other, that I could place my faith in the indeterminacy of meaning and thus feel free to believe in anything at all. If all ways of living were considered equal and no true consequences stemmed from my ideological decisions, what difference did it make if I became a banker, a lawyer, a ballroom dancer? A Buddhist, an atheist, a Jew?

—

Of course, we forgot about the children. They start appearing in trickles and drips toward the end of February, but by the first week of March, scads of college students pour into the city, their rusted low-slung cars clogging every inlet and roadway. One morning, I go for a jog along the boardwalk only to discover that they've colonized the beach. Shirtless boys in straight-brimmed ballcaps migrate down the shoreline in groups as large as ten, jostling one another and razzing other beachgoers like some great cloud of hubris.

In the middle of this bedlam, I pull out my phone and text my wife—*Noooooooo*, I type. *They're here*—and after a volley of commiserative messages, we agree to meet near Trump Tower, where she arrives a few minutes later in what has become her standard outfit of muumuu, shades, and sunhat.

I flourish my arms like a gameshow assistant, as if showcasing the beach.

"Oh, God," she says. "It's an infestation."

Whiffs of coconut sun-oil and Axe body spray, of watery pilsners and dried vomit, assault us as we veer toward the encampment. Thousands of collegians are here, loitering under wind-tossed flags that bear their school's name: Ohio State, one says. Indiana University, says another.

As my wife escapes to a more serene vector of the coastline on the thin premise of getting some midday exercise, I turn around and begin swerving through the mayhem. The beach teems with incident, and the reigning mood is comparable to *The Garden of Earthly Delights*. There are beer bongs and quarters and rounds of beachside shots. Dozens of students are cavorting through the turquoise surf in a way that for some reason reminds me of a T-Mobile commercial. I walk so far. When I finally turn around to measure the distance I've traveled, Trump Tower is merely a smudge on the horizon, and the Boschian chaos of spring break stretches into the distance as far as the eye can see—a blur of flesh and indulgence.

Heading back toward the boardwalk, I somehow find myself dragooned into a conversation with a quartet of bros from Indiana University, all of whom have corn-blond hair, impeccable orthodontia, and apostolic names: Matthew, Paul, Luke, and John. The boys are all wearing Fitbits, and when I inquire about their devices, they become ecstatically animated, maundering on and on about their features and apps. To ask about this technology is to send them into reveries of self-improvement. They tell me about optimizing their workouts. They tell me about saving time. They tell me about sleep schedules and REM cycles and the Superman diet. For a minute, I toy with the idea of bringing up the idioms of Zarathustra, of mentioning offhandedly something about the perils of the Übermensch, but the fervor with which they speak about these self-bettering regimes makes it seem like they'd be impregnable to my concerns. They've fallen hard for the gospel of self-determination, of Dataism and enhancement, and I know better than to contend with hardcore zealots and challenge foundational beliefs.

Scarcely are the boys alone in their fervor. It seems to infect every last visitor to this cloudless swath of South Florida. It hovers over the poses of the sunrise yoga club, a group of hotel guests who contort themselves on the beach every morning, and pervades the temple of the South Florida Dharma Punx, a posse of young people with mohawks and narrative tattoos who aim for mindfulness without dulling their countercultural edge. More often than not, these promises depend upon a faith in materialism. Exercise becomes a conduit for self-invention, which suggests that a sculpted midsection can be an emblem for a sturdy identity.

In hindsight, the injunction to optimize ourselves has been hounding us since we arrived. Earlier this month, while spending a day in Miami, my wife and I came across something called "The Self-Mastery Gym," where a horde of true believers inside a banquet hall clutched flutes of prosecco and watched a bald man in Jeff Goldblum glasses stand behind a lectern and wax capably about Eckhart Tolle. And in the cereal aisle of a Whole Foods last week, a redheaded woman in a leotard and show-horse braids handed my wife a flyer for something called "The Real You" retreat. The glossy brochure boasted "four days of fun & fitness," including workouts with celebrity instructors, makeovers and fashion shows, and an "All White Beach Party," which sounded like a soiree hosted by the KKK.

My wife responded with a polite half-smile, equal parts derision and amusement. "I'm not sure I'm ready, spiritually, for this kind of commitment."

"I get that," the woman said, "but sometimes we have to go beyond our abilities." Our willowy spirit guide then flashed a runic smile and retreated down the aisle in soundless ballet flats, which were coated in ruby-colored glitter.

Not since the Sophists have there been so many spiritual consultants—chakra experts, biorhythm specialists, and vision quest advocates—all of whom are willing to sell you a certain version of your life. We used to have counternarratives to defend against these chimeras, to curb the tendency to see ourselves as omnipotent—as gods. But today, tech prophets in headsets forecast the arrival of our digital bodies, which in due time will no longer suffer from illness and decay. Instead, we will "hack" our lives, programming new efficiencies, our defects coded away. In a moment. In the twinkling of an eye. We shall be changed.

The boys invite me to join them for a "boot-camp workout" on the beach tomorrow morning, and I feign interest and give them my number.

"It was a pleasure to meet you," Luke says. "Yeah, drop us a line," says Paul, "and hopefully we'll touch base tomorrow."

Dusk settles over the shoreline, a hallucinogenic wash of infant blue and lewd pink, and the students gyrate to a song that blares from someone's speaker. Darkness is upon them, but the students are a thousand strong. They lift their hands exuberantly, a roil of limbs and exaltation, and they bellow a faithful mimesis of the lyrics, a great communal roar that sounds somehow both jubilant and desperately pained. "And we can't stop," they cry. "And we won't stop."

—

Of course, there is a point at which self-determination veers unavoidably into self-delusion. In March, the news breaks about an eighteen-year-old kid named Malachi Love-Robinson who apparently has been posing as a doctor at an outpatient clinic in West Palm Beach. For nearly a year now, the kid has been running something called the "New Birth New Life Medical Center," which offers a gamut of dubious services, including air and water treatments, phototherapy, and many other "natural remedies." On the walls of his New Life office, Dr. Love exhibits a fraudulent diploma from Arizona State, along with a doctorate of theology that is, apparently, authentic. While still in high school, the boy completed a PhD from the Universal Life Church Seminary, an online degree that can supposedly be purchased for $29.99.

One evening the pool in the courtyard is humming with gossip. The old ladies play judge and jury while fanning themselves with sunhats, wearing long sheer robes over one-piece swimsuits.

"Did you hear he's a Christian?" one says.

"It says here," says another, her face tented by the *Sun Sentinel*, "that he treated an elderly woman for severe stomach pain and charged nearly thirty-five hundred dollars. Imagine if that had been one of us!"

Later that night we gather in a neighbor's apartment to watch an interview with Dr. Love on the nightly news, and I'm struck by the manner in which he conducts himself, a veritable theme park of bluster and prevarication. "The situation I face now is accusations . . . I'm not portraying [myself] as an MD. I've never said that I've gone to school to be an MD . . . Accusations are merely accusations."

"Don't you just think that's awful?" one of the ladies asks. "Him pretending like that?"

Except I don't. The air down here is too polluted with mythologies, too humid with tales about freedom and reinvention.

—

It is difficult to say precisely when things begin to worsen for me. One morning in the atrium, I run into the debonair Englishman, who proceeds to say one of the most thoroughly British things I've ever heard: "Dreadfully sorry to interrupt you, friend, but I wonder if you're sharing my same trouble this morning. Though I can't say for sure, there appears to be, in my bathtub here, the presence of human waste." Dutifully I follow him into his apartment, where the stench of excrement hangs roguishly in the stagnant air. His bathroom has Kohler fixtures and monogrammed towels, but these luxuries do little to offset the scene of horror inside his bathtub. In it, there is a stew of shit, an ankle-deep gumbo of fecal matter that appears to burble nightmarishly near the drain. A plumber arrives a few hours later and tells us that the septic tank has ruptured beneath the complex. "You overburdened the system," he says. "So now you've got shit coming up through the pipes." It's difficult not to read his statement as metaphorical, as though the stern expression he gives us were inflected with darker meaning.

Eventually, my anxieties become Victorian—Gothic, even. All morning long I sit at the jalousie windows, lost in doleful contemplation, and from this elevated vantage everything takes on a mortal tinge. The octogenarian man who wakes at dawn to sit by himself near the pool, accompanied only by the jargon of morning birds, now possesses a drastic sadness, his torpor bewildering to me. I wonder how he can manage to sit there blinking at the blue nothing, as one hour slips irrevocably into the next. Soon, it occurs to me that our respective postures are shared, that I'm wasting just as much time as he is.

We make a point to get out more. At night, my wife and I walk along the boardwalk in the accretive dark, watching the spangled hulls of cruise ships retreat into the distance—tiered illuminated edifices that, to my wife's estimation, look like wedding cakes. The black water is varnished with the boat's emerald lights, and I think of Gatsby, think of Fitzgerald, think of Zelda going bats. My wife and I sit near the surf, debating the merits of antidepressants and electroshock therapy. Coins of moonlight flicker on the dark waves, and I tell her that coming down here hasn't helped. She knows, she says, and points out that I've been running twice a day. Reaching over to bracelet the girth of my wrist with her index finger and thumb, she says, you're getting twiggy. Marriage, Samuel Johnson once said, is "a continuity of being," and never before have I felt that sentiment with such ardor as when we sat along the lunar shoreline. It occurs to me that the vows we swapped three years ago in that little church in Michigan functioned as the lone instance in my life when I traded the freedom of choice for the burdens of commitment. So I tell her not to worry, that everything will be okay, but there's something in her expression that makes it easy to see that she's not entirely convinced.

—

Near the beginning of March, my wife's sisters visit us from Michigan. We pick them up at the airport, and they come stumbling out the terminal doors with an air of pallid exhaustion, a sluggish Midwestern ennui. Pushing flight-addled toddlers in strollers, they tote diaper bags and Samsonite luggage, which I race out of the car to relieve them of. Our greetings are bright and lilting, everything in falsetto, and on our way to the coast, they bring tidings from back home. They tell us about an acquaintance who has died, a friend who's getting married, and as these facts of life begin to sink in, the illusions of our life here in Florida begin to scatter and dissolve. Such is the way of family. Their mere presence calls into question your entire manner of being and points out the extent to which you'd been living under a mistake.

My three-year-old niece is strapped into a car seat. Around her mouth is a continent of juice-stain. She keeps saying, "This doesn't feel like Florida, Mom."

They ask us how we've been. My wife mentions nothing of my insomnia or my two-a-day jogs in the deadening heat. We don't tell them that I've stopped writing, that we've paged through the Yellow Pages in search of outpatient clinics.

Over the next couple days, my wife's sisters fall under the spell of the tropics. They unwind with pineapple daiquiris and spend whole days beside the pool, abjuring sunscreen because, of course, the scarlet burn will give way to a handsome sienna tan. Absent other guardians, the children fall under our care, and my wife and I ply them with colossal stuffed animals and gadgets that we think are age-inappropriate.

One day, I spend a listless afternoon reading to my nieces by the pool—illustrated books with spare plotlines that are told in faithful terza rima. A young black bear with anthropomorphic eyes hunts for salmon in an overfished river before eventually losing track of his den. It's a smart book, I think, about greed and the perils of a debt economy. We lie on a deckchair, and the girls, who are two and three respectively, have cuddled their heads into my armpits while I hold the book over my chest. It is an old volume, with a battered hardcover and a torn dust jacket, its edges curling like birch skin. My wife sits along the lip of the pool with her feet in the deep end, making little dawdles and splashes, the water cerulean and twinkling behind her. Chewing the limb of her sunglasses, she watches me read to the girls with an attitude of evaluation, as if, despite her aversion to having children, she were measuring my fitness as a father.

Somehow, despite my best efforts, I have returned to the realm of stories, have settled unwittingly into the arcs of conflict, climax, and feel-good denouement. And as I'm reading about the bear's tribulations, some dormant critical reflex is activated in me, until soon I'm interpreting his adventure not merely as a lesson about the virtues of communal life but also as an Iliad of self-delusion, knowing full well that the beasts who haunt our hero are not real threats but figments of his own making. Tragedy, Adam Phillips writes, doesn't show us "the horror of life" as we know it. Instead, the genre aims to dramatize "the horror of life under the aegis of a certain kind of conscience."

But when I turn the page to bring the story to a close, we find ourselves up against the inside back cover, a hard blank surface—empty, inscrutable, showing nothing—at which point I realize the last couple pages have been torn out—it's an ancient and poorly kept storybook, after all, its original owner probably my wife's grandmother. So the story will end here, cantilevered over empty space, uncertain the outcome awaiting our skittish woodland hero. But when I try to explain the missing pages to my nieces, they are not simply flummoxed, they are tearfully indignant. They want to know— what's the story? How does it end? Their expressions are wounded with earnestness, their eyes tear-glinted and full of anticipation. I glance at my wife, who can sense my distress, and who tries to assuage the girls with palliative phrases, with the promise of TV and ice cream, but their unhappiness cannot be contained. I am thirty-one years old, a husband with a lettered disposition, someone who attended grad school to learn the art of telling stories, who knows all about the conventions of storybook endings. But for some reason, I cannot lend this story an ending, cannot give it some final meaning.

—

And without explanation, I get up and run. Because I am stuck in this lousy failing body, I run. Much to the confusion of our nieces, I dash up to our apartment, change into my sneakers, and I'm out the door within minutes, bolting down the side streets, flying past the condos, the resorts, the garish retail developments. The sky above the shoreline looks hazy and provisional, something that will surely darken before it comes to an end. Pageants of tourists maneuver down the boardwalk, families and couples and loutish spring breakers, everyone fleeing the approaching storm, and I am the lone person running among them, my breath audible and gruff. I've grown so tired of stitching this into some orderly narration, when the truth is that I have no more stories to relate, no more anecdotes to decode. The only thing left is the dumb lurch of my body and the vans of this buffeting wind.

I make it as far as Trump Tower, where I stop, hunched over and gasping for breath. The sky over the ocean is forked with lightning and the sidewalk is pocked with rain, and I veer under the hotel's porte cochère, where there are, inexplicably, squadrons of men—workers, presumably—who are barking orders through static-glitzed walkie-talkies, running pallets of boxes into the frenzied atrium. From outside, the glass of the doors reflects the drab, rain-muddled street, but when I cup my hands around my eyes, I'm astonished to find the hotel's interior humming with life. Inside there are sweeping marble floors and trios of low-backed chairs, accented with autumn-colored pillows. It looks nearly finished. How long have they been at work, invisibly but diligently, without ever once drawing notice? Months later, in the middle of that fateful November, it would become impossible not to see this moment as a harbinger of how wrong we had been. Down here, in these balmy climates, one can come easily to think that the world boils down to the whims of the body, that ideology is nothing more than a thing of the past. But these men had been summoned to another calling, driven by some unseen master, and together in these months of vague disquiet, they had erected this formidable structure. We had presumed it was empty, but their work was nearly done.

CONSCIOUSNESS RAZING

You're being reborn," the voice says. "Exiting the womb of your mother. Coming into the earth as a small baby. Everything is new." Right now, it is a Saturday morning in mid-March, and I'm lying on a yoga mat in a hunting lodge in Ohio, surrounded by fifty other men who've come to the Midwest for a weekend of manhood-confirming adventures. The voice in question belongs to Aaron Blaine, a facilitator for Evryman, the men's group orchestrating this three-day retreat. All around me, men are shedding tears as Blaine leads us on a guided meditation, a kind of archetypal montage of Norman Rockwell boyhood. "You're starting to figure things out," he says, in somniferous baritone. "Snow, for the first time. Sunshine. Start to notice the smells, the tastes, the confusion. The fear. And you're growing. You're about ten years old. The world's huge and scary."

Even though it's only the second day of the Evryman retreat, it's worth noting that I've already been the subject of light fraternal teasing. Already I've been the recipient of countless unsought hugs. Already I have sat in Large Groups and Small Groups, and have watched dozens of middle-aged men weep with shame and contrition. I've heard a guy in the military tell me he wants to be "a rock for his family." I've heard a guy from Ohio say that his beard "means something." Twice I've hiked through the woods to "reconnect with Mother Nature," and I have been addressed by numerous men as both "dude" and "brother." I have performed yoga and yard drills and morning calisthenics. I've heard seven different men play acoustic guitar. I've heard a man describe his father by saying, "There wasn't a lot of ball-tossing when I was growing up." Three times I've been queried about how I'm "processing everything," and at the urinal on Friday night, two men warn me about the upcoming "Anger Ceremony," which is rumored to be the weekend's "pièce de résistance."

As we lie there on the floor, I'm vaguely aware of Blaine, a U.S. Special Forces veteran with tattooed shoulders and a corn-silk moustache, who's pacing around the labyrinth of yoga mats, still exhorting us to recall certain touchstones from our childhood. Earlier in the weekend, he'd recounted for us the sense of brotherhood he'd shared with his platoon, as well as the abyss of anxiety and depression he'd fallen into after returning from his deployment. "I had lost my tribe," he'd said. Blaine now serves as Director of Operations at Evryman, which is run by a coterie of guys from the tech and media industries. For the last two years, they've been holding weekend retreats in places like the Berkshires and Joshua Tree, hoping to foster what they call "masculine emotional intelligence." In preparation for the retreat, I did my best to acquaint myself with their rhetoric. Mostly this consisted of spending a lot of time on their Instagram, marveling at the preponderance of Ansel-Adams-type photographs—think: black and white shots of mountaintops overhung by frescoed skies, with smiling guys in the foreground wearing rucksacks and ballcaps. The photos were underscored with heart-rustling captions—about men breaking down stereotypes, about men no longer suppressing their emotions—to which had been appended a whole host of earnest hashtags. #manup, one said. #wildernessmakesyoubetter, said another.

After several minutes, Blaine's meditation transitions into adulthood, and almost immediately, the mood in the lodge has changed. Lots of guys around me are sighing raggedly as Blaine offers a more grueling contemporary update: "Then all of a sudden you're responsible for a lot. Wife, kids, partner—everyone is looking at you. *Dad, dad, dad: What do I do?* And you don't even know if you know yourself. You gotta make the money. You gotta be tough.

"That's great and all," Blaine continues. "But today you're dead. You're going to die today."

—

Early last January, the American Psychological Association released its new treatment protocols for men and noted, decisively, that "traditional masculinity" was toxic. Owing to outworn habits of stoicism and aggression, it argued, men were hurting themselves and others, and were eschewing the care they need. It was difficult not to read this as an understatement. After all, over the last few years, men have been killing themselves in unprecedented numbers and, as of 2017, comprised 76 percent of the nation's suicide rate. Men have also been disproportionately affected by the recent opioid epidemic and account for over 80 percent of the arrests for violent crime, against both women and other men.

I came across this information last winter, but in truth, I didn't need a bulletin from America's foremost corps of psychologists to know that a lot of men are struggling. It's hard to say when it started exactly—two years ago, maybe three?—but most of my conversations with male friends had begun to resemble unofficial therapy sessions. Lots of these guys I'd known since college and were scattered in cities across the country, and whenever we called one another to catch up, the charade of light chitchat quickly devolved into a dirge of existential updates. Several of these men struggled with addiction and depression, or other conditions that could be named, but the more common complaint was something vaguer—a quiet desperation that, if I was forced to generalize, seemed to stem from a gnawing sense of purposelessness. Granted, I myself was no stranger to the bleak terrain of melancholy. I'd weathered a series of Richter-scale depressions in my mid-twenties, and if these friends confided in me so readily, it was probably because they sensed that on some level I could understand.

Then there was my neighbor, the thirty-something man who occupied the apartment next to mine, who lived alone and worked at one of the big tech companies in town—I knew this thanks to his corporate-issued tote bag. I had never exchanged more than a passing greeting with him in the hall, but through the scrim of our ancient, parchment-thin walls, I could hear the war-blitz of his video game console, which began like clockwork each Friday evening and continued without rest—rain or shine, winter or summer, with little regard for holidays—until the end of the weekend. It's difficult, in hindsight, to account for the sadness I experienced listening to him holed up for days on end in front a screen, blasting Elder Dragons or whatever. Sometimes, late at night, he would get drunk, put on indie music from the late 1990s, and sing along in a voice that was full-throated, plaintive, and remarkably on key.

For a long time, I told myself that none of this was new. Probably everyone felt this way as they began the long, slow descent into the doldrums of middle age. And anyway, one is disinclined these days to feel sorry for men, especially considering how adept we've become at feeling sorry for ourselves. One need only take a look online to find the reactionary and often violent ways in which men have responded to their ailments. On the rightmost end of the spectrum are factions like Incels, those pale, misanthropic creatures who contend that feminism has spelled their downfall on the sexual marketplace and who have responded with either "blackpilling" (accepting one's fate) or "looksmaxing" (using extreme plastic surgery to carve oneself into an Adonis). No less odious are the clerics of the alt-right, such as the lantern-jawed Gavin McInnes, the paterfamilias of the Proud Boys, who thunders about the virtues of patriarchy and forbids masturbation among his adherents. And let's not forget the self-help maven Jordan Peterson, he of the all-beef diet and three-piece suits, who relies on fossilized Jungian archetypes to parse the differences between men and women.

Most of the contemporary men's movement, though, isn't so overtly political. For instance, *The New York Times* recently lauded the ManKind Project, which has been enlisting fresh recruits into their "New Warrior Training Adventures" since the early 1980s. There's also Brett McKay's *Art of Manliness* podcast, which has garnered over a million subscribers and which idolizes the bullish virility of Theodore Roosevelt. McKay believes that, just like in the nineteenth century, men have been "glutted with conveniences" and thus suffer from "lack of decision in trifling matters" and "deficient mental control." The panacea for such doleful enervation, McKay believes, is his online training regimen, called "The Strenuous Life," which is essentially just Boy Scouts for men. After completing "Weekly Agons," participants earn "badges" for competence in myriad skills, which are denoted with epithetic signifiers like "Gentleman Scholar," "Social Dynamo," "Lock Picker," and "Sartorialist." The twelve-week program offers participants a snazzy gray and army-green uniform, plus a "handsome, pocket-sized" handbook "styled like the scouting manuals of old," all of which veers into the self-parodic and possesses the zany, boutique aesthetics of a Wes Anderson film.

By far the savviest and most normal-seeming of the new men's groups was Evryman, a benefit corporation founded in New York City during the winter of 2017. I stumbled across their website early in my research and couldn't help scrutinizing their sleek, unfussy aesthetic, no doubt intended to appeal to a more sophisticated gentleman, the kind of guy who might scrub himself with Dove's Men Care and consult Esther Perel's podcast.

What set Evryman apart was that they seemed acutely conscious of the very tradition of men's groups, which have a knotty history of being both reactionary and essentialist. This was most glaringly apparent in the knuckle-dragging machismo of the Iron John movement from the 1990s, when men partook of "hero quests" and occasional nudity to recover their "true" masculinity. More than anything else, Evryman seemed hell-bent on destigmatizing such men's work—to the point where their insistence bordered on preemptive apology or outright embarrassment. The group's most popular ad to date opens with Evryman's Brand & Marketing Director, Ebenezer Bond, offering a "candid" testimonial. Wearing a Williamsburg beanie and a faddish lumberjack beard, he says, "When I told people I was going to a men's retreat, I was like, 'This is going to be fucking awful. If I have to get in a loincloth and dance around a fire and beat a drum, I'm never going back.'" So Evryman isn't that? asks some off-screen interlocutor. "It's not that," Bond says.

Evryman had already received splashy news coverage from *GQ Australia* ("This Men's Camp Is Fixing Toxic Masculinity") and *Men's Health* ("Inside the Retreat Where Men Purge Toxic Emotions"), plus a hagiographic spot on *The Today Show*, where some of the guys got emotional with Carson Daly and Al Roker. And yet I couldn't quite see how a gender-exclusive space would be the best venue for interrogating masculinity. Still, they were promising to provide a "life-changing experience." They were promising to help men get in touch with their emotions. For a thousand bucks, I could spend three days in the woods and find an enduring brotherhood. The condition was I couldn't just be a fly-on-the-wall, they said. "If you want to write something, you have to participate."

—

It's the first weekend in March, and I'm driving along meandering county roads toward the Cedar Grove Retreat Center in Logan, Ohio, a shire of log cabins studded among the quaint Hocking Hills forest. As with most men's groups, Evryman operates from the Thoreauvian premise that bucolic isolation can be good for the spirit, that this kind of "work" can only be performed when one is sequestered from one's family.

Inside the main lodge, I'm bombarded by the roar of fifty male voices that are meeting one another for the first time. Introductions are made with vise-like handshakes, plus baritone recitations of provenance and profession. "I'm Matt. I do finance in Michigan." "I'm Rick, and I'm a scientist from Ohio." Before dinner, I meet a lean, tan man with basset-hound eyes named Robert, who tells me that he's authored over twenty volumes for something called greatbooksforboys.com. "What a lot of literacy folks don't realize is that boys have a different brain structure than girls," he says. Females are auditory learners, he tells me, whereas boys are "more visual." Over the last decade, Robert spent a million dollars on market research, trying to figure out what boys want to read, which consisted of visiting schools and speaking with parents and teachers, all of which yielded an adventure series called *Time Soldiers*. In it, camo-clad tweens defy the space-time continuum, equipped with helmets and skateboards. The series pairs cinematic photos with skimpy blocks of text, creating what Robert suggests is an entirely new type of literature. To me, though, it sounds like your standard picture book. "What do you call this genre?" I ask. "They're movie books," he says. Part of the reason he's joined the Evryman movement is that he lost four million dollars in the venture and has been lugging around a surfeit of anger as a result. Soon he introduces me to Ben from West Virginia. Both of them have previously attended Evryman retreats and freely admit to being "criers."

After dinner, we hunker down in a circle of bone-white folding chairs, where the cambered roof of the lodge has been festooned with Italian lights, an accoutrement better meant for a shabby-chic wedding. For all the enlightened bluster on the Evryman website, I can't help noticing that both registration and the catered dinner were staffed exclusively by women, who subsequently disappear, presumably to some other cabin on the grounds, as the facilitators settle down to business.

On the far side of the room is the Evryman staff, a veritable A-team of "new" masculinity. This includes the movement's éminence grise, Owen Marcus, a man in his sixties who's been running men's groups for over three decades. Next to him is Dan Doty, the public face of the organization and the host of the Evryman podcast. Before serving as a producer for a Netflix hunting show called *MeatEater*, Doty ran therapeutic wilderness adventures for juvenile offenders in Minnesota, leading groups of boys through the forest, discussing coping mechanisms for life's problems, and gathering them around the fire at night for readings from *Siddhartha*. Also in attendance this weekend is Lucas Krump, Evryman's CEO, who made his bones in the tech industry, until the soul-withering demands of corporate life left him isolated and bereft. Now, he's funneled his wealth into the Evryman business, hoping to spawn an international movement. Beside him are the aforementioned Aaron Blaine, as well as Dan MacCombie, whose LinkedIn profile describes him as "Entrepreneur, Coach, Human."

Blaine and MacCombie are leading the retreat this weekend and begin by reviewing the Evyrman "Agreements." These include an indemnifying waiver and a promise of confidentiality. Moreover, in the spirit of getting in touch with our "true, authentic" emotions, Evryman has put a strict embargo on any mood-altering substance. Later, however, I'll get wind of several rogue factions who scuttle into the woods to smoke weed throughout the weekend, and journalistically speaking, this will be kind of a nightmare, since this unsanctioned bowl-smoking will make red eyes an untrustworthy signifier, and it will no longer be clear whether the heavy-lidded guy in question has had an emotional breakthrough or has maybe just returned from hitting some really dank sativa.

Whereas the male liberationists of the 1960s and '70s were inspired by second-wave feminism to interrogate the ways in which modern masculinity was socially constructed, both by the imperatives of Madison Avenue and the fiats of consumer capitalism, today's men's movement tends to focus on emotional intelligence. Instead of "consciousness-raising" sessions, Evryman is big on somatic awareness. "Turn the feeling lever up," Blaine commands at one point. "And turn the thinking lever down." The lynchpin of the Evryman program is something called the "ROC" (read: "rock") method, which stands for "relax, open up, and connect," an acronym whose clear associations to tumescence—think: "rock hard"—seem designed to subvert the notion that emotionality is somehow effeminate. To relax, we perform a brief meditation because, as men, we've supposedly been inculcated with the deleterious belief that we should muzzle our pain as means of proving our toughness. But this, Marcus stresses, only causes our emotions to putrefy and fester. What this weekend will offer, in other words, is a chance to open up the spigot of those emotions.

Blaine and MacCombie then launch into the evening's central exercise, and we're asked to start wandering around the main hall, gazing into the eyes of the men we pass. Soon the room is clotted with male bodies, a haphazard ballet of anxious gaits and pendulous arms. Some men maintain unabashed eye contact, while others are so overcome with trepidation that their eyes are glinting with tears. All around me is an epidemic of Carhartt and Patagonia, plus an impressive spectrum of facial hair, ranging from chic stubble to Talmudic beards. The ages span from early twenties to mid-seventies, and the group turns out to be resoundingly Caucasian.

Finally, after a couple minutes of this anguished waltz, MacCombie tells us to pair up with whomever we're looking at, and I find myself standing across from a short blond man starchily attired in a powder blue merino sweater and loosely fitting pants. We trade restive salutations, and when he glances up at me, his wide searchlight eyes are panning across my face. Mac-Combie then instructs us to take a step closer to our partner until we're facing off at a kissable proximity, at which point we're enjoined to complete the following prompt: *If you really knew me, you'd know . . .* For me, this resembles nothing so much as the forced intimacy of a middle school sleepover, but out of journalistic obligation, I find that I can do nothing but dive right in. "If you really knew me, you'd know that I'm full of self-loathing. That throughout my twenties, I struggled with addiction and depression. That there have been several times throughout my life when I've contemplated suicide." I'm a little surprised by my promiscuous self-disclosure, and I watch now as the man's Adam's apple bobs up and down—a courage-endowing gulp. Then it's his turn. "If you really knew me, you'd know that I've never had any friends, that I've never wanted any. If you really knew me, you'd know that I've recently come out as gay, that I've had sex with over four hundred men, that last October I tried to commit suicide after I confessed everything to my wife."

Switch! MacCombie yells.

Clueless about how to meaningfully end this heart-tweaking interaction, I briskly thank the man for his courage and candor, and proceed to execute this confessional musical chairs with two other men, hugging each one in turn. For the final face-off, I'm paired with a hulking, bearded guy from Ohio, who has boyish eyes and a twangy, land-grant accent, something you only find in rural quadrants of the Midwest. Our prompt this time is *If I wasn't acting out of fear, I would . . .* He tells me he'd finally start his real estate business.

—

The next morning, I am the first man to cry in Small Group. In my defense, I've slept a total of four hours across the last two nights, doubtless the result of the cramped and foreign sleeping arrangements, which involve bunking with five other men, whose nocturnal rumpus of flatulence and snoring has pierced my every attempt at unconsciousness. Plus, I like to think that I'm fairly in touch with my emotions, becoming, as I do, a geyser of tears at the slightest provocation. I confess that, among friends in middle school, my special playground epithet was "The Sprinkler."

Small Group takes place in Stillwater Cabin, a three-story hunting lodge outfitted with a pool table and a hot tub, plus a panoramic balcony overlooking a pond of Kermit green. Right now, we're sitting on a quadrangle of brown Naugahyde couches while a gas-fueled fire sizzles in the corner. The exposed logs of the cabin, together with the elk-themed blankets, lend our discussion a rustic manliness, despite our abundant tears.

First up is Matt, an active-duty Green Beret who reports his passion for "kicking down doors and shooting guys in the head." He speaks uxoriously about his wife but laments his inability to reconnect with her between deployments. Possibly sharing his war stories would help, but he knows they'd give her nightmares for the rest of her earthly life. Next is Tim, an ashen man in his early thirties with a swoop of wheat-blond hair, who confesses that he tried to kill himself in 2017 and that Evryman has saved his life. Apparently, this is his second weekend retreat. But the real emotional acme of today's Small Group occurs when Andrew takes the floor. A scrubbed corporate guy from Cleveland, he is handsome in the bland, sanitized manner of Ken dolls or newscasters. In all his relationships, he explains, he suffers the habit of always putting others before himself.

"Can I help you with that?" Owen Marcus says. He's helming our Small Group and has settled into a rakish posture on the couch. "You're very articulate, and you're very good at describing those emotions, but see if you can slow down and just feel them."

At this point, Andrew is squirming in his chair, his hands flexing like anemones. "Um, in order to do that, I think we'd have to go outside."

"Let's do it," Owen says.

Soon, we're gathered on the balcony overlooking the scum-laden water, and Andrew clutches the splintered railing, quaking with disquiet and grief. I'm standing directly behind him, giving him the widest possible berth, and so forcefully is he juddering that it looks like he's manning a jackhammer.

"OK," Owen says. "Let it come out. From your balls all the way up."

Andrew rears back and screams. "FUCK IT ALL!"

We listen as his echo booms desolately across the forest. Disturbed by the uproar, a flock of mallards erupts from the shrubbery near the pond, flapping as it ascends, the birds' honks dull and metallic. I glance at the other guys, all of whom watch Andrew's purgation with bemusement and approval, like flinty-eyed onlookers at a boxing match.

"Let it overwhelm you," Owen says.

The intervening silence is woodsy and tranquil. Somewhere across campus, the female staff members are preparing food for lunch, and I picture them all looking up from pots and pans to identify the source of this commotion.

Pausing between each syllable for emphasis, Andrew yells, "FUCK. IT. ALL." Then, after a brief caesura, "IT STARTS NOW!"

When we get back inside and perch beside the fire, Owen commends Andrew on his "work," while the other guys are smiling and slapping him on the thigh with chummy jocularity. The atmosphere in the room is primal and festive, as if we were celebrating a rite of passage—a cliff summited, say, or the vanquishing of one's enemy. What baffles me, though, is the utter lack of a postscript. Scarcely do we wonder whether Andrew's impulse toward selflessness is actually a virtue, nor do we conjure solutions to his interpersonal dilemmas. Instead, what takes primacy is the outpouring of his emotions. That these discussions are resistant to broader considerations won't fully hit me until later that day, during our second Small Group, when I'll share feelings of isolation and disenchantment as a result of teaching university students, whose sadness and despair is so rampant that, on my evening commute, I often find myself in tears. Audibly, I wonder whether we, as a culture, are doing enough to furnish them with meaningful systems of belief, or if their only recourse has been to the dictates of corporate success and the soft nihilism of self-improvement. Yet even this attempt to discuss larger social phenomena gets trampled, because Owen will ask if I've ever heard of "Mirror Theory," suggesting that perhaps my characterization about my students is actually a funhouse reflection of my own sadness, so instead of talking about the culture, why don't we talk about that maybe?

—

Notions of American masculinity have long drawn on a shallow pool of familiar tropes, most of which we tend to associate with fictionalizations of the frontier: the lonesome swagger of John Wayne, the gruff reticence of the cowboy. But up until the end of the nineteenth century, the ideal of American masculinity was far more communal. The historian E. Anthony Rotundo has observed that the masculinity of the colonial era wasn't defined by chest-thumping machismo or brawny, entrepreneurial pluck, but was measured instead by a man's willingness to forfeit his time and resources for the betterment of his community. Hardly was this a matter of "emotional intelligence." Rather, his duties were fulfilled through "publick usefulness." Often this led to nascent forms of mutual aid because in a world where "creditors were neighbors and kinsmen were clients, a man's failure at work was never just a private concern." Meanwhile, those men who saddled up and lit out for the territories were roundly condemned as "frontier wastrels," as historian Vernon Louis Parrington called them, princes of thoughtlessness who pursued their own agendas and roamed the country as they pleased.

Yet the rise of industrialization and the birth of modern capitalism rewarded precisely those attributes that colonial communities were prone to denigrate: aggression, guile, and an overwhelming will to power. Even when men failed to thrive in the marketplace, they nevertheless succumbed to its sanctioned forms of masculinity. The feminist scholar Joseph Pleck notes that during the Great Depression, men no longer had access to the sorts of external achievements that once granted them a stabilizing dose of virility—wartime brawn or financial independence—so they deferred instead to psychological or behavioral attributes to restore their sense of identity. Lacerated by the dehumanizing conditions of the factory, male workers typically responded with a cocksure "hardhat culture," as the scholar Pankaj Mishra calls it, whereby heavy drinking, coarse language, and prurience became tokens of masculinity, a conception that Mishra believes has "reached deep into blue-collar workplaces during the decades-long reign of neoliberalism."

Rather than confront these structural changes head-on, men were often encouraged to blame other culprits: usually immigrants or women. In *Back-*

lash, her mammoth history of antifeminism, Susan Faludi notes that the antagonism toward women in the 1980s coincided with lackluster growth of traditional male industries, which caused a precipitous drop in real wages in households where men were the sole breadwinner. In describing this era, she writes, "The 1980s was a decade in which plant closings put blue-collar men out of work by the millions, and only 60 percent found new jobs—about half at lower pay." And yet instead of interrogating the economic woes behind their fear and instability, the powers that be put the onus upon women. "Part of the unemployment," Ronald Reagan suggested in a 1982 address on the economy, "is not as much recession as it is the great increase of people going into the job market, and—ladies, I'm not picking on anyone but—because of the increase in women who are working today."

Such outpourings of essentialist machismo have always accompanied surges in feminism. Even before the acquisition of female suffrage, in fin-de-siècle America, men reacted to the entrance of women into politics with wariness and hesitation. Theodore Roosevelt, for instance, famously added women's suffrage to his Progressive Party platform, but he compensated for this by doubling down on testosteronic rhetoric and championing football and boxing. Then there was the Iron John movement from the 1990s, when men responded to Third Wave feminism by resuscitating their inner "Wild Man," a term coined by the Minnesotan poet Robert Bly. Bly founded the "mythopoetic men's movement," and his book *Iron John* spent sixty-two weeks on *The New York Times* bestseller list. Invoking Jungian archetypes about masculinity and relying upon harebrained interpretations of Brothers Grimm fables, the Iron John movement believed that the Industrial Revolution sequestered fathers from sons and created an environment in which patriarchal authority became rotten and suspect.

Though Bly's Iron Johns and Roosevelt's disciples claimed to be in sympathy with their era's feminist movements, most critics saw in their objectives an attempt to reclaim the patriarchy. Sometimes even Bly himself let the mask slip. At a 1987 seminar in San Diego, a male participant asked

Bly what he should do if he revealed his true feelings to women and they dismissed him, to which Bly responded, "So, then you bust them in the mouth." When a flabbergasted audience member accused Bly of condoning battery against women, he tried, fruitlessly, to walk back his statement. "I meant, hit those women verbally."

It's easy to see how this revanchism has played out in the Trump era. And yet even when men aren't exhorted to engage in such blatant Otherism, the American male has been inculcated with the belief that the culprit behind his woes is either psychological or biological. Keen ironists will note that when biological factors like testosterone are pegged as the locus of toxic masculinity, such an argument relies on the same sort of essentialism that gets invoked by chauvinists who claim that women are biologically determined to be more emotional or diffident. Moreover, when the APA noted that "traditional masculinity" is "toxic," they were suggesting that this hardnosed disposition causes men to reject therapeutic assistance. Scanter attention gets paid to the structural forces behind their reluctance, which include not only the steep economic costs of therapy but also the paucity of resources in certain rural communities. Around the time the APA released its new guidelines, a number of other, less-talked-about articles recounted the shortage of psychologists and counselors in America's heartland, with stories of rural men sometimes traveling several hours to receive the care they need. Oddly, in supposing that men's lone motivation for eschewing mental health services is toxic masculinity, we are assuming that their hesitance is a personal choice rather than a structural impediment, thereby perpetuating the Marlboro Man myth that each guy is in control of his destiny.

Of course, it's breathtakingly naive to think that therapy alone would be enough to redress the larger systemic forces behind a problem like toxic masculinity. But this hasn't stopped a whole plethora of personalized remedies from getting pitched to men as a tonic—a new membership with Cross-Fit, a cathartic jaunt to Burning Man, a weekend retreat in the woods to recover his "deep masculine." "Popular accounts of the male crisis and male confusion," Faludi writes,

> are unrelievedly ahistorical. The conditions under which men live are ignored and men themselves are reduced to a perennial Everyman . . . How would men's problems be perceived, though, if we were to consider men as the subjects of the world, not just its authors?

——

The rest of day two is a derby of self-expression. We take a mid-afternoon hike through the woods and "reconnect with Mother Nature." It's a ritual, we're told, that's been performed in the Middle East for thousands of years, with roots in early Judaism. It involves staggering through the wilderness and "speaking to the universe." While I don't remember the Torah mentioning anything about Moses's unbalanced chakras, I can't help noticing that, for all their attempts to distance themselves from the mythopoetic men's movement, Evryman nevertheless embraces essentialist precepts (gender exclusion, for one), as well as the Iron Johns' impulse toward postmodern sampling. While Robert Bly pulled from Teutonic folklore and African fables, the new men's movement relies upon Gestalt therapy and Eastern traditions, as well as lush strings of corporate slogans and the frothiness of wellness bromides. I can't tell you how many times I heard guys, when struggling with vulnerability, say they really wanted to "lean in."

Still, the carnival of openness affords me a chance to learn more about my Evryman brothers. I hear about lost jobs and unfaithful wives, gambling problems and squandered ambitions. One man, during a "connection" ritual in the woods, confesses to me that he's grown addicted to massage parlors, a meager compensation for his etiolated marriage. Another guy named Rick, who works as a life coach in Ohio, disclosed his earliest memory: his stepfather trying to drown him in a bathtub when he was only two years old. Up until he started doing this work, he mitigated this trauma with a whole menu of iniquitous behavior: pathological overachievement in high school, visits to brothels in the Air Force, to say nothing of his monstrous eruptions at his kids and spouse. "My son has not spoken my name in eleven years. Will not say my name," he says. "I was kind of a bear when he was growing up."

Like Rick, a few of these guys have gothic backstories and are dealing with unresolved childhood trauma. But more consistently the men report feeling spiritually lost or existentially adrift. High achievers in their professional lives—CEOs or team leaders, tech moguls or restaurateurs—these men feel wary about their status in the workplace and are searching for more meaningful interpersonal connections. Again and again throughout the weekend, the guys will sing arias about the soul-withering effects of corporate life, claiming that all the benchmarks of neoliberal achievement—"big salary," "sexy title," "an office in the C suite"—have not conferred upon them any sense of lasting fulfillment.

After yoga that morning, I meet Francis, an oaken-voiced man with an Anderson Cooper haircut, who tells me, "My career has been a fucking mess." A graduate of the Wharton School of Business, he worked for a long time on Wall Street, where he avers "you don't have time to be a human being." Yet while he was checking all the boxes from a professional standpoint, "making my parents happy and doing what I was supposed to be doing," he was vitiated by the cutthroat wagers of the job, and when the markets failed in 2008, he decided to become an entrepreneur. First, he tried to buy a tortilla-manufacturing plant, and later he started a frozen yogurt shop in Florida, but when both ventures crumpled, so did his mental health. "At the time, I was living in Miami, with the balcony overlooking the ocean, and I kept having visions of going over. And that really scared me. That was when I hit my bottom. So I pulled myself up by the bootstraps and made the best of my situation." What he proceeds to describe is a regimen of self-curated therapies: reading books on psychology and neuroscience, experiments with acupuncture and massage, as well as a revolving door of self-actualization trainings through corporate platforms like Landmark. And yet, despite this pageant of self-renovation, Francis says, "there's somebody different who shows up at work. I'm not the guy that's there. I get stressed and fall into a war-like mode and become a different person, which leads to loneliness and disconnection." You'd be forgiven for thinking that such callousness was at least partly due to his vocational situation. But when I innocently posit this, he is quick to personalize the issue, saying the onus is upon him to recalibrate his temperament.

Back in the Main Lodge, it seems like everyone's defenses have been lowered. One consequence of having overactive tear ducts is that the other guys keep assuming that I'm having a slew of emotional breakthroughs and keep sidling over with tender voices to ask how it's going, jokingly wondering if I'm maybe getting more out of this reportorial assignment than I had initially bargained for. At one break, Owen totters over and rubs my back encouragingly, saying, "Wow. Way to show up in Small Group." But if you spend three days in a claustrophobically isolated environment with four dozen other men, all of whom are reckoning with childhood trauma or existential dissatisfaction, then see if you, too, aren't shredded and raw. See if you, too, aren't strangely moved.

The relevant question for me, though, by the end of day two is whether this torrent of emotion is a meaningful intervention into the debate about masculinity, whether Evryman is treating the symptom or the cause. So insistent are they about auditioning and accepting each man's grief, that sometimes I find myself alarmed by the statements that go unaddressed. At a Large Group check-in on Saturday, after a hike through the forest, one man says, "I found an animal bone in the woods. And I put mud on my face. And I missed the meeting." He starts crying. "And I realized that I'm a wild man unfit for modern society. And for that I feel shame." Another man named Tom tells me that he came to Evryman because he felt timid and unassertive but that during his initial Small Group the first words out of his mouth were *I hate men*. "And I looked around and I'm like, fuck, I just ruined the whole weekend. They're going to chase me out of here with burning sticks." Instead, his Small Group facilitator looked him in the eye and invited him to elaborate. "And I said, 'I hate the way men can take up all this space.' And I threw my arms out, and one of the other guys in the group asked, 'How does that feel?' And then I sat with it for a second, and I was like, 'Actually, this feels really good.' And he was like, 'Right. Yeah, take it up and enjoy it.'"

That such comments might benefit from feminist scrutiny seems too obvious to mention, but the docket is so chock-full of activities that we're soon shepherded to the evening's next event, which is the Evryman Talent Show, during which one of my bunkmates, Steve, sings Tom Petty's "Learning to Fly," a sterling tenor rendition that left several men (okay, me) in tears. It's worth noting that by this point, unabashed fraternal PDAs have become rote and commonplace. Two men during the second half of the Talent Show—one a real estate broker from Canada and the other a construction worker from Illinois—take turns tenderly resting their heads on each other's shoulders, looking very much like high school sweethearts.

This is mostly nice, and in this climate, who could possibly complain about well-intentioned men partaking in fulsome acts of affection? After all, is this not a herald of our masculine emotional intelligence? Except I remember that I have paid for this open-armed embrace. I've shelled out good money for a domain in which I can say anything without fear of judgment, where I can wail and caterwaul without batting anyone else's eye. And because the Evryman protocol asks us to refrain from sharing our "stories," and because I have offered only thumbnail sketches of my isolation and despair, there's no meaningful sense in which these guys actually know me, apart from having a vague understanding of my most tender psychological wounds. What else could result from this but the thin simulacrum of brotherhood, a bond based not upon the specifics of my life but upon the shared condition of a Y-chromosome? That there might be more important similarities or differences between us—that our respective ideological, spiritual, or political commitments might actually be radically divergent, if not downright antithetical—none of this matters at Evryman. What matters is your pain.

—

Sunday morning, pre-dawn darkness. The men of Stillwater Cabin lumber through the gloom of our bunkhouse, looking for jackets and boots. We've been asked to report to the Main Lodge in outdoor gear, and soon we're trudging across campus, shuffling under a dark lavender sky still salted with stars. Inside, the coffee tastes like a brown crayon and does little to remedy my exhaustion. Sifting through my emotions, "holding space" for other men, plus the gauntlet of hikes and exercises, has left me ragged with fatigue. I can barely uncurtain my teeth for a smile or a morning hello, and in the bathroom mirror, I observe with interest that my eyes and jowls have begun to sag like those of second-term presidents.

Pretty soon we're told to congregate in the central hall and find a place on the ground. Fifty men now lie supine on the floor, their arms splayed out messianically to the side. Leading this exercise is Tom, one of the Evryman facilitators, a svelte, handsome man from New York City who moonlights as a photographer. "So we're gonna do some pranayama breathwork," Tom says, "I just want you to know that there's nothing dangerous about what we're doing here."

The doth-protest-too-much quality of Tom's proviso already makes me uneasy, even before he explains the technique. It consists of two huffy in-breaths and one violent out-breath, a labored respiration that, when performed, sounds vaguely Lamaze-ish. "In-in-out," Tom intones, snapping his fingers, keeping us in time, occasionally pelting us with varsity-coach commendations: "Good!" "You've got it!" "Listen to the cadence of your brothers!"

I now confront the problem of conveying just how discomfiting this gets, how unnatural it is to respire so forcefully while exerting no other physical effort. The result is a self-imposed hyperventilation. The result is a vertiginous nausea that sends me pinwheeling toward the bathroom, though the men still breathe at a decibel level loud enough to permeate its heavy chestnut door. *Sip-sip-ah,* they breathe. *Sip-sip-ah.*

I don't quite know how to describe what happens next. Tom instructs the men to pick up the pace and says, "If there's a noise that wants to come out, let it come out." One man unfurls a woozy bellow, a sound that recalls the zigzagging deflation of an unknotted balloon. Another man groans Neanderthalically—the first croak a zombie makes after it's been disinterred.

"Let your body do what it wants," Tom yells. "Nothing is wrong here. Make noise. Get primal!"

Now the men become loudly unglued. There are ferocious growls and unbridled sobs, anguished shrieks and boyish gasps. It sounds Dantean in its anger and pain.

"Almost there," Tom says, after a half hour. "Just a few more minutes. Let it scare you."

"I need help!" one man cries. "Please! I need help!" Quickly I dash over, whereupon I discover that the anguished man is Steve, one of my Stillwater bunkmates, and already he's been swarmed by Doty and two other facilitators, one of whom says, "He's hyperventilating. Does anyone have a paper bag?" I hustle toward the nearby kitchen and scan the storage cubby, but there's nothing in either cabinet. Yet when I glance back at Steve, it looks like he's calmed down while Doty lies beside him, whispering assuagements in his ear. Meanwhile, the floor is covered with several dozen men who still writhe and weep, like figures in a *tableau vivant* of a Hieronymus Bosch painting. Once I settle back on my mat, it proves difficult to reenter "the cadence of my brothers," and so I mostly just try to wish myself elsewhere. No matter how daffy and potentially dangerous I find this exercise, I can't help observing that the pain unleashed by these guys is bone-deep and very real. The man to my right is sobbing full-throatedly, his limbs tangled in a fetal position, and he's rocking back and forth in a lost, desolate way, his face violet with woe.

Things reach some sort of apogee when the boy to my left, an undergrad from Ohio State who's spending his spring break with Evryman, whimpers, "Holy shit. This is everything."

Owen Marcus comes over and kneels beside the boy, putting a hand on the kid's chest. He talks now in a fatherly, pastoral way. "Let it come out. You've been holding that for a long time."

"This is insane," the kid says. "I feel like I'm on acid right now."

"Yeah," Marcus says. "Just let the acid take over. Enjoy the trip."

The analogy turns out to be startlingly accurate. For while the Evryman crew alleges that this breathwork derives from the pranayama tradition, which Tom later tells me he learned about in "a class at a yoga studio," it is actually a form of Holotropic Breathwork, a method developed by Stanislav Grof, a Czech-born transpersonal psychologist who influenced the New Age movement throughout the 1970s. In fact, Grof came up with holotropic breathing after lab experiments with LSD were outlawed, and he found that hyper-oxygenation of the blood could produce similar results. Participants underwent oneiric visions, muscle spasms, and hysterical crying jags, all of which induced near-death experiences and helped participants uncork long-dormant emotions. Setting aside the technique's possible salutary effects, it bears noting that over the last few decades the strategy has received no small amount of disapproval. A 1993 report on the practice, for instance, found that it could often trigger seizures in participants or lead to psychosis in vulnerable people. To be fair, Evryman isn't alone in resuscitating this technique. Holotropic Breathwork has become popular at many wellness junkets and spiritual retreats, the sorts of places where muumuus are worn without irony and people sip kombucha on tap.

Huffing on a yoga mat, I'm now in a position to grasp the contemporary men's movement's fundamental appeal. Far from interrogating masculinity head-on, these groups are approaching the issue at a dodgy, sidelong angle and are trying to pitch men's work as a hip, new wellness therapy, no different from any of the other practices that have become faddish in Silicon Valley. See, for instance, Jack Dorsey's regimen of weekend fasts. Or witness Elon Musk's use of nootropics. Later that weekend, Evryman's CEO will tell me that he wants men's groups to be regarded as "CrossFit for your insides," which is precisely what so confounds me about the weekend thus far. They are operating from the premise that men's work can be depoliticized and dehistoricized, that all men need is a good old neoliberal catharsis. It is a worldview that persists under a kind of end-of-history insouciance, a belief that because the system cannot be changed, the best that one can hope for is the chance to blow off some steam.

—

Even though many of us are still visibly attenuated from the Holotropic Breathwork, we are immediately shunted outside and told to walk toward the copse of distant trees, for what activity, exactly, the facilitators will not say. In single file, we tramp across blond, withered grasses, with low velveteen clouds scudding overhead, their edges pink-tinged by the dawn. Several men are still glassy-eyed from the purge, and so our procession into the woods has thus attained a somber, funereal aspect.

At long last, we enter a clearing and wordlessly gather into a circle. Some of the men have put their arms around each other's shoulders, sort of in a band-of-brothers-ish way, and all of our faces are woebegone and depleted. Overhead, birds spew their jargon from the trees, a cheerful rebuke to our sorrow below. Eventually, Aaron Blaine says, "OK. This is the Anger Ceremony. It's your chance to be a victim and let things come up."

In case any of us are confused about what this might mean, Owen Marcus elucidates, "This is a chance for you to let it rip. So, a few things: Be safe. Use your body, but don't throw things or break things, because there might be other guys around." The goal, in other words, is kind of a volcanic expulsion. "Choose someone to get mad at. So who is that person in your life that you're pissed at? It could be your partner. It could be your business partner. It could be your father. Just start with that one person, and if it goes somewhere else, fine. But not you!" he says. "The earth can take it. Grandmother Earth, and all the four elements. Actually, it's a release. The traditional people say, 'Give it away to the earth.'"

Aaron then explains that we should spread out across the forest but stay in view of a partner, presumably for safety purposes. "Once everyone's in place, we're gonna howl. Like a wolf. That's when it starts."

"Don't start howling on your own," Dan MacCombie says. "No false howls."

After all the early morning activities, I can't imagine who might be feeling constipated or repressed, but before I can ask what we're supposed to do if we're already feeling well-ventilated, Aaron says, "Go ahead and find your spots."

With this, we disband and disperse crunchingly through the forest, weaving around a wasteland of sclerotic-looking trees. Eventually, I stumble upon a clearing that faces a flaxen-tinged meadow, at which point Dan and Aaron unleash the inaugurative wolf-call, one that ricochets crisply across the forest. In the distance are the sounds of men stirring with pent-up rage, the tentative throat-clearings of long-suppressed ire. Out of a sense of jour-nalistic obligation, I do my best to participate in the exercise and train my mind on a figure for my anger. But flipping through the Rolodex of possible subjects—my wife, my parents, my students, my siblings—I find myself wholly devoid of the impulse to, as it were, "let it rip." Whether this reveals my habits of suppression and self-blame, or whether this exposes Evryman's false assumption about the exigency of catharsis, I cannot say. All I can tell you for sure is that over the next twenty minutes, I'm made to endure the catacombs of the male psyche, an opera of full-throated pain.

"I'm not your fucking parent! Take care of yourself!"

"Stop fucking laughing at me!"

"Get out! Get the fuck out!"

"Pay attention to me! Fuck me!"

"I don't want to be fucking dead!"

"Be a parent!"

Notwithstanding the troubling implications of this exercise, I can't help wondering whether this aural hellscape might be triggering for some of the men in our company, several of whom are Special Forces veterans, and others of whom have confided to being victims of abuse as children. For a while, in the interest of not going to pieces here in the forest, I turn away from the ceremony and stare at the sylvan resplendence of the clearing, watching the early morning sun peak through a raft of fast-dispersing clouds. Here I find my buddy Tom, a general contractor from California, not screaming but down on his knees, his hands threaded in prayer until he eventually presses them to his ears. Whatever else I might feel about the virtue of this exercise, I find myself choking up at the sight of this man praying for, and terrified by, this outpouring of human emotion.

It turns out Tom and I aren't alone in our trepidation. After the terminating wolf-call and the group reassembles for a round-robin of check-ins, several men reveal their skepticism about the purpose of the Anger Ceremony. "Having grown up with all of that in the house," one man says. "I had a hard time with those noises." Another man says, "Anger just isn't in me." Other men, when asked to describe how it went, are far more enthusiastic. One bullnecked man named Tony, who ascended the glade and rejoined the circle shirtless and glistening, says, "Mother Earth took a beating today. And for that I'm grateful." Later that day, I'll notice that his knuckles are gashed and bleeding, grim relics of the pummeling.

—

After the Anger Ceremony, we're given a much-needed respite, and since this is the final day of the retreat, lots of us are engaged in last-day-of-camp valedictions, swapping hugs and phone numbers, tentatively expressing the kernel of new friendship. I, myself, in the weeks and months to come, will trade emails and texts with Rick and Matt, trying to stay engaged in the switchbacks of their lives. Matt wants to set up a monthly phone call and work on "staying connected," and Rick wants to apply to MFA programs, so I offer to lend advice. This is part of what Evryman calls the "re-integration" process, a term with a pungent whiff of the military, like Odysseus coming home from the Trojan War, now a civilian, once a soldier, still pining for his brothers.

At lunch, I sit with a group of guys to whom I haven't spoken yet. One is a redheaded Aussie who works in corporate branding. He tells me that he came to "the wilds of Ohio" on a fact-finding mission. One of his clients is looking for "an institutional response to masculine challenges" and with Evryman, he believes he's found the best bet. It turns out the Aussie isn't alone in thinking so. Evryman has already been approached by several marquee corporations who are looking to run workshops for their employees. While loath to give specific names, the Evryman crew does tell me they've been approached by a tech colossus in Silicon Valley, as well as one "large-scale blue-collar industrial giant." And yet I can't help thinking that by focusing so monomaniacally on the crusade of emotional intelligence, Evryman has ignored the extent to which these institutions themselves can be instruments of injustice. After all, we may have good reason to be wary of kinder, gentler men, particularly when they're willing to let the structures of capitalism do the work of patriarchy for them. And in failing to address how some of these men are themselves victims of patriarchy, Evryman has erased the potential for men to see their plight as bound up with other communities, particularly those who've long suffered, in far greater ways, under the yoke of this arrangement.

That afternoon, we reconvene in the Main Lodge and gather into one last scrum, with our arms hitched at the elbows or threaded over each other's backs. And as Owen Marcus proceeds to put us into a kind of trance, gruffly exhorting us to "feel what it feels like to be supported," I myself begin drifting off into my own internal hypnosis, feeling myself float to some removed point overhead, and I'm remembering ten years ago when I put a leather belt around my neck. I was living in a garden apartment on the north side of Chicago, where my life had contracted to something dismal and small, a reality trivial enough to abandon. And yet in the waning afternoon light of the retreat center, arm in arm with my Evryman brothers, I am skeptical of dwelling exclusively in the bog of my own sadness. After all, when we shed tears for the veteran Matt, we're ignoring the extent to which his grief has been caused by his armed service, that his inability to connect with his wife stems from the foreign policy decisions that we civilians have tacitly endorsed. Or when I lock arms with this smart-home entrepreneur, I'm invited to ignore the fact that the automation of Silicon Valley will eventually put some two million truck drivers out of work, an impending structural shift that no doubt runs the risk of increasing toxic masculinity. It is an insidious habit of our time to assume that personal deprivations don't have social or political dimensions, that the cure-all can be found in the detour of a retreat or the ablutions of self-care. But what I feel most acutely in this moment, and during the long drive home across the byways of the Midwest, is loneliness. We had talked of an enduring brotherhood, and yet as soon as I leave the retreat center, I realize these men are strangers to me. I try to imagine them making similar journeys home, drawing divergent routes across the country, waiting out layovers in airport lounges, standing under the sickly lights of convenience stores—each man returning to his private grief.

OKAY FOREVER

I find the video buried deep in the C: drive of my father's computer, in a folder called "ANDY: LEGAL." It plays six and a half minutes from December 24, 2005 that were recorded by the front-entrance security camera at a Water Street bar in Milwaukee. The file is called "XMAS05_SWANSON _ACCIDENT," and I'll watch it hundreds of times in the coming months.

The video is at first grainy and blurred, bearing more or less the cinematographic quality of a home movie. Dark figures migrate across a cadet-blue backdrop, and it's during these first ten seconds of the video that you can just barely make out two faceless figures standing toe-to-toe in the center of the frame. There's no audio. The figures mug it out while other daubs of color scuttle here and there, ghosting from one end of the bar to the other, but everything is wholly silent. The two figures could be dancing, exchanging intimacies, kissing even. But around the half-minute mark, the tracking tightens, the dimensions resolve, and the images get pulled into clarity. Here are two men, drunk, spitting taunts and admonitions through gritted teeth. Occasionally they point, at one another's face, or outside toward the sidewalk, where herds of barflies are swerving to and fro, some wearing

Santa hats and ugly knit sweaters. A few people have drifted over to watch the argument, and some of the braver witnesses start pulling on each guy's elbow, offering what must be all the relevant exhortations—*take it easy, let it go, have another one on me.* The crowd thickens in this interval. The paradox of a crowd is that the larger the crowd grows, the harder it becomes to see the inspiration of its origin.

My brother, Andy, is the beefy guy on the right, wearing the black backward cap, a matching muscle shirt, and two earrings in each lobe. In a few hours, the ICU nurses at a nearby hospital will give my mother a Ziploc baggie containing these dented metal hoops, along with two nipple rings, a leather choker-necklace, and an argent chin stud. The camera, though twenty feet above the floor, still conveys Andy's fullback stature. He has the build of a Mason jar, stout and rounded and strong. Right now he's wearing his usual pre-punch expression of what almost looks like sadistic glee, a clown's meretricious grin. I know this expression from childhood, when he used to pummel me with gusto whenever our parents left the house. He wants the other guy to know that he's got exactly zero problem with trading blows if that's what this is going to come down to. In the video, he's acting under vague professional pretenses as a bar bouncer, a job for which he gets paid handsome cash, under the table, and one that has rather unsurprisingly supplied him with extensive knowledge about the many permutations of human aggression. He once told me about dragging some poor sot out of the bar by his ears after the man in question had groped a female patron, and that by the time they made it to the sidewalk, the guy's ears were starting to rip away from his skull. He once described the foul sound his carpal bones made that one time he landed a concussing punch. He has shown me how to take down a guy twice my size by slamming the butt of my palm into the assailant's thorax.

Earlier that evening, only half an hour before what takes place on the video, Andy called me from the bar, using his friend's cell phone so that I wouldn't recognize the number.

"Hello?" I answered groggily. I was home from college on winter break, lying in my childhood bedroom and staring up at the phosphorescent stars I'd once pasted onto the ceiling in haphazard constellations.

"Mr. Barrett Swanson?"

"Who is this?"

"Mr. Swanson, this is the U.S. Census Bureau. We've just been reviewing your information and wanted to know: How do you live with yourself?"

"Andy?"

"Sup, dippy?"

"Where are you?" The reception made it seem like he was traipsing through a wheat field during a windstorm. "Sounds like you're getting buffeted by some real precipitous gale-force winds there, guy."

"Are those real words or Barrett words?"

"Don't be a dick," I said.

"Come down to the bar. I'll buy you shots, find you an older woman."

"I'm in bed. We have to be at Grandma's in like ten hours."

"I know. I'm supposed to glaze the ham."

"Why is it that when you say 'glaze the ham' it sounds like a euphemism for masturbation?"

"Because that's what I meant," he said. In the static-glitzed background, I could hear a dulcet female voice call Andy's name, telling him to hurry up. "Come on, it's Christmas. Show your brother some love."

"You're out of cigarettes, aren't you? You want me to stop at the Mobil and bring you smokes?"

"Maybe I do. Maybe I don't."

"See you tomorrow, Andy."

Around the video's one-minute mark, it looks like the other guy is attempting détente—he holds out his hand as if to shake and make up. In response, Andy grabs himself meaningfully and points. The crowd seems to swell as the other guy rears back and snarls in response, his arm cocked not with forfeiture but intent, but his friends grab him, deactivating the attempted jab. At this point, you can only see his head, there are so many people holding him back. That the whole muddled tableau of my brother and the drunken patron and the anonymous watching mob is entirely silent somehow makes everything worse. In the face of the guy's theatrics, my brother stands firm, and, brazenly, stupidly, kisses his palm and waves. It's the exact same gesture my dad makes whenever angry motorists honk at him for cutting them off. It's the exact same showy semaphore I used to razz linebackers with after I split a cover-two defense and threw a corner fade for a touchdown as a high school quarterback. I understand acutely the delicious mix of peril and pluck that prompts a male from my family to behave this way, to have the gall, the temerity.

Finally, the other guy's friends corral him out of the frosted-glass doors, whereupon they all migrate down the street until they disappear from view. Soon, the bar seems to heal itself. A few coworkers come over and make sure Andy is all right, and after engaging these fellas in a rather complicated-looking sequence of high-fives and fist bumps, he's left alone and the holiday's ambient good feeling seems to resume. Seconds later, a woman wearing a Santa hat and a short leather skirt swivels through the front door, and Andy turns to watch her. It's odd to see my brother like this—confident and cocksure, blustering around the bar like he knows he's being filmed.

He walks outside, where he leans against the front window and lights a cigarette. A feathery plume jets out of his mouth, rises, and disappears. A police car swooshes past, its lights going kaleidoscopically, washing the street with infant pinks and the blue of the long dead. Flurries have started to fall, and within a matter of minutes, the sidewalks look confected. Andy glances left and then right, inhales and exhales, the smoke unspooling, rising. Cars blur by. A group of barhoppers passes him on the sidewalk, and they look like they're singing Christmas carols.

But then it's just as Andy stomps out his cigarette and turns back to the bar's entrance that there's a visual disturbance in the right periphery of the frame, a strident streak of gray, bleary movement, and at this point, the camera's transmission glitches and loses its feed for half a second, a dark blink, but restores itself in time to see the patron who left the bar only moments ago—the other guy—a pace or two away from my brother, who himself is just now beginning to sense and register something racing toward him and now turns to look at the exact moment the guy fires his clenched fist, the impact of which lifts my brother what I swear must be two feet off the ground, so that for the briefest of instants it looks like he's levitating, and as his head arcs down toward the street before his feet follow him, he looks momentarily graceful, majestic, the snow falling in eerie slow motion behind him, but the hideous beauty of this moment ends abruptly when his skull flails back and cracks against the building's brick wall. For the remainder of the video, before the bartender finds my brother splayed out unconscious on the frozen sidewalk, before someone calls the cops, before the ambulance arrives, for these two full minutes before the video runs out and the computer's media player tells me I have the option to PLAY IT AGAIN, the man stands over my brother's body and points, taunting him.

—

The Glasgow Coma Scale is one of many ICU scoring systems used to determine the neurological capacities of persons who present signs of traumatic brain injury (TBI). Both EMTs and emergency room doctors are instructed to assess a cranially injured patient's eye (E), verbal (V), and motor (M) responses, which are then ranked on a scale from 1 (least responsive) to 5 (closest to normal function), meaning that, say, an E1 score would denote a patient's inability to open his eyes; a V2, that his linguistic range amounts to the screech and garble of a smart ape; and an M3, that in response to painful stimuli the patient exhibits a decorticate posture—bending his arms inward to his chest with clenched fists and locking his legs into full extension, a pose that doctors colloquially (and rather cruelly) call "the mummy baby" posture. Any total GCS score less than 9 ranks as a Severe TBI. During his ambulance ride from the snow-dusted sidewalk outside the bar to the entrance of the nearest hospital, nearly seven miles away, my brother's GCS score was very low. Upon their arrival at the ICU, my parents were whisked down to the hospital's little prayer room/chapel to meet with the chief neurosurgeon and a social worker—the hospital's way of informing the family that the patient's prognosis is dire and perhaps fatal.

I imagine Andy's emergency room arrival as a high-octane sequence from *ER*: harried but good-looking doctors in unblemished smocks jog beside his stretcher and shout abstruse medical commands. Tributaries of fresh blood trickle down his face while a female resident asks him whether he can understand what she's saying. His neck is in a foam brace, and his eyes are closed. The right side of his face is already swollen, the skin around the eye bearing the shape and elasticity of a blown bubble of gum. Even though he's unconscious, his hands fidget at his sides, his fingers bending and swooping across the air, which the nurses misinterpret as involuntary muscle spasms resulting from cerebral edema but which are actually finger spellings of ASL, a language that Andy has been studying with a kind of monastic intensity for the last few months. Later, when the nurse points out his odd digital movements, my mother will lose it. A few months ago, Andy, very eager to share his new knowledge, taught us all how to sign the ASL alphabet, and in the intensive care unit, around 4:30 a.m. on Christmas Eve morning, my mother will have watched her oldest son, unconsciously, autonomically, finger-spell what she swore was the same word over and over again: "no."

———

We're not supposed to be here. It's Christmas Eve, and we're all supposed to be at my grandma's lake house, getting drunk on my uncle's old-fashioneds and singing woozy renditions of Bing Crosby songs. We're supposed to be unwrapping presents and *oohing* enthusiastically at the ugly sweaters we've gotten for each other. There's supposed to be eggnog and snickerdoodles and honeyed ham. There's supposed to be a filigreed explosion of Yuletide kitsch: stuffed reindeer with googly eyes hanging from doorknobs, plastic decals of snowflakes plastered to the windows, a toy train orbiting the base of a heavily decorated tree. Someone should be asking us to remember what we did last year. But, instead, there is only this: my brother lying unconscious on a hospital bed, his face beaten and bloodied, a crown of gauze adorning his temple, little highways of tubes snarling up his arms.

Right now it's about 7:30 p.m. on Christmas Eve. My sister, Cat, and Mom flank Andy's bed, and they take turns soaking a rag in a bowl of ice water and scrubbing away the dried blood from his temple. Something about this scene—the silent ablutions, the stoic grief—reminds me of the *Pietà*. Cat is headlong into the sort of adolescent rebellion that will make her cringe in just a few short years but that right now finds its most obvious expression in her portmanteau wardrobe. She wears a gray Mohawk, thrift-store acid-washed hip huggers, a red leather vest (whose origins are wholly unknown), and does her makeup in a way that can only be described as Ancient Egyptian, the collective effect of all of which makes her resemble Pat Benatar if Pat Benatar ever dressed up like a Pharaoh. She reeks of menthol cigarettes, a sick, minty miasma that both Mom and Dad ignore.

Dad sits next to me in one of the comfier chairs that the nurses brought in when they realized the rules about visiting hours weren't going to apply to our family. They have arranged the furniture around Andy's bed stadium-seating style, a feng shui that somehow invites spectation, as if the room itself were suggesting that all we can do is just sit here and watch Andy's brain decide whether he's going to live or die. His room is huge, with large city-facing windows and potted plants. Beige machines with black-and-green monitors draw the horizon line of his pulse. A respirator, which is connected to the oxygen mask he wears, huffs and wheezes, asthmatically.

Mom and Dad's marriage has been in a state of slow attrition these last few years, and as is so often the case during these sorts of familial schisms, the parental alliances have been decided by gender. I am thus the de facto advocate of Dad's marital grievances, and Cat is Mom's, which means that she and I have been regarding one another for the last few months with the casual malice of divorce lawyers.

"Hungry?" Dad asks. He hasn't slept in twenty-four hours, and little psoriatic pouches have gathered under his eyes, lending him the look of a hound dog. Since before I was born, Dad has worn the same neatly trimmed Pancho Villa moustache to distract from his horseshoe hairline.

"Not really." Earlier in the day, Mom insisted Cat and I open our stockings, which she brought to the hospital. Unsure of what to do after we dutifully nibbled at our chocolate Santas, Mom urged us to open a couple of presents, to as best we could carry on with the traditions of Christmas, until someone—I can't remember who—dropped a bulky and extravagantly wrapped box on Andy's stomach, which didn't at all rouse him or make him flinch, and which reminded us of why we were there, prompting us all to agree that it would be better to hold off on presents until later, after Andy woke up.

Above me, the TV broadcasts a Christmas marathon of MTV's *The Real World*, which Cat watches absently, her chair pulled up real close to Andy's bed, her head resting on the edge of the mattress, as if she and Andy were watching the antic shenanigans of hip twentysomethings—people his age—together. Cat's position next to Andy has a *Weekend at Bernie's* falseness to it. On the other side of the bed, Mom looks raddled. Around her eyes are webs of broken capillaries, and her auburn hair has the tousled coiffure of someone who's recently awoken from a nap. She wears big square glasses and a pilled turtleneck.

"So the guy just came up and sucker-punched Andy, that's all we know?" I ask.

"He went outside to smoke a cigarette, the bartender said, and the guy ran up and punched him," Mom says. Her voice is brittle from too much crying.

"Lighting up seems like a pretty innocuous thing to do for someone to put you in the hospital."

"What are you saying?" Dad asks.

"You know how Andy can get."

"What, you think, like, Andy provoked him?" Cat asks.

"I'm just saying that there's probably a reason."

"Guys like that," Dad says, "don't need a reason. They go out *looking* for a fight."

"Andy wouldn't do something like that," Mom says. She looks back at Andy lying on the bed and breathing into the oxygen mask.

One thing Mom and Dad do when one of us kids has either failed to achieve something we really wanted or has fucked up in an appallingly monumental way is that they explain the circumstances of the situation in such contortionate ways that they effectively erase your culpability in the respective failure or fuckup. Dartmouth's application requirements were excessively high; your friend's neighbors were being priggish and unreasonable when they called the cops on the party; you are a young, handsome guy and shouldn't yet tie yourself down to one girl. It's hard to ignore the fact that their airbrushing of the truth, their making you look better or less at fault than you really are, is their way of maintaining their sinless mental image of you. The frequency of these charitable excuses has increased commensurately with the worsening of their marriage, as if Mom and Dad needed to convince themselves that their festering relationship hasn't at all prevented their children from becoming consummate model citizens. To be a good parent of suburban American children then is to be forced into a wholesale bargaining of reality, where one must continually whitewash the faults of one's progeny in order to preserve the daydream of raising the perfect child—as if wishing made it so. It occurs to me that Andy, Cat, and I are thus, perforce, supposed to serve as sterling instantiations of why it's important to *stay together for the kids.*

What I haven't admitted to anyone yet is that I'm not scared. Even though the nurses keep reminding us that even if Andy does wake up, it's all but inevitable that he will suffer from debilitating brain damage that could impair his motor skills, his speech, and his ability to comprehend reality, I remain unfazed, emotionally immobile, frozen inside. I don't know whether this is a manifestation of some sort of deep sadistic pathology lying dormant within me since birth and that I'm just now beginning to realize that I'm some kind of unfeeling sociopath who regards his brother's unconsciousness as just the next thing that has happened in his life, or perhaps it's that Andy's accident has hurtled my brain into such a state of shock that I'm unwilling to register the ghastly realities unfolding in front of me, but the truth is that I'm not worried, that I have maybe chosen to harbor the fanciful delusion that everything will eventually be OK.

One of Andy's nurses—the one who has been tending to my brother with an almost maternal sedulousness—enters the room. Even though we've only been here for fifteen hours, we have grown comfortable with these strangers intruding on our little bivouac of bereavement, carrying out their ministrations while we whisper and weep. Mom is quick to get out of the way and help out if she can, but the nurse says she just needs to quick-change Andy's gauze. A light over his head deepens his features in a way that reminds me of a Caravaggio. And just like that, with exactly no momentousness whatsoever, Andy stirs, groaning full-throatedly, which for obvious reasons—i.e., the persistent worry that he'll surface from this horror with the intellectual capacities of a baboon—unsettles me. He opens his eyes and is swiftly resurrected into a state of total confusion, his face wounded with concern. Then he starts thrashing around the bed, convulsing and screaming. He tears the IV out of his arm. He hikes up his hospital gown and tugs the catheter off of his penis in a way that I assure you does not look painless. "Andy, Andy!" the nurse yells. Dad and I are up from our seats and stand at the edge of the bed. Mom mutters something devout. Cat covers her face with her hands and is looking through the web her fingers make, saying at intervals and with increasing volume as Andy's movements become more frantic, "Mom? Mom?" The nurse hits a button on the gadget near his bed, and within seconds, a few more nurses race into the room. They all work to restrain his arms and legs, a process which, given his considerable hulk, is not executed easily. But before they can even tighten the restraints, Andy relents and lies back, huffing raggedly. An eel of fresh blood squirms down his face.

"Andy, listen to me, honey. It's OK. You're in the ICU, you're in the hospital. Your family is here. I want to ask you a quick question, honey. I want to know if you know what today is. Do you know what day it is? Talk to me, Andy. What day is today?"

His chest rises and falls. His mouth is twisted up, his expression rueful, almost childlike. He looks like he's on the brink of either hysterical laughter or a crying jag. His eyes pan from Cat to Mom to Dad and then to me, where they settle for a minute before they close. The silence is alive, a presence in the room. Then he opens his eyes and looks up at Mom and says, "Presents?"

—

Here's a memory. Andy is about twelve years old, which makes me nine, and we are watching our parents get ready for one of those rare date nights when they gussy up in their nice clothes and head out sans children and drive to their favorite Japanese restaurant where they'll split a bottle of bad wine and eat some weak suburban hibachi. Right now Mom sits on the edge of my parents' bed, looking into a compact and wiping a mar of lipstick off her front tooth, humming along to the Bette Midler playing from the bedside's tinny stereo. She wears her hair in a loose chignon and her perfume reeks of mildewed fruit. Swaddled in a hatchling-yellow blanket, a four-year-old Cat is barnacled to Mom's side. Andy and I sit on the floor and watch Dad titivate in the bedroom mirror, futzing with his moustache and the knot of his Windsor, and because he can sense us watching, he hams it up for us, doing his Rodney Dangerfield impressions, all throttle-popped eyeballs and raspy exclamations of disbelief—*Hey, I don't get no respect!* Andy and I eat this up, not because we've seen *Caddyshack* or *Easy Money*, but because this is our father being silly, performing with Vaudevillian animation, just for us. It's one of those few times where he's cut-loose happy, giddy at the prospect of having a night alone with his wife. But even as I'm laughing, I'm growing acutely conscious of the fact that soon our ranch-style suburban home will be empty of parental authority and the sensible code of conduct it enforces, including such provisos as NO FIGHTING, which, of course, means that my brother, riled from an adolescently fraught week at middle school, is going to be able to evoke and cathart his rage on the putative human punching bag little brothers everywhere are supposed to serve as. It's not like I don't understand the child-raising bromide—*boys will be boys* (a tautology that I find about as reasonable as it is poetic)—or that my brother's roughhousing *always* wandered out of the realm of sibling roughhousing and into the vaguely demarcated territory of torture, but I will say that as an inveterately sensitive young boy, in the sometimes hour-long throes of grunting struggle against my brother, I had a very tricky time parsing the differences between the expected fraternal horseplay and the diabolical violence in which my brother seemed to revel.

Sometimes my fear would be unwarranted, and we would end up watching *Big* or *The Sandlot* on the couch while our parents were out. But other times were of course different, darker. I forget how these epic brawls began. The scenes emerge out of the film-fade of memory, in medias res, disjointed and gauzily edged, fragmented by forgetting. And yet, during their dramatic zeniths, they do take on a high-definition clarity, a plasma-screened pixelation—that one time Andy pretzelled his legs around my stomach and squeezed until I screamed so loud that I popped blood vessels in my right eye; the time he jumped off the top of the couch and landed on me, breaking my arm; the time he and his friend locked me in a closet with the light off for an hour; the time he threw me down the stairs because I wouldn't tell him what Mom had gotten him for his birthday.

Sitting here next to the hospital room's window, in the wine light of a molten sunset, what frightens me most is there were times when I was a kid that I actually prayed to my puerile idea of God—a kind of cosmic genie who would grant my every wish and cede to my every demand—and asked for something like this to happen, for Andy to get hurt so disastrously that his proclivity to beat me up would be, in turn, concussed out of him. I imagined him bloody-faced and crying. I wanted to see him hurt and puling, crawling toward me, begging for clemency. I fantasized about standing above my brother, looming, pointing. Asking him how he liked it.

—

It strikes none of my family members as odd that the chief neurosurgeon has decided to hold Andy's X-ray against the window, blazed to a golden foil by the early morning sun, instead of just using the lightbox on the wall. It's Christmas Day, about thirty hours since Andy was wheeled into this room. The doctor has a little bejeweled Rudolph brooch clipped to his lapel. He points to the image's amorphous shapes: the dark areas indicate infarction (tissue death) or edema (abnormal accumulation of fluid), and the bright, diaphanous portions signify calcification, hemorrhaging, or the displacement of bone. There's a hideous gorgeousness to the pictures. Seven contusions bleed across my brother's brain in dark blotches that are somehow reminiscent of those black scourges of communism and fascism that overtook world maps in those old duck-and-cover films. Mom asks about our options. The doctor says that depends on a number of factors, but right now we need to let his brain heal on its own, as best it can. He tells us with professional alacrity to sit tight and keep praying. There's an odd apparitional quality to the shapes that have developed on the celluloid sheet that the doc still holds pressed against the windowpane, as if what were being displayed here were not so much an index of the damage done to my brother's brain, but an imprint of his ghost, a scanner-blast of his soul.

—

Here's the truly distressing double bind about hospital gift shops: usually you purchase a gift because you want to surprise the giftee with something heartfelt and special, an emblem of true affection, but because the medical events that bring someone to the hospital typically occur without warning, you have no time to dash out and select something useful or thoughtful or etc., all of which is problematic because, of course, any sentient convalescent is going to know the various merchandise that a standard gift shop carries and will thusly be able to surmise that you picked out the sea-salt chocolates and the "Get Well" Mylar balloon and the Calvin and Hobbes sympathy card you gave them *at the hospital gift shop*, meaning that the whole act of giving the gift is going to look obligatory, carried out in deference to trite social conventions and just so that you could say you brought the person something, which maybe isn't that big of a deal if the person is just a friend or a colleague or some distant relative you never much see, but when the person is your brother and his chances of survival are touch and go and his cognitive abilities at this point are on par with a drowsy infant's, the paucity of gift choices can run you down to the point where you're sobbing in public with your face pressed against the stuffed pectoral of an oversized Foghorn Leghorn, which of course draws concerned looks from the other gift shop patrons until eventually the kind lady behind the register offers you a diet soda and crackers, allowing you to sit on a stool in the shop's back office where a little black-and-white TV is playing the Packers game, which makes you feel better for a little while, even if we're down 21–17 at half.

—

No one who knew Andy well would have thought that at twenty-three years old he'd end up bouncing at a Water Street bar. In high school, he cultivated an image of himself as a brooding *artiste*, a sensitive type who eschewed any and all displays of machismo. Aside from being an indispensable part of the high school's award-winning choir, Andy was also in a professional performing group that did shows at events and festivals all across Wisconsin and to which he contributed a winning stage presence and a syrupy baritone.* Along with his thespian achievements, Andy was also a prodigiously gifted painter, influenced by the controlled technique of Cézanne, the creative caprice of early Jackson Pollock, and the theoretical pursuits of Jim Dine. As a high school senior, Andy had exhibitions at privately owned galleries and even sold some of his work. His was a talent so refined that he was accepted to the Minneapolis College of Art and Design (MCAD)—one of the best art schools in the country—on a full scholarship. And the truth was that Andy couldn't wait to get out of there. Growing up in an affluent suburb of Milwaukee, which was known for its big shopping plaza, was for him variously like walking around the soundstage of *Leave It to Beaver* and the set of *Blue Velvet.* Around town, in grocery stores, denizens regarded one another with a kind of caffeinated cheeriness that I can now only describe as a model for customer service. For Andy, a flannel-wearing, teenaged misanthrope who rode skateboards and smoked Camels and sometimes drank vodka out of Evian bottles before school, this was a suffocating environment, one that he started rebelling against by the time he hit puberty. But at MCAD he thrived socially and excelled academically. By the end of his second semester, his work was so roundly admired by his peers and the faculty that one of the printmaking professors asked him to be his TA for the following fall semester, an unprecedented achievement for a freshman, according to the school's lore.

But then one night, in one of life's weird, unforeseen peripeteias, Andy

---

* Full disclosure: I, too, was a member of this group in my more impressionable early teenaged years, when the group's uniform of jazz shoes, pink cummerbunds, black tuxedo shirts, and chartreuse silk vests didn't seem like that big of a threat to one's reputation as a tough-guy jock.

went to his studio, threw on the newest Spiritualized album, and apparently got so intoxicated that the world contracted to something bitter and small, a reality trivial enough to abandon. At some point that night, he destroyed most of his paintings, kicking holes into canvases, using his hands to shred sketchpads. Then he went to a party in Uptown, by Lake Calhoun, and no one's exactly sure what happened after that. He surfaced the next morning, at around 7:30 a.m., while walking down a residential road in St. Paul, nearly seventeen miles away from where he lived, and as he watched joggers huffing down the sidewalk and a delivery man toss newspapers out of a slow-moving car and a sprinkler spray a helix of dawn-glinted water onto a nearby front lawn, he looked down at his bleeding hands and his torn shirt and realized that he needed to come home.

Ruined and then annealed by his misfortunes at MCAD, he lived in the carpeted room of our home's flood-damaged basement, got a job as a sales associate at Restoration Hardware, and started hanging out with some of his old friends, whose puny ambitions didn't take them very far from home. He got a tattoo and pierced his lip. I rarely saw him during this period, but when I did, we would occasionally engage in drunken, bumbling tête-à-têtes. Whenever I brought up those fights from childhood, he would misremember the episodes or contend they weren't as bad as I had characterized them. "Besides," he said, "that I beat you up probably made you more sensitive, which is why you're such a good writer. So, really, you can thank me for that." He'd usually punctuate these aperçus by tipping the top of his beer bottle toward me, as if we were coming to some sort of agreement.

When he saved up enough money, he moved out. Having worked in restaurants while going to school in Minneapolis, he was quickly hired as a sous-chef at a posh trattoria on the East Side and soon fell into the cash-burning rhythms of the late-night service industry, which is to say that whenever he wasn't working, Andy was eating at friends' restaurants, out partying at the local bars, or inviting his service-industry friends over for dawn-seeing parties. The owner of the bar, whom Andy met during this period of heavy carousing, asked Andy to do some part-time bouncing work, under the table, to which he ultimately agreed.*

On the night of the assault, before he showed up at the bar, Andy had been dancing in the halftime show of a Milwaukee Bucks basketball game. The incongruity of these events startles me—one minute he's doing a round-off at the Bradley Center wearing spandex and jazz shoes, and the next, he's grabbing his unit and telling a bar patron to go fuck himself. It turned out that one of his old friends from the performing group had become a Bucks cheerleader and asked Andy to dance with her because that night's choreography featured a lot of complicated lifts and gymnastic maneuvers, which a guy of Andy's strength and stature could execute effortlessly. After the show, as he and the rest of the male dancers drank celebratory beers with the cheerleaders, toasting one another on a job well done, Andy got a call from his boss at the bar—an oleaginous guy who every time I saw him wore tortoiseshell glasses and a Boston Red Sox cap—asking that he come in to help with the Christmas Eve rush. An hour or so later, Andy showed up and was informed about a patron who'd been making lewd advances toward the female bartender all night. Andy tapped the guy on the shoulder, and the two had a conversation near the entrance, the mute surveillance camera version of which I watched hundreds of times a few months later. I never found out what exactly was said between them—whether my brother stepped outside the ambit of his professional duties as a bouncer and provoked the guy. In fact, it seemed any possible culpability on Andy's part was rinsed away by the fact that he ended up unconscious in the hospital.

—

* Andy's failure to sign a contract was something I later regarded as breathtakingly stupid, especially since it allowed the bar owner to wangle his way out of paying Andy's workers' compensation, thus causing all sorts of financial/legal migraines for my parents. When Andy finally left the hospital, the boss had the gall to visit our house and bring Andy an Xbox 360 as a gesture of apology and recompense. What a guy.

At night, there's an odd, oneiric quality to the ICU. All the overhead fluorescents have been turned off, but the galaxy of power indicators on everyone's
machines are of course still on, so that when you walk down the hallway
and peek into other people's rooms, it looks like each person is recumbently
manning the switchboard of a space station. All the nurses shuffle here and
there in their sensible sneakers, whispering to one another updates about
this or that. I drift back to Andy's room with an intoxicated listlessness,
my body still humming with the memory of the cigarette I stole from Cat's
purse and sucked down in the underground parking lot only moments ago.
Inside the room, everyone's asleep. Mom lies on the cot next to the window,
using her peacoat as a blanket. Cat is crumpled up like a crustacean in the
chair, her hands clasped together prayer-like and wedged between her knees,
her Mohawk mashed against her pillow. Dad lies collapsed on the floor like
he fell through the roof, using a rolled-up jacket as bedding. Andy is awake.
His right eye is still swollen to a slit, the bruise around it the color of a wine
stain, its shape no more symmetrical than a Rorschach blot. But his left eye
is trained on me in the sort of way children under two will stare dazedly at
you when you make little gaga faces at them. He looks like he's trying to
figure out who I am, but he doesn't seem alarmed or concerned about my
presence in the room. I walk over to him and hold his hand, acutely aware
that I'm reenacting just about every hospital scene from every TV drama,
major motion picture, and novel that I have consumed in my heavily me-
diated nineteen years. I resist the urge to say something genre-appropriate
like *we're gonna get through this.* He looks down at our embrace, indifferent,
just curious. The machine beside him aspirates and contracts. I can feel my
father's snoring in my chest, even from across the room.

"How are you doing, guy?" I whisper. "Do you know who I am?" The
nurses have encouraged us to ask him this question, to get him to tell us our
names. Even though it feels ridiculous—it's the type of thing you quiz your
friends' children on—the nurses say it's important we test his memory with
easy ones, as if our identities were simply a matter of trivia. I keep meaning

to ask the nurses what we should say on the off chance that Andy can't answer this question. What are we supposed to ask him then?

"Andy, it's your brother," I say, right up close to his ear. "Do you know my name?"

The machine behind him beeps as it draws the green cliffside of his pulse. He closes his eyes, inhales and exhales steadily, a sound I've grown to covet.

—

For an entire day, the guy who did this to my brother ran free. He went home that night, slept, and woke up on Christmas morning. Throughout the first day in the hospital, I spent what turned out to be an unhealthy amount of time imagining what sorts of Yuletide fun was being had by my brother's assailant. Maybe he wore something festive, a red cable-knit sweater and green chinos. Maybe he styled his hair with pomade. Maybe he visited his grandmother in the nursing home. Maybe he and his father reconciled after years of strained communication. Maybe he ladled out chili at a soup kitchen, or washed bedsheets at a homeless shelter. Maybe he sang Christmas carols at the VFW. Maybe he drank more. Maybe he masturbated. Maybe he played football in a snowy park with a group of rowdy friends. Maybe he and his girlfriend had gentle sex next to a dawn-facing window. Maybe he was a good person. Maybe he wasn't normally like this. Maybe he was just blotto and made a bad decision. Maybe he went to church and was washed with little geodes of light beaming through the stained glass. Maybe he prayed that my brother was OK.

But it turned out that on Christmas night, my brother's assailant was at a family party, eating shrimp cocktail and standing with some of his male relatives in front of a big-screen TV. At a certain point, after all the small talk (and what I imagine had to have been more than a judicious amount of brandy-laden eggnog), the guy began cheerfully alluding to knocking someone out at a Water Street bar. In one of the incident's weirder twists of fate, my uncle, who's something of a socialite and has a long roster of friends and just so happened to be at this party, overheard the assailant's bluster. My uncle excused himself from his conversation, walked over to the scrum of men by the TV, and asked the assailant whether this incident had occurred at Andy's bar. The guy nodded, smiling. My uncle then gave him a rather merciful ultimatum: either the guy turn himself in or he would do the honors and call the cops. When he related the story to us an hour or so later, he said that never once in his life had he felt more like Columbo.

—

It's only when I'm urged to get out of the ICU for the night and told to go see some friends, and thus leave these hallways fumigated with grief and disease, and finally exit the hospital's automatic sliding doors that open along their tracks with a respiratory hiss, that I am overwhelmed by an incredible soaring relief. I'm nineteen and on winter break from my second year at college, and even though my brother is in the hospital, I'm still able to go out into the December evening and find a friend's party and drink watery beer and forget the vertiginous events of the last two weekends. It's only after I call my friend Sam, and learn that another friend's parents are out of town and that she's having a party, and drive over to her house and enter without knocking and am swarmed by friends and strangers alike who, I shit you not, form a little line to greet me with their sympathy and concern that I begin to understand the unbelievable advantages of having a moribund brother in the hospital. *Barrett, take a quick pull of this scotch I got here. Have a ciggy with me, Swany? Give me an update about yer bro's prognostication, guy. Yo, b-man, what's the story with your bruh? Your brother's in the hospital, that must be horrible, huh?* After a few drinks, I'm feeling better, shined-up and mercurial, able to converse prolixly with everyone, and I explain the dire state of Andy's condition with an anesthetized fluidity. I realize that

I'm the god of this story, that I can make it seem as bad as I want, that I am in control of my brother's life in this moment. I consider telling them about the contusions and the post-traumatic seizures and the one pamphlet I read about dealing with a brain-damaged loved one, but as the scotch marinates my bloodstream, my summary of his prognosis takes a markedly optimistic turn and instead I tell everyone he's nearly back to normal and the doctors say he'll be out of the hospital in just a few days. As long as I can convince them of this story, as long as people think Andy's going to be OK, then at least for the night, he will be.

—

Spend a week in the ICU and roam the hospital's scrubbed and sanitized hallways and you'll eventually notice the squadron of janitors and cleaning people who wear khaki jumpsuits and assiduously wax and sterilize just about every linoleum surface until all the hallways are lemon-scented and gleaming, lest the perfume of blood and carrion waft into other rooms and remind the ill and infirm of their ultimate fate. As much as the doctors and nurses and staff work to facilitate convalescence, there seems to be a tandem and equivalent effort to expurgate death from the hospital's interior-decorative arrangement. Looked at closely, a hospital—with its white walls and white-coated doctors and white-smocked nurses and white bedsheets and white towels and white glinting floors and white Formica surfaces—appears to be one large contrivance toward the heavens, a huge portal through which the diseased and dying can pass seamlessly into the white light.

Sleep-deprived and commensurately bereft, I begin to resent the hospital for this curatorial effort, because the truth is that at a certain point in this line of thinking, you begin to associate the monochromatic environment with the very thing its sterility and cleanliness and homey ambiance are trying desperately to conceal—namely, your own mortality—which makes the whole thing a lot like listening to a car salesman tell you he's offering a real sweet deal while you test-drive a Buick without brakes. Exacerbating my anger about all this is the fact that nearly every doctor, RN, CNA, resident, and intern looks hale and happy and gorgeously complected, their skin untouched by any blemish or mole or liver spot, their bodies gym-fit and libidinous.

Cosmetic discrepancies between staff and patients notwithstanding, the true root of my outsized anger stems from the fact that my brother can't remember my name. Every night, when everyone else is asleep, I return to his bedside and ask him to tell me who I am. Invariably, he just stares and stares. At times, his confusion is so total that it looks contrived and I almost think he's putting me on. I have to restrain myself from smacking his head and shouting, *Come on, do it, asshole, say my fucking name!* It occurs to me that what would be way worse than Andy dying would be Andy living and having no memory. Because if he surfaces from this neurological oblivion with no recall of who I am or what we've been through together, then in a certain way it'll be me who has died as a result of that punch. He won't associate my face with the person who came to every single one of his gallery openings, the person who used to beg him to perform that skateboarding trick one more time in the driveway. Maybe it's selfish, but the truth is that during these moments I begin to grieve the loss of the person who lived inside my brother's head, the person I was to him.

—

By the 30th of December, almost everyone has stopped by—family, friends, coworkers, his boss. When his ex-girlfriend stops by and massages his feet, Andy wakes up and smiles at her knowingly, as if the sensation were an inside joke between them. And yet he doesn't respond when she calls him by his pet name, "Mister." Everyone brings him an offering, but given his prognosis—i.e., a traumatic brain injury—it's hard not to see most of their gifts as cruel: board games, crossword puzzles, the new Lincoln biography. When one of his friends hands me a one-thousand-piece jigsaw puzzle (which I know that motherfucking asshole bought in the gift shop; I saw it), I say, expressing my nineteen-year-old-little-brother indignation, "Dude, seriously?" For the most part, though, I labor hard to hide my contempt for their thoughtlessness, to return their words of concern with appreciative hugs. Everyone brings flowers. Whole nomenclatures of tulips and daffodils and water lilies line the windowsill and tables. The room blazes with these little bonfires of color to which Andy, when he's awake and trying to stay engaged, will point and say things like "What's with that dog?" or "Gimme that nova there." Most of the time, though, he just sleeps.

And yet he has made substantial progress. The doctors keep our expectations in check by reminding us that just because Andy can recognize Mom and Dad and knows what day it is, it doesn't mean that his will be a full recovery. They warn of aphasia, post-traumatic seizures, ataxia, depression, and memory loss. We try to exercise cautious optimism, but it's difficult not to be heartened by his improvements. Yesterday, our aunt, fresh in from Las Vegas where she lives, stopped by to check on Andy. A few months ago, Nancy paid for Andy's veneers—all his life his teeth had huge gaps between them, going all the way back to his molars, which somehow made him look feral or malnourished. When she came over to Andy's bed and said, "Hiya, sweetheart, how you feeling?" Andy looked over at her and opened his cheeks really wide—it was a smile without emotion, like a monkey's—to reveal a mouth full of teeth so straight and pristine they could have sold toothpaste. Nancy screamed with laughter and Mom started to cry, both of them realizing that this meant Andy not only knew who Nancy was but could remember something from a few months ago, which suggested that his long-term memory was still in working order.

But the true bellwether of his progress occurred earlier this morning when Andy was scheduled for a shower. The youngest of his nurses—who goes to UWM and who laughed at my joke about Andy's boss looking like a sober Robert Downey Jr.—approached Andy's bed, brandishing a little scrub tub and loofah. "Looks like I'm the one who's washing you today," she said. I squeezed Andy's arm until he looked at me with a kind of resigned weariness—the way everyone looks when they're in line at the DMV—and I mouthed, *You lucky bastard.* No response. "Do you understand me, Andy? I'm gonna help you take a shower today." He looked at the woman and then looked at me, clearly confused, as if she were reciting Dadaist poetry. "Andy?" A silence followed, a brief interlude of beeping machines and voices coming from another room. I could already see the joke hanging in his eyes. Without any facial expression or vocal affectation whatsoever, Andy said, "I think you should meet my mom first."

—

My tuxedo shirt is too tight and Andy's pant legs are too long. He's fixing his cufflinks while I tend to his crooked boutonnière. It's late August, years later, and it's his wedding day. We're standing under an amber sky in the little rhomboid of grass outside his house on the East Side of Milwaukee, waiting for one of Andy's other groomsmen to arrive before we head over to the Astor Hotel, where Andy will swap vows with his fiancée. (Andy will buy Cat and me tequila shots at the cash bar, and Mom and Dad will be amicable for the night, despite their recent divorce.) Birds chitter overhead and the wind is like something out of Tarkovsky, strong and tidal-sounding, a portent of obscure meaning. The yard's trees and shrubbery are so green they look like they've been treated with food coloring. He keeps his hair Agassi-short, and his stocky stature fills out his tux rather sharply. His face and neck are lightly shellacked with sweat.

"Nervous?" I ask.

He frowns and then feints a jab at my face, and I flinch, and for half a second I think he's serious, but he breaks into a smile, so I lasso my arms around his neck and bring him in for a hug.

"Big day," he says, smiling. "Huge day."

The straggler arrives and we all get into our cars. Andy and I ride together, in his crummy, grumbling Taurus, and soon we're speeding down Kinnickinnic Avenue, past the hipster thrift stores and fair-trade cafés and organic pet depots, and we cross the bridge into the Third Ward, with its boutiques and its spas and its aura of opulence. We're on Water Street when we hit a red light. Broken glass speckles the cement and coruscates in the sun. Crushed beer cans pock the sidewalk. A discarded stiletto is stuck in a nearby sewer grate. The street has an eerie evacuated quality, as if God made a mistake and only the frat boys and party girls got raptured.

There's not one scar on his face. The last vestige of the assault was the scar tissue that mottled his temple like cottage cheese, but it disintegrated about a year ago. That's not to say that his recovery was without hitches. His was an Iliad of cognitive rehabilitation. After getting discharged from the hospital, Andy spent nearly two months on the couch, slack-jawed and sedentary, and watched staggering amounts of syndicated TV. *Star Trek* and *Seinfeld* were among his favorites. At times, his confusion was precocious— adorable even. When someone called the house for Andy and I'd hand him the phone, he would stare at the device for upwards of thirty seconds, seemingly perplexed about what he was supposed to do with this odd gadget. I had to show him how to hold it against his ear. Other times, he'd walk into a room, forget why he was there, and utter non sequiturs like "Well, how do I fashion *this* news report?" In the middle of the night, he took to sneaking into Cat's bedroom, and without expression, throwing his balled-up socks at her sleeping face, trying to be funny, but actually sort of freaking Cat out. But there were moments where he'd look at you with a kind of abused confusion and then say something cryptic like "You don't look like you." He went to physical therapy and cognitive therapy and slept on the couch. In spits and spells, he had memory lapses, the most disturbing of which involved him forgetting that he had been beaten up and then trying to leave the house. Because of his neurological fragility, we were forbidden from letting Andy go out on his own, lest any slight bump or chance bop of the head trigger a hemorrhaging afterclap. One time he got so insistent about leaving that he pushed Dad, who was blocking the front door, to the ground. Still, after nearly six months, he recovered. As the civil and criminal trials were being adjudicated, if at a glacial pace, my brother decided to drop the criminal charges against his assailant. When I asked him about this act of strange mercy, he said, "At that point in my life, that could have been me on the other end of that punch."

The red light is long, but we don't mind. The wedding can't start without the groom and his best man. Andy has put on *Purple*, the Stone Temple Pilots album, which is one of those records that's so thematically perfect that you never have to skip to the next song, since each one has a kind of anthemic quality, as if Scott Weiland were eulogizing every hue and nuance of your sad, disastrous adolescence.

The light turns green, but Andy has his eyes closed as he belts the song's chorus. He's drumming the wheel and swaying his head back and forth, and I laugh as cars start honking behind us. It could be his buzz cut or his late-summer tan, but Andy's face retains a youthfulness so stark that he looks younger than I do. And maybe it's the occasion and his pre-wedding jitters, but for a minute, I feel like the older brother and am momentarily overcome with the urge to tell him a story, to assure him that he's ready for this, that he need not worry about what comes next, that no matter what, I'll be right here and everything will be okay forever and ever. Things that during the crisis of childhood I wish he would have said to me. The truth is, of course, that the story does not end here at the stoplight beneath the clear blue wash of a Wisconsin sky, does not end as I close my eyes and join Andy in this moment of willed blindness. Nor does it end in this darkness, as I listen, among the blare of music and beeping cars, for the sound of my brother's voice. And though this is not the ending of our story, it's the one I keep telling myself, the one I think that, in the wake of all that has happened, my brother and I just might be willing to believe.

THE SOLDIER
AND THE SOIL

At the beginning of the summer, in the middle of the country, dawn breaks over the heartland. The village of Waunakee is minced with lonesome county roads, a town where men sport Carhartt and chew Skoal, where women don teased bouffants, where the little ones play football even though everyone knows it will ruin their brains. To the north sits the Holy Wisdom monastery, where a circle of Benedictine women nurture a community garden and recite the Liturgy of Hours every weekday at noon, and to the south is Wisconsin Scaryland, a haunted house that used to be a Stop & Go fueling station but now frightens carloads of Wisconsinites on frigid October evenings. Between these cosmic polarities, the land of Waunakee is dominated by garish rows of corporate corn, which are as tall as a man and so meticulously arranged they seem to resemble a military formation. But after a couple miles something goes wrong. There is a break in the pattern, a mutiny in the landscape. In the center of these steroidal, chemically treated cornfields are eleven acres of plush organic farmland, the perimeter of which has been buffered with a wall of fulsome sunflowers.

"I planted them," Steve Acheson tells me, "because that sharecropper next door drenches his corn with Roundup, and the last thing I wanted was my produce getting soaked with the same shit they sprayed on my buddies in Vietnam." While Steve is only thirty and fought in Operation Iraqi Freedom, many of the workers on his veteran-led farm served in the Tet Offensive and were exposed to Agent Orange. Whenever these curtains of pesticide drift into Steve's fields, their skin undergoes an allergic reaction called chloracne, a nasty crimson rash of blisters and boils. As we walk the borders of his farm, Steve's eyes are lowered under a faded brigadier cap, and tendrils of black hair sprout from its brim. He wears an *Iraq Veterans Against the War* t-shirt, and his skin is teak-brown, dark as syrup. He points up at the sunflowers, whose broad golden-rayed blossoms seem to have absorbed the worst of the sharecropper's toxins. Now they hang limp and withered, the posture of a dejected person. "Within a couple weeks, they died," Steve says, "which kind of sucked, since they're pretty, but that's what they're supposed to do."

—

I first heard about Peacefully Organic Produce at the beginning of the summer while playing pickup basketball with some colleagues from work. I teach English at a small Dominican college in Madison, Wisconsin, serving as an adjunct instructor, which is essentially the academy's version of a fry cook. As we dribbled under yolky sunlight, my friend Josh gushed about his weekly CSA parcel, a topic of conversation that is, I confess, totally unremarkable in a granola-crunching town like Madison. An incorrigible foodie, Josh raved about the vegetables, praising their bold colors and intricate mouthfeel. The farm was called Peacefully Organic Produce, "and the guy who runs the place," Josh said, "is absolutely incredible." He proceeded to describe Steve Acheson, a young Iraq War vet who had been something of an eminence in the contemporary antiwar movement and had apparently thrown away his service medals at a 2012 NATO summit in Chicago. A few years ago, Steve withdrew from activist circles and moved to Waunakee to start the veteran farm, trading the rancor of dissidence for the tranquility of the plains. "Sometimes in the furrows, out of nowhere, he'll blurt things like *Fuck the Koch brothers!*" Josh said. "And I'm like, *what?* And then he explains that the twine we're using to trellis the tomatoes is actually manufactured by Koch Industries."

Over the previous couple years, I had developed an abiding interest in veterans' issues, mostly because so many of my students were veterans of the Iraq War. These men and women would sit stoically in the back of my classroom, unamused by my standard dog and pony show, my wretched attempts to be the "cool professor." They'd joggle their knees at insane speeds and stare out the window with faraway expressions, recalling the "thick-eyed musing" that Lady Percy accuses Hotspur of in Shakespeare's *Henry IV.* Still, their prose often stood head and shoulders above the standard freshman drivel, exhibiting a certain rigor of thought and depth of feeling that perhaps comes from having witnessed whole anthologies of trauma—entire villages razed by fire, wide-eyed children draped in gore, wives screaming beside mutilated husbands.

Many of these vets were as old—if not older—than I, and seemed like uncanny incarnations of the kids I had known in high school. I had been a baby-faced junior when the Twin Towers fell—during Algebra 2, the principal came over the PA, delivering the news in a soft, grief-cracked contralto—and many of my classmates would eventually enlist out of revenge, economic necessity, or a marrow-level sense of civic obligation. (*Ask not what your country can do for you*, and so on.) Over a decade later, face-to-face with these students, who had been halfway around the world and back, who often stared at me with spooked eyes and a squirrelly intensity, I was forced to confront certain aspects of myself that I'm reluctant to admit. The fact of the matter is that while I went off to college and attended keggers, these men and women were devoting their lives to certain fleecy abstractions that would make most of the civilians I know roll their eyes: duty, honor, and country.

In the U.S., it's customary to honor our veterans with the following shibboleth: "Thank You for Your Service." If you see uniformed individuals in airports or checkout lines, it's proper decorum to sidle up and offer this brusque hosanna. But for some reason, whenever my students would talk about their service, I could never bring myself to utter this phrase. It wasn't that I didn't feel some measure of gratitude toward them, nor was my silence some kind of artful partisan complaint. Rather, "Thank You for Your Service" struck me as sterile, a neutered term, the type of grandiose abstraction that implies everything but doesn't actually mean anything. After all, what exactly was I thankful for? That it wasn't me who had withered in the deserts of a foreign country and risked head and hide for a cluster of eighteenth-century ideas? That, adjusted for inflation, gas prices have remained relatively constant over the last forty years?

Throughout the early days of summer, my friend Josh kept mentioning Steve, and one evening in early June, I found myself googling the farm. Peacefully Organic Produce, it turned out, had a slick, well-curated website, teeming with photos of vegetables that were so lurid and engorged they verged on being pornographic. One photo showed Steve—a tan, darkly featured guy with jam-band hair and a rakish smile. In the photo, he's back-dropped by sunflowers, his arms outstretched beatifically, as if to say, *can you believe this?*

—

The packing shed at Peacefully Organic Produce is a temple of antiwar sentiment. Its walls are papered with dissident posters, most of which resemble the homespun covers of pamphlets and zines, with grayscale illustrations drafted in black Sharpie marker. *War Is Trauma*, one reads. *Support GI Resistance*, says another. Right now, Steve is rummaging through the storage cooler while bragging about the time he met Tom Morello of Rage Against the Machine.

"He was up front marching with us at a protest in D.C. At some point, he turns to me and is like, *Hey man, can you get my guitar?*" Steve beams at the memory. "So I haul ass backstage and fetch his acoustic."

Ever since I arrived at the farm, Steve has been zooming hill and dale through his morning chores: harvesting salad greens for a wholesale order, delegating jobs to his veteran staff, and tilling the cabbage beds for new seedlings. I keep offering to help, but he consistently begs off in a distinctly Midwestern fashion, saying, "Aw, thanks, man," but then never actually assigning me any tasks. Throughout these errands, he offers an unbroken stream of autobiography—about his deployment, about his activism, about his middle school wrestling career. One of my best friends from childhood had been all-state, and when I mention this, Steve pokes his head out of the storage cooler and asks, with mortal seriousness, "What was his name?"

I tell him, and he says, "Oh, yeah. I remember that kid. I beat the shit out of him."

At the rear of the packing shed, the doorway glows with torrid sunshine, and I follow Steve through it, swiftly entering a nirvana of color. Rambling out to the distant wood line, the farm is lush and mesmerically green, bearing a whole nomenclature of organic vegetables—from chard to arugula, beets to patty pans, basil to summer squash. Flocks of volunteers pluck thistle in the furrows, their brows stitched with concentration. Smedley, the farm's jovial yellow lab, appears beside us, dragging a tree branch that is the size of a dinosaur bone, the jagged broken end of which digs a rivet in the grass, prompting Steve to say, "Showoff."

As we meander toward the potato beds, he tells me about growing up at his stepdad's dairy farm in the boondocks of Wisconsin. "It was like a Tim McGraw video," he says. "Friends would park their cars in the pasture and sleep in tents. We'd pull dead trees out of the forest and build forty-foot fires and drink tons of beer. And I didn't discriminate. Everyone came out. The jocks, the stoners, the smart kids. Everyone was invited."

It's easy to identify Steve in this lineup of John Hughes archetypes—the affable, razor-witted kid who belonged to no clique but slid easily between lunchroom hierarchies, liked by everyone. After high school, though, Steve felt cramped and restive in his small Midwestern town. His post-graduation prospects weren't exactly lambent either. For a while he worked as a deejay, mixing playlists for school dances, followed by a landscaping gig and an engineering internship, but nothing seemed like it would extract him from this Podunk setting. "When the recruiter finally called me," he says, "it seemed like the right thing to do."

Upon his arrival at Fort Stewart, he was trained as a forward observer. So formidable was his performance during basic training that he was named the Distinguished Honor Graduate in his class, and he was eventually chosen to be the lead driver for a three-truck convoy tasked with protecting a U.S. Brigade Commander in Sadr City. He accompanied this colonel wherever he went—meetings with ayatollahs, talks with the interim government. At one point, he even had Petraeus in his truck; General Casey, too. During his eleven-month deployment, he completed over four hundred missions, piloting his convoy through Sadr City, the Green Zone, and the insurgent stronghold of al-Salman Pak. Those roads, some of the most heavily bombed in the country, were edged with drifts of rubble—perfect hiding grounds for IEDs—and though he attended more than sixty funerals for fellow soldiers, he and his platoon somehow managed to emerge physically unscathed.

Psychologically, though, Steve was shaken. Something had been sundered, his receiver was on the fritz. "We saw everything," he says. "Everything." Though we are ensconced in bucolic splendor, his expression turns pensive and haunted-looking for a second, a woeful pall moving across his face. What follows is a long, carbonated silence, with insects humming in the furrows with electric stridulations and a mobile of barn swallows wheeling across the pasture. You can see it gather in him, the weight of some unutterable burden.

He came up with the idea for Peacefully Organic Produce with his partner, Steph, whom he met while finishing a civil engineering degree at the University of Wisconsin–Platteville. Dreamily they spoke of starting a farm—one where vets with disabilities could find a place to work and recuperate after their tours of duty. Operating as a training facility, Peacefully Organic Produce would serve as an incubator program for other veteran farms and would forge partnerships with nutritional specialists at the VA, allowing eligible veterans—such as those with diabetes or heart disease—to receive insurance vouchers for Steve's produce. And at a time when many civilian employers were wary of hiring veterans with mental illness, they'd hire folks with drug addictions, schizophrenia, and more commonly, PTSD.

Their timing couldn't have been better. With a majority of American farmers nearing the retirement age, the USDA was looking to recruit a million new growers over the next decade to keep the industry viable. And since nearly half of the soldiers returning from Afghanistan and Iraq had grown up in rural areas, the USDA pegged them as prime candidates for the job. Which thus explains the 2014 Farm Bill. Seven years ago, Congress appropriated roughly $450 million in grants and low-interest loans for new veteran farmers, which could be used to buy animals, tractors, and other startup equipment.

It was one of those atavistic news stories that somehow managed to hit all of America's patriotic sweet spots—the heartland in trouble, the ever-gallant war vets who were up to the task—to say nothing of the fact that it was a rare instance of Congress actually doing something. Unsurprisingly, the media had a field day. The dailies were in hysterics, and NPR aired a few stories that were the rhetorical equivalent of a wet dream. Regardless of the venue, the articles invariably focused on the serenity that life on the farm would offer the one in five vets coming home with post-traumatic stress. At times, these pieces took on the lallating tones of a resort brochure, describing agriculture as if it were a kind of vocational spa treatment. *Feeling a bit ravaged from all that serving of your country? Why not come on down to the farm, where you'll harvest arugula under mimosa-colored sunshine and get reacquainted with the earth?*

In the end, much of the Farm Bill was a deft bit of scapegoating, a two-birds-with-one-stone approach to veterans' issues, whereby we furnished vets with new job prospects while claiming that the nature of the work would also redress their psychological turmoil. Perhaps it was yet another way of downplaying the epidemic levels of post-traumatic stress among our armed forces. Few of these pieces mentioned the fact that twenty-two veterans commit suicide every day, a statistic next to which even the most cheerful article about veteran agriculture would dim. It seemed, in short, that civilians were all too eager to wash their hands of veterans and the moral challenge these returning soldiers present to American culture at large.

Steve himself seems to see farming as a more complicated venture. For him, it isn't just a pastoral antidote to the traumas of war, nor is it simply a suitable profession for veterans raised in the hinterlands of the nation. Instead, the farm itself is a form of activism, a cunning method of protest. By its very existence, Peacefully Organic Produce points out the deprivations of civilian society and the failures of the VA, and in this way, these veterans share a bloodline with latter-day Black Panthers, those who eschewed radicalism and saw themselves as community organizers, furnishing their neighborhoods with medical clinics, bus systems, and meal programs for kids. In this light, the farm could be seen as creating a parallel world—one in which veterans are actually provided with the social services that were promised to them: a stable job, a recuperative environment, a safe place to stay. Instead of railing against the system with placards and chants, it is attempting, however gradually, to midwife a new one.

All of these aims are admirable, and yet as I leave the farm that day I can't help but wonder how Steve's political idealism will work in practice, particularly in a social climate that seems so intent on whitewashing—or ignoring completely—the stories of veterans who have served in our nation's most controversial wars. In the coming months, it will occur to me that the success of the farm depends, in large part, on the wider community—that its fate is bound up with the willingness of civilians to contend with the legacy of violence that has been enacted in their name.

As we stroll back to the farmhouse, where I parked my car, Steve tells me most of his CSA customers live on the east side of Madison. I remark casually that East Siders, with their love of fair-trade coffee and free-range poultry, must make for loyal customers. People on that side of town are paragons of conscious capitalism—they like knowing that their economic choices have an ethical bent.

"Seems like they'd be sympathetic to your cause," I say.

"Because that's exactly what I want," Steve snorts. "Their sympathy."

The reproach unnerves me, but before I can respond, he's reaching in for a guileless handshake and smiling broadly. He says he's looking forward to my visits this summer and, without another word, turns and marches back into the brume of the fields.

—

Iraq Veterans Against the War (IVAW) essentially started as a book club. Fueled by six packs of beer, a cadre of marines at Camp Lejeune would stay up until dawn discussing the finer points of capitalism and U.S. hegemony, using *Chomsky for Beginners* as their vade mecum. Soon their syllabus included *Manufacturing Consent, A People's History of the United States,* and the work of Daniel Ellsberg. After falling under the tutelage of some Vietnam vets in Philadelphia, this ragtag cluster of young veterans announced the formation of IVAW in 2003. Nervous, indignant, and clad in street clothes, they sought to erode consent for the war primarily by sharing their stories, since they saw no better way of subverting the Bush administration's platitudes about liberating the Iraqi people than to enumerate the atrocities they had carried out in-country. While these narratives would comprise the bulk of their protest tactics, they also tried to sow dissent within the military itself. One strategy for doing so was "Befriending a Recruiter." This involved an IVAW member feigning interest in combat service and hogging a recruiter's time so he couldn't pitch to actual prospects. Other efforts included IVAW barbeques on active-duty bases where they plied soldiers with free food and beer while outlining the perils of reenlistment.

It was at one such barbeque that Steve first learned about IVAW. One day at Fort Stewart, after returning from his deployment, he found himself strolling over to the cookout under a spell of curiosity. He insists there was no road-to-Damascus moment, no parting of the heavens and shock of white light. Instead the process of becoming antiwar happened gradually. He was haunted by scenes of Iraqi children tiptoeing barefoot through rivers of sewage, all because the U.S. military had decimated their public infrastructure. And he couldn't understand why he risked his life every day when civilian contractors, who loitered behind the gates of the cozily appointed military base, were paid three times as much as he was. Increasingly, he began to feel that he'd been duped into a senseless war, a safari of gratuitous violence.

Upon his honorable discharge, he left Fort Stewart wearing an *Iraq Veterans Against the War* t-shirt, and when he returned home to the Midwest, he spent four years crusading for peace with a cabal of likeminded vets, joining demonstrations that went some way toward airing his grievances and reconciling himself with the Iraqi people. In 2012, he helped organize the antiwar protest in Chicago, during which he and dozens of other vets threw away their service medals, echoing a gesture made some forty years earlier by VVAW (Vietnam Veterans Against the War) during the Operation Dewey Canyon protests in Washington, D.C. The Chicago event culminated in Steve holding hands with Jesse Jackson and belting "We Shall Overcome" while marching down Michigan Avenue.

Of course, when a soldier renounces his service, he refuses to settle down into the jacuzzi of civilian appreciation. Instead, doomed to a sort of ideological purgatory, the antiwar vet is called a traitor by red-state conservatives and is made a protest stage-prop for beltway liberals. More fundamentally, though, the antiwar vet disrupts the feel-good narrative of the American war hero, a myth so pervasive in this country that even those who decry our hawkish interventionist policies still subscribe to it, still stand up at the Super Bowl tributes, still consume those SEAL-Team-Six memoirs by the hundreds of thousands. But soldiers like Steve are staunchly opposed to using the term. "So many vets fall prey to the idea of the war hero," he says. "So they never talk about the things they witnessed. They never let themselves weigh the moral costs of their actions, even if some part of them is bothered by what they've done." So vehement is his conviction that he eschews the term even when it could help his business. Recently, the Farmer Veteran Coalition—a nonprofit organization that Peacefully Organic Produce is a member of—discovered that their farmers can label their produce with "Homegrown by Heroes" stickers. But Steve won't do it, believing the term a misnomer. "It's unfortunate because it would probably help me out with the bigger grocery stores, but there's no way I'm putting that shit on my produce."

While the ferocity of his convictions is undoubtedly stirring, the decision to forgo the stickers seems risky, pitting the farm's financial success against his own unswerving principles. The extent of the risk becomes clear to me one morning in June when I come for a visit. The farm is desolate and eerily quiet. Gravel crunches under foot as I roam the lot, looking for signs of life. I walk up to the farmhouse, past the runty wooden sign that reads *Trespassers Will Be Composted*, and rap gently on the front door. After several minutes, Steve appears, rubbing his eyes with his fists, looking haggard, barely there. He mutters something about having forgotten that I was coming out today, and invites me inside where he needs to finish washing dishes before heading to the fields. Steve variously calls the house "Humpty Dumpty" or "Frankenstein," since he's in the process of renovating and doing add-ons. Opaque plastic sheets have been taped over an unfinished patio door, and they inflate like lungs as we hustle into the kitchen. Speaking in ballistic cadences, he tells me he's been up all night scouring the Internet for grants, and veering from one complaint to another, he rattles off an inventory of this week's misfortunes: a defunct mower, a broken spindle, and a tractor that won't start. "What's depressing is that the repairs will probably cost more than the damn thing's worth."

Over the past few weeks, it's become clear to me that the farm is teetering on the edge of solvency. Capital-heavy investments in equipment have forced them into debt, and in the meantime, Steve is shelling out thousands of dollars to keep the farm operational. The faulty tractor will mean renting one for two thousand dollars a week, and Steve recently maxed out his Menards card, which he'll have to pay off with the profits of his slaughtered chickens.

To cover the shortfall, Steve has been applying for nonprofit grants and governmental loans, a maddeningly tedious process that has been made all the more cumbersome due to the farm's antiwar associations. After Steve received a recommendation for full funding for a grant through the Department of Vocational Rehab, some bigwig at the organization—whom Steve suspects is "probably a Heritage Foundation member and a Governor Walker appointee"—put the kibosh on his application.

"Why?" I ask.

Steve shrugs. "Maybe someone googled me." With the faucet going at full-bore, he pumices a frying pan with a loofah of steel wool. "They claimed that we were a 'hobby farm,' saying that we only made nine thousand dollars a year, but that was just our farmers' market earnings. That didn't include wholesale yields nor what we make in CSA shares. So I told the guy that if he thinks our place is a hobby, he can climb out of his cubicle and come shadow me for a day, if he can keep up."

Steve has decided to appeal the decision, but with all these applications in limbo, the farm is just barely breaking even.

—

Outside, rafts of mackerel-colored clouds have amassed in the distant sky, and the farm is veiled with rain. As we head to the fields, Steve tells me I'm going to "link up with" Crystal, an Iraq War veteran who lives on the farm and whom Steve is helping with an application for Mission Continues, a nonprofit organization that provides grants for vets who participate in community programs. We grab gloves from the barn and meet Crystal in the onion beds, which are clotted with ravels of unkempt thistle. Crystal is short and compact, with the prim carriage of a ballerina, her nose bearing a constellation of freckles.

Though she seems somewhat guarded around me, leery of my questions, she literally wears her politics on her sleeve. A tattoo on her right forearm reads MAKE PEACE in chunky black letters. And the left arm says NOT WAR. "And then, on my pinkie," she says, "I have a paperclip." I noticed this when we first shook hands, figuring it was some sort of hipstery aesthetic statement à la Magritte: *c'est un paperclip*. Turns out I'm wrong. She tells me the symbol dates back to World War II when Norwegians affixed paperclips to their lapels as an emblem of resistance to the Nazi occupation, evincing solidarity with the plight of the Jews. During Vietnam, draftees against the war similarly sported paperclips on their uniform collars to alert other soldiers that they were antiwar. Some of Crystal's fellow soldiers in Iraq did this too.

"Then I heard about this one soldier in Vietnam who'd tattooed FUCK YOU to his right hand, his saluting hand, so every time a superior went past, he'd basically be announcing his protest," she says. "I thought that was pretty cool, so when some other soldiers and I went to get the paperclip tattoo, I decided to get mine on my right hand."

Apparently, there's an acronym for it: **P**eople **A**gainst **P**eople **E**ver **R**eenlisting. **C**ivilian **L**ife **I**s **P**referred. Eventually, she wants her whole body to serve as a gallery for tattoos, culminating in a huge mural depicting the Tree of Life on her back. Her next tat will be a giraffe stretching its long neck across her deltoid, where it will snack from the tree's fruit-laden boughs.

Since her honorable discharge in 2010, Crystal has agitated for peace with organizations like Under the Hood Cafe, Ft. Hood Disobeys, March Forward!, and IVAW, but the apogee of her activism occurred in 2011, when she joined five other vets in barricading Highway 190 in Killeen, Texas—an interstate used by Fort Hood for mass deployments. Garbed in black *Disobey* t-shirts, she and the other demonstrators arranged themselves across the road and unfurled a homemade banner that read: *Tell the Brass to Kiss My Ass, Your Families Need You More.* Their efforts stalled six busloads of soldiers deploying to Iraq, and even though it was a crime punishable by up to six months in federal prison, she felt the cause of peace was worth it.

When I ask Crystal why she left IVAW for organic farming, she speaks of activism much in the way Steve did, noting wearily that performative protest seemed increasingly impotent, little more than mass catharsis. "It doesn't do much good to hang around a street corner with a sign," she says. "Now, I'm feeding people nutritious food. There's nothing more fundamental than that."

Later that day, we tramp down to the hoop house where Steve is watering the sweet corn seedlings. Crystal's phone buzzes in her back pocket, its screen glowing through the denim. "It's probably Mission Continues," she says.

"Right, because who else would be calling you?" Steve jokes.

He and I walk toward the packing shed to give her some privacy.

"She's gonna get it," he says. "This will be great." When I ask what the grant entails, he says it'll provide her with a nine-hundred-dollars-a-month stipend, a nice complement to the three-hundred-dollars-a-week he can afford to pay her now, a pittance considering she works twelve- to sixteen-hour days.

She comes out of the hoop house. Even though the phone is still pressed to her ear, she's shaking her head, mouthing, "It's no."

"Fuck," Steve says, kicking at the dirt. "Fucking bullshit." He stalks off toward the edge of the tomato plants, his eyes roving across the fields, panning quickly, assessing everything he sees. The spirit of some dark contemplation gathers in his expression as he considers all the fronts on which he seems to be waging a losing battle.

Crystal finally hangs up and walks over. "They said my situation was too unconventional. She said that three times. *Unconventional.*"

Steve snorts. "It's probably because you didn't say *guns* and *freedom* enough in your application." He storms toward the onion beds and fetches a crate glutted with tools. When I offer to lend a hand, he says, "No, that's okay. When I'm pissed, I need to lift things."

Halfway there, he halts abruptly and drops everything, falling to his knees beside a row of summer squash, whose broad frond-like leaves are spattered with pale spots. "Is that blight?" I ask.

"Yeah. Shit," he says, running a hand over his face. "I knew it was coming, but not this soon."

Smedley emerges from the cornfields, his fur strewn with leaves and burrs, and he weaves around Steve's legs, sensing distress. With a jeweler's scrutiny, Steve inverts the leaves of the squash plant to inspect their veiny underbellies, which insects have munched into doilies. When he finally speaks, his voice is just shy of a whisper. "You know, sometimes I consider getting out of veterans' advocacy."

I ask him what else he would do.

"I don't know. I have other passions. Environmental sustainability. Civil engineering. Politics. I could do other things. Maybe run for mayor?" he says, smirking.

In a futile attempt to leaven his mood, I offer a blizzard of look-on-the-bright-side comments. Maybe the Department of Voc-Rehab will approve his appeal and the grant for new equipment will come through. Maybe the farm will get approved by the FairShare Coalition, which would allow his customers to buy produce through their insurance, which would undoubtedly increase his business.

"Something better work out," he says. "Because if one of these grants doesn't go our way, there might not be a year three."

———

Despite these significant financial woes, Steve continues to set up a farmstand every Wednesday at the local VA. One morning I wait for him in the humming fluorescence of the hospital gift shop, amid a garish accumulation of candy and snacks. There's also aisle upon aisle of patriotic clothes—collared shirts silkscreened with bald eagles, windbreakers emblazoned with undulant flags. If you've ever wondered where veterans get those Legion caps stitched with phrases like VIETNAM VET and PROUD TO SERVE, the answer is the VA gift shop. Near the back of the store, a wall of TVs plays Will Smith's *I Am Legend*, and for a few minutes, I watch the Fresh Prince unload rounds of artillery into a grove of approaching zombies.

Steve shows up in a tense mood. At the hospital portico, he storms out of his truck and races to set up the vendor tent. As we begin removing crates of produce, a dyspeptic man in a blue Honda comes barreling down the driveway and screeches to an abrupt stop right behind Steve's bumper, shouting through an open window, "This is supposed to be a cleared entrance!" Steve replies, "I know. Sorry, I'll be out of here in a second. I'm just unloading for the market." The guy snarls, "I don't care! I don't care! Clear the fucking driveway!"

As the car peels out of the parking lot, Steve mutters, "Yeah, yeah, yeah, I'm a fucking veteran, too, buddy."

It takes fifteen minutes to set up the farmstand, and by the time the first customer approaches, the tables offer a horn of plenty: there's swiss chard and russet potatoes, kale and broccoli, carrots, beets, kohlrabies, garlic scapes and turnips, cauliflower and patty pans, strawberries and sweet corn. Soon, the market does brisk business. Manning the farmstand, Steve is garrulous and chipper, complimenting folks on their attire, dispensing suggestions for possible recipes, and razzing younger vets with coded military jokes (apparently, marines and naval officers are famously antagonistic). It is a vaudeville of customer service. After completing his first sale, Steve quips, "We're here every Wednesday. We hope you're not, but if you are, we'll be here," after which he turns to me with twinkly eyes and a conspiratorial grin, whispering, "I've got tons of these one-liners." He seems truly happy to be here, and the first hour of the market proves to be an exercise in consummate retail service.

After an hour, a yeti of a man ambles over to the tent, apologizing for his truancy. This is Ron, one of the Vietnam vets who works at the farm. (Later, Steve will tell me that Ron is "pretty much [his] best friend.") Ron is enormous, with kind, mirthful eyes, and wears a puckered ballcap with a frizzy white ponytail sticking out the back. His wispy beard is the indeterminate color of old snow and his customer service approach is that of a carnival barker. The man can shrill with alacrity. "Welcome, welcome!" he shouts. "We are Peacefully Organic Produce. Everything you see here is USDA-certified organic. Our farm is owned and operated by veterans, and if there's anything we can get you, just let us know."

Later, I will learn that Ron served in the Special Forces during Vietnam. When he returned home, he was so wracked with anxiety that he couldn't be around other people, which prompted him to retreat into the north woods of Wisconsin for fifteen years, buying a tract of land so deep in the forest that the township had to build a road to his property so the school bus could fetch his daughter in the morning. The waggish city planners named the street *Middle Earth*. When Ron finally emerged in the early 1980s, he joined a local chapter of VVAW that carried out a series of performative protests, even at one point occupying the roof of the VA from which they dropped hand-painted banners across its façade to raise awareness about the dangers of Agent Orange. (Ever since, the hospital has maintained a strict proviso about any roof-related activities.)

One hospital patient hobbles past the farmstand on crutches, and Ron tries to empathize. "Hey, man, I can identify. I've got two stents here," he says, pointing to his heart. "And a fake knee here, and a fake hip there." And with a finger at his temple, he says, "And PTSD here." He chuckles brightly, then claims that veterans, by their very nature, are professional gripers. "Yeah," Steve jokes, "all we do is bitch and moan." Then he winces and slaps his forehead.

"What?" I ask. "What is it?"

"I've been trying not to do that."

"What?"

"Say," he pauses for a second, then lowers his voice and spells "*B-I-T-C-H.*"

He tells me that his partner, Steph, who is completing a graduate degree in education, has recently started interrogating the subtle misogyny of his language. "It's an interesting time for us," he says. "She's being exposed to all this new stuff through her program. Feminist theory. And sometimes it's hard for me to acknowledge my privilege as a cis male with white skin. For whatever reason, I used to think that there was a difference between calling someone a 'bitch' and saying something like 'stop bitching at me.' But it turns out there isn't, you know, a difference."

As we start to pack up, an elderly veteran leans on a metal walker and inches his way down the sidewalk, with his wife at his side. Both of them have parchment skin, pendent jowls, and the smiles of old people still in love. As they enter the parking lot, Steve turns to me and says, "I really hope I'm like that one day. Kicking around with my wife."

—

There is a difference, Lawrence LeShan writes in *The Psychology of War*, between "mythic" and "sensory" war. "Sensory war" is the carnal experience of combat, the psychological whirlwind that a person endures when he or she is steeped in violence. "Mythic war," on the other hand, is the fable we construct to justify the depravities of battle—the gauzy-edged daydream where freshly buzzed recruits defend our Constitution from shadowy foes, soundtracked by proud trumpets. But what happens to the soldier who sacrificed his life for the myth? What happens when the horrors of combat do not jibe with the redemptive saga he was promised? How should he interpret the charred bodies, the ruined streets, the children aproned with blood? These are the leitmotifs of a story he's not familiar with, one in which he is the protagonist and the pages seem to go on forever.

One cloudless Sunday in June, I receive a harried email from Steve, titled "EMERGENCY TOMATO SITUATION—HIGH WINDS, POSSIBLE TORNADOES TOMORROW." The message reads: *I know it's a gorgeous Sunday, and I really hate to ask, BUT tomorrow is supposed to be a significant weather day, with high winds, possible tornadoes, large hail, and torrential downpours. I could really use a hand from anyone that is available with trellising the rest of the tomatoes to provide extra support for tomorrow's storms. I'll be starting around eleven, and going until I drop, or the mosquitoes carry me away.*

I check the weather, which hardly seems to warrant this level of concern: a few thunderstorms on the horizon, but nothing out of the ordinary for midsummer Wisconsin. Still, I decide to lend a hand. The crew and I spend the afternoon kneeling in the tomato plants, but when morning comes, the storms are temperate, emitting soft burps of thunder, posing little threat to the farm.

It's easy to chalk it up to a simple mistake. But over time I begin to sense in Steve's vigilance a kind of disproportional concern, a preoccupying desire to avert any and all disaster. Farming was supposed to resuscitate him, its rigors and burdens serving as a reliable detergent for the mind. During the farm's first year, Steve posted a note to Facebook, testifying to the farm's exonerative potential, effusing with all the ardor of a true believer: "You should all try it out sometime. Get back in touch with your roots, get some soil on those hands. If I had a soul, it would be healed." But lately the work seems spiritually corrosive, pumicing away the last flecks of an identity not already given over to being a veteran.

One afternoon, while sitting at a local market, I ask Stephanie whether she thinks farming has had a palliative effect on him. "Uhhh," she says hesitantly, turning to look at Steve on the other side of the market, where he leans against his truck and extracts a splinter with a pocketknife. "Well, it's the height of the summer season, so things are pretty stressful." Never a great sleeper, she tells me, he's been logging only three or four hours a night. And sometimes he doesn't even come to bed, but camps out in the utter darkness of the packing shed, scribbling notes to himself about chores to complete the next morning. They hardly ever go out anymore, and when they do, Steve insists upon sitting at a booth in the back of the restaurant so he can monitor the exits—"like a mob boss," Steph says. Usually, he becomes so agitated that they have to leave before the food arrives.

In current medical parlance, veterans haunted by their deployments are diagnosed with post-traumatic stress disorder. But Steve, like a lot of antiwar vets, argues that the term is Orwellian, insinuating that afflicted veterans are responding "abnormally" to the degradations of battle. In the packing shed, Steve has tacked up an IVAW poster that reads: *What part of being emotionally and spiritually affected by gross violence is a 'disorder'? How about going to war and coming home with a clear conscience disorder? I think that would be far more appropriate.* It is now common among antiwar soldiers to refer to the condition as "post-traumatic stress," a term they feel describes a normal response to war. All of the veterans at Peacefully Organic Produce emphasize this subtle linguistic distinction, and in a certain sense, you can see how there are clear political ramifications for this term. By understanding "post-traumatic stress" as a suitable response to combat, it not only treats soldiers as competent moral agents capable of feeling remorse, frustration, and shame—which flies in the face of our pieties about soldiers being stouthearted heroes—but also impels civilians to recognize the egregious combat orders that soldiers are often forced to execute under our flag.

What's clear is that farm life hasn't "cured" Steve of these mental harassments. If anything, the farm has become a proxy for battle, an outlet for his hypervigilance. What keeps him going, though, is the dreaded scenario of letting someone down. And the roster of people who are counting on him is long: Steph, his stepson Alex, Crystal, and Ron, to say nothing of the whole community of veterans and volunteers who rely on him for fresh produce. One afternoon, I arrive to find Steve stomping around the farmhouse in a frenzy, folding a pile of laundry. A hummock of clean clothes had been sitting on the family room couch for the better part of a week, and while he's been trying to help Steph with housework, it's hard to stay on top of domestic chores with so much to do on the farm. "It's usually because of where my priorities are," he tells me. "You know, Sergeant Steve steps forward and wants to do it his way. And I was trained to think 'Mission First.' And now, here, it's always 'Farm First.' And so she gets on me about that."

I wonder whether, after a few years of being out of the military, he's figured out his post-deployment identity, or if he still finds himself straddling that murky border between civilian and soldier.

Placing a dun-colored bath towel on the arm of the couch, he looks up at me appraisingly, and there's this second where it seems as though some sort of neural gate has unlatched, and all of his defenses have been lowered. His eyes are glittering and fervent, full of petition. "Honestly, man," he says. "I'm still trying to figure that out. I'm trying so fucking hard to become the person I want to be."

—

Over the Fourth of July weekend, my wife and I visit her parents in a small lakeside town, where Independence Day means nothing more than apple pie, ubiquitous flags, and bikes festooned with patriotic streamers. At a family barbeque that afternoon, I tell some of my relatives about the farm, and upon hearing that Steve and the other veterans suffer from post-traumatic stress, several family members utter slogans of obligatory dismay—"That's so sad," one says. "It *is* really sad," says another, her voice swollen with ersatz concern. But the conversation pretty much ends here. No one uses this as an opportunity to discuss U.S. foreign policy nor does anyone issue an antiwar complaint.

Ever since Nixon repealed the draft in the early 1970s—which he hoped would neuter the country's antiwar movement—the military has been composed of volunteers. And to a large extent, their deployment only affects the small, localized communities of their families and friends, remaining luxated from the fates of other Americans. This has triggered a seismic shift in public opinion. Whereas in the 1960s the Selective Service program made it pretty much impossible to remain neutral on the question of Vietnam, it's now much easier for civilians to regard foreign policy as another matter of soapbox fervor and partisan bias. And as our veterans return home, it is similarly easy to dismiss the debts we may owe them, since, after all, they signed up for this. They knew what they were getting into. Perhaps out of a latent sense of guilt, we civilians cuddle the myth of the American war hero, labeling anyone who's seen combat with this valiant designation.

I'm weighing all of this while my family and I watch fireworks detonate over Lake Michigan on the night of the Fourth. Splinters of Honolulu blue incinerate the sky, accompanied by yawps of disgruntled thunder. I try to imagine how Steve might react to this sound and fury, try to trace the associative logic that would cause a person to clutch his ears at the sound of these celebratory reports. My initial impulse is to feel bad for him, to regard his suffering as unfortunate, terrible, sad. Perhaps I'm drawn to Steve because he reminds me of the guys I knew in high school, back when our best idea of a good time was to get drunk in our parents' basements and make each other laugh. Perhaps such pastimes were stamped with provincialism, a kind of prairieland idiocy, a flyover state of mind. But the pastures of Wisconsin are long, seeming to go on forever, and we boys had to find some way to pass the time. Perhaps if I had grabbed a different branch as I climbed my way through childhood, then maybe right now I, too, would be carrying a cache of dark memory, my heart racing at the lurid sky, my hands twitching at loud noises.

Of course, I know this is false projection, that Steve would bristle at my sympathy. He doesn't want my attempts at identification. He doesn't want my pity. And the last thing he wants is for me to thank him for his service. Perhaps the greater favor I can offer him is to simply listen, to try to understand what causes a man to become an antiwar veteran. There have been times at the farm when Steve harangues U.S. foreign policy and his words remind me of sentiments expressed by Ernest Hemingway after the Second World War: "We have come out of the time when obedience, intelligent courage, resolution and the acceptance of discipline were most important, into that more difficult time when it is a man's duty to understand his world rather than to simply fight for it."

Perhaps in understanding this world, we owe veterans the duty of listening, of not placing upon them the terrible burden of heroism, of allowing them to be more complex and conflicted, of granting the possibility that they're currently grieving for what they've done. If antiwar veterans unsettle us, it's because they force us to encounter a version of war far from the star-spangled gallantry promulgated in textbooks and Hollywood blockbusters. Think of how much nerve it takes to admit your complicity in immoral actions. Witness that kind of valor. If in the end a man decides to renounce his service, if he finds that the story he'd been telling himself was a lie, if he chooses to live out his days in enduring protest, might we find in such a man no small measure of courage? Might this be heroic?

—

August arrives with a bolt of clear blue skies. On my last day at the farm, Steve greets me with some good news: they recently heard back from the

Department of Voc-Rehab and were awarded full funding for their grant, which means Steve will soon obtain a flotilla of new equipment, including riding mowers and a waterwheel tractor, all of which will help mechanize the farm and expedite its operations. This update couldn't have come at a better time, since the team has had trouble keeping up with chores. Earlier that week, I noticed that the thistles in the potato beds were positively colossal, with stems as thick as baseball bats. One worker was hacking them down with a machete, swirling the implement like a samurai.

"You guys are really doing it," I say.

"That's why I started the farm," Steve says, positively glowing with optimism, falling into raptures of self-congratulation. "I was so sick of other activists talking about what they wanted to do. But veterans like us—we're doers. It's a cliché, but it's true. I always say, don't talk about something, *be* about something. And that's what we do."

As the fall semester kicks into gear, my days are overrun with lesson planning and student emails. Most mornings, I camp out on the couch, retooling my syllabus or clipping articles for my course reader. Yet despite the change in scenery, my mind remains rooted in the furrows. I'd been hoping the end of the harvest would temper Steve's anxiety, but if his web presence is any indication, he seems just as bothered and preoccupied as when I left him. In a recent Facebook post, he writes:

I've found a healthy way to vent my pent up aggression . . . There's a group of radical catholics that are constantly protesting outside of the planned parenthood in Madison. I happen to drive by there to pick up coffee chaff for our poultry bedding from the Just Coffee roaster right next door. I've begun protesting the protestors every time I drive by, it's healing, tongue-whipping the shit out of them for about five or ten minutes . . . I don't usually get lunch breaks throughout the day, so this is how I spend my 'five minutes alone' (my Pantera reference for the day). So far, better than any group therapy I've tried. I figure, most of the rest of society is either too afraid or too unaware to confront these lunatics, so, fuck it, I'll be your huckleberry.

There is venom here. That seems difficult to deny. But beneath the cheeky bluster of the prose, there is something else, a desperation, a certain questing spirit, a call for an intermission, a few minutes to extinguish the agitation in his head. Later that day, as I prepare for a lecture on the philosophy of Thoreau, I find myself distracted and preoccupied, sitting at a desk strewn with lesson plans and an open volume of Stanley Cavell, where I have underlined a passage from the King James Bible: "The summer is over, the harvest has ended, and we are not saved."

—

In late September, I return to the farm for Veggies for Vets, a fundraiser that Steve hosts in conjunction with Warrior Songs, a Madison-based nonprofit that aims to heal veterans through arts and music. Last year, the event raised enough money to provide fifteen veteran families with a weekly share of produce, and this year, Steve hopes to double it.

All afternoon, the farm thrums with activity under vast chlorinated skies. Near the tomato beds, clans of joyful suburbanites partake in "family yoga," giggling at their contortions. Toddlers queue up in the barn to get their faces painted, and moments later, they transform into scrawny cheetahs and diminutive kittens who harass Smedley with their hands locked into menacing claws. A few visitors go for a spin on something called the "salsa bike," where a food processor has been rigged to a Huffy. At the center of the commotion is Steve, leading clumps of visitors around the farm, wearing his standard uniform of boots, jeans, t-shirt, and ballcap.

My wife and I wander through the labyrinth of tomatoes, trying to catch up. Steve hasn't noticed us yet and is spewing invective about the sharecropper next door, doing little to tailor his statements to the temperament of his audience, which includes a bevy of seven-year-old girls. When Steve plucks a habanero pepper from its plant and claims that it could "melt your face off," one of these girls tugs on his shirt, looks up at him and says, with unblinking earnestness, "I bet my dad could eat that."

"No he could not," Steve retorts gruffly, claiming that most restaurants use a single pepper for a vat of chili sauce.

The tour ends in the packing shed. In the corner, there's a commemorative shrine to a man named Jacob George, one of Steve's close friends, an IVAW member and a veteran of the Afghanistan War who, as Steve tells us, committed suicide almost a year ago today. He was thirty-two years old. Tonight's concert is dedicated to him. On a small sideboard table, there's a spray of Jacob's photos, grainy printoffs from Facebook. One shows a handsome shaggy-haired guy playing banjo. Another depicts the same guy, except now he's a scrawny dude in a swimsuit, sporting a buzz cut, and he's screwing up his face into a loony scowl, an attempt to make his photographer laugh.

Someone claps me on the shoulder, and I turn to find Steve grinning broadly. "What's up, man?" he says, his breath perfumed with booze. Exiting the shed, I introduce him to my wife, and we make idle, wandering chitchat. While we try to catch up, a constant parade of people come up to greet him. A bearded guy in a fedora and sunglasses slaps him on the back with affectionate gusto. Another woman—a doctor from the VA—introduces Steve to her family. I get an eerie premonition of Steve on the campaign trail, pressing palms with prospective voters. Perhaps a mayoral run isn't so far-fetched. But he looks tired. His eyes are raccooned from little sleep, and he seems wound up and agitated. At a certain point, he apologizes for the bedlam and says, "I'm fucking exhausted and need a beer. Let's catch up later, after the concert." But we never do. After pulling a foamer from the keg, he retreats to a beige RV parked near the farmhouse, where a close friend is spending the night. Even though there are dozens of people by the barn and loitering in the fields, Steve spends much of the afternoon hunkered in the lee side of this camper, lounging in the shade of an opulent jade tree.

Soon, dusk settles over the farm, and the fields look hazy and distilled, as if frozen in amber. I decide to walk the grounds one last time before we leave, and the furrows are a vast chromatic spectacle: rubicund tomatoes, emerald peppers, burgundy eggplant. To my surprise, even the sunflowers—wizened and wilted all summer—have bloomed again. The perimeter of the farm is ablaze with them, their bright yellow blossoms meant to serve as a bulwark against dangers both tertiary and atmospheric. As I stand there in the spectral quiet, amid the hum of crickets, I'm reminded of the fact that even the land out here had to heal. Organic certification requires that farmers must let their fields go dormant for three years, allowing the soil to cleanse itself of pesticides and toxins. In that time, the loam grows rich and piquant, abounding in minerals that amplify its fecundity. Standing at the edge of his pasture, I'm wishing Steve a similar recuperation, that these days of hard labor and psychedelic sunsets might afford him a respite, a reprieve, because I know how far he's come and how tired he's getting.

MIDWESTERN GOTHIC

When I was twenty years old, in the fall of 2006, the body of my best friend was found in the Mississippi River. The discovery had come at the end of a long weekend search. Crews of police officers and volunteers, his friends and family among them, had combed through the streets of La Crosse, Wisconsin, a moribund rust belt town where Luke was attending college on a basketball scholarship. Rumor had it that on Friday night he had been out partying at the annual Oktoberfest celebration; on Saturday morning he failed to show up for a golf outing. Surveillance footage from the night before showed him eating a hoagie at a local Jimmy John's, but the trail of breadcrumbs ended there. Mutual friends later told me that by the end of the weekend the search party had grown so weary and desperate that they'd taken to peering into dumpsters and ripping open trash bags, hoping they wouldn't find him buried among the ruins. That level of savagery, in other words, was no longer outside the remit of their concerns.

At the time, I was going to school in Chicago, and on the morning my father called to say that they'd found Luke's body, I drove back to our hometown, chain-smoking and aphasic with grief. Throughout four years of high school football, Luke and I had both played quarterback, and every practice we ran drills in perfect symmetry. We'd call hike and drop back to pass, firing spirals at targets downfield, our arms mirrored at identical points of release. Often our coaches called us by each other's names. In the intervening years we had drifted apart, owing as much to geography as to diverging vocational interests—he was studying business, I fancied myself a writer—and though we still drank together over winter break, our phone calls throughout the rest of the year had grown stilted and brusque.

There was a vigil that night at the old high school. Family and friends congregated around the flagpole of the front quad. And with their expressions flickering in the bronzy light of votives, old classmates offered halting tributes to my friend, heartfelt remembrances about good times in study hall or at school dances. All of it struck me as mawkish and premature. Luke had been dead for all of thirty-six hours, but already my peers were engaged in the ho-hum business of eulogy? I was haunted by more basic questions: How was it possible that he had lost consciousness at the precise moment he wandered down to the river? Had I ever known Luke to drink himself beyond basic motor skills? And why had the authorities settled on "accidental drowning" before they even received an autopsy report? Without sturdy answers to these questions, the patness of our grief felt indecent: a mummery, a desecration.

Over the next few days, as the funeral came and went, I canvassed my friends to see whether anyone else was entertaining similar ideas, but it seemed a taboo subject. I had to present my doubts as simple bewilderment, softening them with analgesic swear words and casual syntax. *It just doesn't make any fucking sense*, I said. *It's like, why would he even go down to the river?* I could tell that on some level they shared my reservations, but my questions stoked a palpable unease, as though everyone feared that diverging too far from the official explanation would lead us into some benighted wilderness where any horror was possible. Better to stick to the consolation of a tidy ending: once upon a time our friend drank too much and fell into a river. An accident and nothing more.

Only Luke's mother seemed to believe darker forces were at play. A sun-wrinkled woman with a poof of frazzled hair, she was a beloved figure in our friend group, largely for the way she liked to embarrass her son by dancing clownishly at family parties, sometimes doing the splits just to make us laugh. Luke covered his eyes at her theatrics, but I always sensed he enjoyed her presence, the radiance of her charm. After his body was found, she underwent a spiritual defoliation. You could see it right away: the lights had dimmed. Something had narrowed behind her eyes. Asking her outright would have been unthinkable, but in those days, I assumed she had trouble accepting the essential absurdity of the incident. Certainly her boy liked to drink and have a good time, but Luke would never be so stupid as to traipse down to the river by himself. He'd been brought up in the hardscrabble pragmatism of the rust belt, which always favored prudence over adventure. No way her son would lose control of himself like that. Over the next couple of years, I heard stories of her deterioration: that she had trouble getting out of bed, that she'd toyed with the idea of hiring a private investigator. Some of my friends made conciliatory gestures. One asked her to be an honorary mother-of-the-groom at his wedding. Another phoned her twice a week and took to calling her "mother"; eventually he asked her to adopt him. Of course, all of this failed at remediation. One night her only son had vanished into darkness, and no one could account for that.

—

I first heard about the Smiley Face Killers in the fall of 2008, two years after Luke's death. At the time, I was in graduate school at the University of Wisconsin–Madison, living in a decrepit bungalow on the east side of the isthmus, an esophagus of land that runs between two lakes. My life during those years was cloistered and small. Afternoons I holed up in my arctic library carrel, boning up on the urtexts of poststructuralism, and at night, I met my colleagues at dive bars, where we geeked out over heterotopias, summoning Derrida and Foucault to substantiate our most outlandish theories. One friend, a New Historicist with lines from Ezra Pound tattooed on her forearms, argued that the bondage scenes in *The Story of O* symbolized the consensual exploitation of neoliberal contracts. Another suggested that *American Psycho* offered a trenchant indictment of female objectification in contemporary America. In those days, even the most harebrained conjectures could be passed off as viable readings. I myself was not immune. The previous semester, I had written a paper on Henry James's *The Turn of the Screw*, arguing that the protagonist's ghost visions are meant to signify the horror of subjectivity experienced by early Americans, who were no longer bound to the preachments of the clergy or the fiats of kings.

At some point that autumn, I received an email from a high school friend with the subject: "Have you seen this?" The message was blank except for a link to something called *Footprints at the River's Edge*. This turned out to be a poorly designed website with a dull, earth-toned palette and a discussion forum riddled with ads for rancid pornography. Naturally, I was skeptical, but just as I went to minimize the window, one headline caught my attention: "5 EYE WITNESS NEWS breaks The Smiley Face Killer Theory."

If I could somehow return to that moment, I would close my browser and get on with my day, because whatever tenuous closure I had found since Luke's death was swiftly torn open by the contents of this website. Its authors claimed that the official explanation for my friend's drowning was feeble and bogus. Luke hadn't fallen into the Mississippi River during the stupor of a blackout, as the La Crosse Police Department had alleged. Rather, he was a victim of "a cross-country plot to kill young college men." Since the late 1980s, the bodies of nearly fifty males between the ages of eighteen and thirty had been surfacing, under bizarre circumstances, in the waters of the Midwest. In college towns across Minnesota, Ohio, Michigan, and Wisconsin, authorities declared the incidents "accidental drownings," nothing more than the mortal cost of binge drinking. But two retired NYPD homicide investigators, Kevin Gannon and Anthony Duarte, were now challenging this theory, believing darker forces to be at play. The similarities between the cases were too extensive, too peculiar, to ignore, they said. The victims were almost always young white males who excelled in school and athletics, nurturing strong bonds with their communities. But there were also more disturbing correlations. Touring the riverbanks where the bodies were found, the detectives couldn't help noticing a recurring symbol: the image of a smiley face. In town after town, throughout the cankered landscape of the rust belt, the emoticon was graffitied onto trees and bridge abutments, railcars and dumpsters—leading the detectives to conclude that it was the logo of the killers.

Initially, I regarded this theory with a wry academic smirk, dismissing it as morbid catnip for conspiratorial goons and wackjobs. But over the next couple of hours, as I tried to distract myself, a gnaw of curiosity brought me back to the computer. Falling headlong into the rabbit hole of online conspiracy, I came across a story about the Alford brothers of Van Horne, Iowa, who had been tried in 2005 for murdering their roommate with a barbeque fork and kitchen knife. In his statement, the older Alford brother claimed he was the ringleader of an outfit called the Dealers of Death, the Minnesota chapter of a much larger criminal organization that was based in Chicago. Allegedly, the Dealers of Death had over three hundred members, many of them desperadoes and drifters whom Alford had recruited in downtrodden parts of town. Some dwelled in tents by the Mississippi River. Others busked in urban plazas, toting signs of flaccid cardboard. Rumor had it these vagrants were ensorcelled by the exploits of serial killers and that Alford had branded them with hand-drawn pentagrams to mark their induction into the group. After tracking down other Dealers for questioning, Gannon and Duarte came to believe, at least for a time, that the older Alford brother was also responsible for the murder of Chris Jenkins, a University of Minnesota student who disappeared on Halloween in 2002. Four months after his disappearance, Jenkins's body surfaced on a bank of the Mississippi River, his costume snagged on a welter of downed tree branches, his corpse mostly unscathed.

The FBI found little evidence to confirm the testimonies of the Dealers, and ultimately wrote them off as the drug-addled crowings of disenfranchised youngsters. Skeptics on the Internet, however, weren't so easily convinced. On what grounds, precisely, were these testimonies deemed erroneous? And why did a propensity to brag disqualify the statement of a pivotal witness? And if the Dealers of Death weren't responsible for the drownings, then who were the Smiley Face Killers? The commenters wanted answers, and so did I. Or maybe that's putting it too mightily: the truth is I didn't know what I thought. I was blowing on the embers of fear and paranoia during a moment of unutterable grief. No matter how hard I tried, I still couldn't accept the fundamental idiocy of Luke's drowning, that a few rounds of pints were to blame. Surely some part of me knew these theories were rickety and unsound—I was bereaved, not stupid—but maybe something else *was* going on here. Maybe something sinister was afoot, a malevolence so shrewd and resourceful it could kill boys across the country and get away scot-free. The detectives had endowed the mystery of my friend's death with the properties of literature, after all, and who better than me—a grad student immersed in critical theory—to entertain these speculations?

After several more hours online, I came across a crime-scene photo of a concrete wall with a runic message scrawled in crimson spray paint:

YOU CAN'T SEE
WHAT YOU'RE NOT LOOKING FOR

Only later would it occur to me that, at this moment, the cord of my rationality had begun to splinter and fray. At the time, I had no such perspective. I can remember shutting my laptop and glancing outside, where the grackles were screeching in the mauvish dusk, and thinking that the drownings were nothing more than a vast and sprawling narrative, one that defied banal interpretations and conformist readings. On the patio of my apartment complex, neighborhood children were playing night games, but their arpeggios of laughter struck me only as a gothic symbol—an omen, a dark warning.

—

To a certain cast of mind, the prevalence of conspiracy theories in the industrial Midwest confirms the stereotype that only clodhoppers and Babbitts make their homes here. A boggling credulity, mingled with a quaint Protestant nostalgia for grand narratives, makes the cowpokes and suburbanites of the rust belt especially easy targets for scams or sophistries—or so goes the wisdom. Indeed, conspiracy theories are often regarded as a holdover of medievalism, the mindset of witch-hunting peasants that still persists in remote parts of our otherwise enlightened country.

Though often pegged as an enemy to rationalism, it's worth noting that the conspiratorial mindset saw its greatest flowering in the wake of the Enlightenment. The historians Emma Jane and Chris Fleming argue that while thinkers like Locke and Spinoza often issued gusty bromides about the importance of science and reason, they also urged individuals to reject the wisdom of conventional powers, leaving them adrift in a bardo of subjective opinion. "Dare to reason," Kant boomed, "for yourself!" Once early Americans repudiated the Catholic Church and the British crown, they were left on their own to determine the meaning of existence, which created an epistemological free-for-all. This had been the principal concern of the gothic writers I was studying around the time of Luke's death: novelists like Charles Brockden Brown and Henry James, Edgar Allan Poe and Nathaniel Hawthorne, all of whom dramatized the torsions of mind that could send a rational person down the gutter of madness. They believed that, without the lodestars of collective meaning offered by religious and political institutions, citizens of the new continent would soon doubt their own perceptions and begin hearing stray voices in the night. Even as Enlightenment principles laid the groundwork for modern democracy, the French and American revolutions fostered rampant paranoia about secret orders like the Freemasons and the Illuminati.

In the twentieth century, postmodernism would deal the final blow to the notion of collective meaning. And by the time I entered grad school, Derrida and Foucault had so thoroughly decimated grand unifying narratives that paranoia was no longer pathologized as a hallmark of obsession, but was championed instead as a viable mode of critique. Readers were urged to extract from canonical texts any ideas and allusions that were subversive, counterintuitive, or incendiary. While these habits of mind no doubt fostered a lush intellectual climate, this spirit of "radical relativism" ultimately came at the expense of preserving a baseline consensus for democratic rudiments like truth, facts, and objectivity. As fate would have it, the hermeneutics of suspicion, which were originally intended to tear down the edifice of white patriarchal narratives, have now been weaponized by conservative factions who want, at the very least, to deny the science of climate change and, at the very worst, to contort "facts" to the point where they no longer mean anything.

When you're supposed to be working on your dissertation—its own arduous search for meaning—your days are a wilderness: unscheduled, improvised, free. You can spend whole afternoons trawling Instagram or binge-watching prestige television. In my case, entire days were lost to conjectures about Luke's death. For hours on end I would watch clips of *Larry King Live*, *Anderson Cooper*, and *Geraldo Rivera*, all of which featured interviews with Detectives Gannon and Duarte, who often mentioned Luke by name. On *After Hours AM*, a true-crime podcast whose aesthetic could be described as *Dude, Where's My Car?* meets *Unsolved Mysteries*, a retired FBI agent named John DeSouza maintained that the Smiley Face Killers were a cult of psychopaths who drowned alpha males as sacrificial offerings to the ancient dark gods of Moloch and Baal. This is how my days passed: afternoons in the echo chamber of television and the thickets of comment-board conspiracy, evenings dedicated to *The Archaeology of Knowledge* and *Simulacra and Simulation*. Flipping through my course texts at night, I often highlighted any passage that seemed even tangentially related to my headspace. "If in life we are surrounded by death," Wittgenstein writes. "So too in the health of our intellect we are surrounded by madness."

Curiously, those amateur sleuths I encountered on the Internet often deployed the same literary frameworks that guided my seminar on critical theory. Several *Footprints at the River's Edge* commenters riffed on nautical folklore, suggesting that perhaps, like the sirens who tempted Odysseus, covens of attractive females were luring victims to the rivers with tunes of smutty cajolery. One East Coast gumshoe, posting under the screen name "Undead Molly," offered a Marxist interpretation: perhaps a mob of blue-collar workers, resentful of rich college students, was carrying out the drownings as an act of class warfare. One company in particular had come under Undead Molly's suspicions: a manufacturing outfit called Trane Heating & Cooling, whose headquarters were based in La Crosse, Wisconsin, where six of the bodies, including Luke's, had been found. "Trane technicians travel in vans," Molly wrote, "and have access to substances which could stun a healthy young man into unconsciousness."

It's perhaps not coincidental that these conspiracies tended to reflect, with funhouse distortions, the dominant cultural anxieties of the time. In addition to an act of proletarian revolt, the drownings were also conceived as a loose proxy for global jihad. In his book *Smiley Face Killers: Coincidence, Conspiracy, or Cover-Up*, C. Symons notes that this conjecture developed in 2008, after the FBI grew curious about the abrupt disappearance of twelve Somali men who lived in Minnesota. Eventually, the Bureau determined that the men weren't abducted, as their families had feared, but had been recruited into al-Shabaab, a terrorist network of Somali Islamists who orchestrated attacks on local governments and sought to implement sharia. On the thin premise that many U.S. al-Shabaab members were based in Minneapolis, several conspiracy theorists ventured that the group may have carried out the Midwest drownings—going so far as to point out that *sharia*, in Arabic, means "path to the water source."

This is precisely the sort of erratic leap of logic upon which this kind of reasoning depends. Wildly incongruous elements—Somali terrorists and college-aged Midwesterners, say—must be meshed together into a seamless, glittering whole. This is what makes conspiracy theories so charismatic: the air of total coherence. "There is an intellectual function in us," Freud writes in *Totem and Taboo*, "which demands unity, connection, and intelligibility from any material, whether of perception or thought, that comes within its grasp; and if, as a result of special circumstances, it is unable to establish a true connection, it does not hesitate to fabricate a false one."

What states of mind—what *special circumstances*—could condone such famines of reason? The more time I spent on these discussion boards, the more I noticed that the commenters were almost always the fathers or mothers, or sometimes the friends, of a boy who had drowned. I could almost hear the plaintive desperation in their posts as they groped for a resolution to what any sane mind could see was an irresolvable problem. Perhaps part of the reason I spent so much time on these websites, part of the reason I let my imagination run wild, was that doing so allowed me to exist among "siblings of the same darkness," as philosopher Robert Stolorow calls them—people so thoroughly gored and gutted by sadness that they could only recourse to the sturdier plotlines of Greek myths, Marxists narratives, or post-9/11 suspicion to explain their private calamities. Sitting in the glacial blue glow of my laptop, I imagined us as an army of amateur detectives united against some nameless—though not exactly faceless—menace, one that had snatched our boys from our homes and dragged them into the dark.

That winter, my thoughts took a doleful turn. I started noticing smiley-face graffiti around town. Some were spray-painted onto the pylons of campus buildings. Others were scrawled on the oxidized lids of industrial dumpsters. Not far from my house, a cheerful visage with Xes for eyes was frescoed to the brick wall of a rundown bodega, like some sort of jaunty retail mascot. I began taking pictures of these icons without quite knowing why, and soon, during idle moments, found myself inspecting their nuances, trying to decipher commonalities. Was it possible the Smiley Face Killers were operating in my neighborhood? Did the faces augur future drownings? A snippet from Agent DeSouza burbled into my memory: "Sometimes there is advanced preparation of sites for where a killer knows he's going to be operational."

At the time, I couldn't account for the force of this obsession. Since Luke and I had shared so many similarities in life, I suppose my logic ran, it was not unreasonable to assume we'd suffer kindred fates in death. In terms of victim demographics, I fit all of the relevant traits: a young white male who was bright and athletic, I lived in the Midwest and kept an assiduous schedule of heavy carousing. This admission will probably move you to contempt, but I began to suspect I was being followed. Most nights I went to a faddish dive bar called the Crystal Corner and walked home along the shoreline of Lake Mendota, whose surface was tinseled with moonlight. I hopped along the moraine of boulders marking the water's edge, sometimes skipping stones or muttering drunken nonsense at the waves. At a distance of ten years, this behavior seems more indicative of survivor's guilt than of grief, a salve against my creeping suspicion that my fate was bound up with Luke's in ways that remained tenuous to me. The primary allure of the Smiley Face theory, I recognize now, was that it eclipsed any obligation to face the unalterable fact of his death, and instead allowed me to heave the bulk of the responsibility onto a network of elusive villains, their actions as intractable and unstoppable as a force of nature or an act of God.

—

Growing up in the Midwest, you end up cultivating an eerie premonition, an awareness that the wholesome landscape—its polychromatic farmlands and serrated bluffs—belies the region's more unsettling history: failed utopias, tent-meeting revivals, asylums for feebleminded children. If the Smiley Face theory failed to strike me as ridiculous, it was because Wisconsin offers a whole catalog of creepy occurrences and lurid killings—from the cannibal Jeffrey Dahmer, who stored the bodies of his victims in his refrigerator, to the two teenage girls from Waukesha who paid homage to their demonic overlord, the Slender Man, by knifing their friend to near-death on the outskirts of a prairie. Through the scrim of these horrors, it didn't seem impossible to me that an A-team of psychopaths had conspired to drown college-aged boys throughout the region.

What gets lost in discussions about conspiracy theories is that they almost always derive from actual conspiracies. The historian Timothy Melley argues that in the twentieth century conspiratorial skepticism became a justified habit of mind, owing in part to two world wars and a slew of governmental scandals. Once citizens could no longer buy into that famous Enlightenment guarantee—that their lives were self-determined, that they were masters of their own fates—they faced a fundamental rupture, to which the contagion of tinfoil hats over the last sixty years can be seen as a traumatized response. Conspiracy theorists are not wrong to sense that their lives are at the mercy of a vast matrix of obscure forces. But the form in which they perceive those forces—everything from false-flag operations by renegade governments to the sinister dealings of corporate entities to surreptitious invasions by extraterrestrials—is usually deluded.

Here, too, the academy has helped legitimize larger cultural anxieties. In the 1970s, the semiotics of Saussure and the poststructuralism of Foucault popularized the idea that human agency is a myth: that an individual is nothing more than a Frankenstein of social forces, sutured together with a patchwork of received wisdom and stale ideologies. Marx argued that we are all products of social relations. Richard Dawkins held that humans express only the stubborn whims of DNA. As these notions became increasingly accepted, there was a parallel effort to anthropomorphize inanimate social forces, a custom that lives on in the thesis statements of every bad college-freshman paper—"The larger culture tells us we must succeed at all costs" or "Society is making young girls into anorexics"—and perhaps reached an apotheosis with the *Citizens United* ruling, which gave corporations the same legal rights as human beings. To its credit, this intellectual framework rightly accounts for the baffling complexity of social problems, but as Jane and Fleming note, it also undercuts the importance of individual accountability. If people are just recombinant manifestations of various social forces, it's easy to lose sight of who's responsible for a warming climate or economic injustice, a toxic housing market or racist policing.

Over the last couple of decades, rust belt politicians have almost always explained the region's inoperative factories and rampant foreclosures as the byproducts of an economy trending inexorably toward globalization and disinvestment. In town halls across the Midwest, the economy is made out to be a chimera whose conduct cannot be tamed, as if deindustrialization weren't the handiwork of a thousand shoddy trade deals and greedy corporate decisions. Under the duress of crumbling infrastructure, minimum-wage jobs, and failing public schools, it's no wonder disenfranchised voters in the Midwest find conspiracy theories so persuasive. Despite their botched logic and insular worldview, these theories can be read as tragic attempts to preserve the principle of individual culpability. Of course, the impulse to find a villain can often breed rage, prejudice, and kneejerk scapegoating. But at its root is, perhaps, a legitimate suspicion that there are actors behind every system; that someone, somewhere, is responsible for our misfortunes. That there's someone to blame.

—

I keep seeing Luke in various bodies of water, bloated and gray in the shallows, bumping against the berm. Ten years he's been gone, and still he comes back to me like this. Last month my wife and I were driving through Michigan's Upper Peninsula, wending our way through vistas of alluvial forest, when suddenly the road opened up beside a river, and there he was in the water, face up near the shore. A few days later, at a dinner party with friends, I recounted this sighting and found myself explaining the Smiley Face Killers and my dalliance with the competing theories. But as I recapped the minutiae of these narratives and as the expressions of my listeners grew more cynical and bemused, I glimpsed the story for what it was: a delusion, a bad dream.

Speculation about the Smiley Face Killers has lessened appreciably over the last couple of years. There are many reasons for this, but chief among them is the revelation that a New York–based detective had fabricated evidence to make the theory stick. (During the investigation of an East River drowning, he spray-painted *Cayuagawt* on a cement wall not far from where the body was found, insisting the graffiti was a clue to a different drowning, one that had occurred along the Cayuga Wilderness Trail in Ithaca, New York.) Of course, such chicanery shouldn't necessarily upend the entire case, but as criminal profiler Clarissa Cole and others have pointed out, there are other facts that should give us pause.

Roughly thirty-eight hundred people drown each year in the United States, and seventeen- to twenty-four-year-olds are the most common age group, after unobserved children. Drowning on a weekend is 48 percent more likely than drowning during the workweek, and almost all of the men thought to be murdered by the Smiley Face Killers were found on a Saturday or a Sunday.

La Crosse is home to three colleges within one mile of a thriving riverfront district, where heavy drinking is not at all uncommon.

Finally, the smiley face is one of the most ubiquitous symbols in America, appearing on everything from the hippie era's Have a Nice Day meme to

Walmart's price-rollback ad campaign. As one discussion-board skeptic put it, "If you walk within five hundred yards of any body of water in America, you'll probably discover a smiley face."

I graduated from my master's program in the fall of 2010 and took a teaching gig at a small college that is, like many institutions in this neck of the country, rimmed by a freshwater lake. Some afternoons I stare out my office window, watching students retreat down leafy campus footpaths and disappear into the forests that embower the residential buildings. If I've become less prone to conspiracy since Luke's death, I've also become more keenly aware of the real dangers to which undergraduates are vulnerable. Deaths like Luke's are often ruled accidental, as random and unforeseeable as a cleft of lightning. But there do seem to be responsible parties, even if they lack the sensationalist appeal of a roving band of killers. After all, is it unreasonable to expect a riverside college town to fence off hazardous stretches of shoreline after even one drowning? And given the boozy reputations of Midwestern campuses, would we be naive for hoping that administrators would do more to curtail overconsumption? Of course, the self-service of these questions is not lost on me. In the end, my foray into the underworld of conspiracy was just an elaborate attempt to avoid thinking about my own share of the blame. After all, how many times had I gone out drinking with friends, only to let them wander off with attractive women or cohorts of decent-seeming strangers, never once checking up on them? A decade later, I still chide myself for not calling Luke that night, for not heading to La Crosse that weekend, for not keeping him safe.

The other morning, I was jogging near my apartment when I noticed, tagged on the facade of an ocher-colored warehouse, a huge winking smiley face. It was maybe sixty yards from a riverbank. I wish I could say I trotted past it with a mind unadulterated by terror. But something inside me broke open, and I found myself succumbing to a familiar anxiety. When you dwell in these thought patterns long enough, it becomes ever easier to regard each day through the cracked looking glass of fear. "You behold in me," Stephen

Daedalus says in *Ulysses*, "a poor example of free thought." In certain frames of mind, I know the feeling all too well.

I turned and kept running down the elm-studded boulevard. It was late October, the clouds low and gothic, and my thoughts swerved to a long-forgotten memory, of a football practice where Luke and I had raced each other. All afternoon we'd been mouthing off about who was faster, two showboats reveling in aimless competition. At the end of practice, we hunkered down in the end zone and our teammates formed two lines, making an alleyway for us to run through. I can still feel Luke beside me, even now, a mayhem of legs and arms. For twenty yards, maybe thirty, we ran stride for stride, the thunder of his body mirroring my own. But at some point my will faltered, and soon the distance between us lengthened, until he was no longer within reach.

PROPHET OF THE SWAMP

To get to the future, you must leave the coast of South Florida. Head inland on a county highway, one that penetrates the flat, mind-numbing expanse of the Everglades—past rock mines and Sequoia stands and faded billboards hailing defunct tourist traps—all the way to the community of Venus, population 1,043.

I'm driving a rented minivan down a long gravel road, my tires creating a roostertail of dust. The air conditioning stopped working around the limits of Fort Lauderdale, and the van's interior has become muggy in the March heat. Something I learned rather late in my travel plans is that Florida has no interstate that runs across its interior. All major highways meander up the coast—channels of sunshine and commerce—which makes this trip into the state's industrial core feel a bit like going off the grid, wandering backstage on the great American production that is spring break. Outside the window, there's a montage of orange groves and decrepit barns, trees bearded with Spanish moss. Clusters of scrawny cattle plod across a withered pasture, swatting flies with their tails.

I glance at my phone, scanning the email I received from a member of the Venus Project earlier in the week. *If you're early, please wait in or near your car*, it says. *Don't walk around the land or down to the water as there are alligators.*

After a mile, the road becomes a lunar surface, cratered and wrecked and gray. A colonnade of palm trees lines the road, at the end of which stands a large gate that reads:

THE VENUS PROJECT.

JACQUE FRESCO AND ROXANNE MEADOWS.

I hop out of the car and futz with the rusted latch until the gate swings open, and after puttering down the long driveway, I finally see a group of cars parked haphazardly around a sun-glazed pond. At least fifteen people have already arrived, milling around and shaking hands. No alligators are anywhere in view.

I meet a young, hippieish couple from Stuart, Florida. The man, whose hair is speckled with dried paint, nods at me in the brusque, self-assured manner of alpha males everywhere. His companion wears a mirror-plated skirt and ballet flats, her hair blond and sculpted, like the bouffant of a Lichtenstein print.

"So, how'd you guys hear about Jacque?" I ask.

"*Zeitgeist*, originally," the guy says.

"Me too! *Zeitgeist*," says a gangly man who steps out of the shade wearing Jesus sandals.

I nod decisively even though I have no idea what they're talking about. The next visitors to arrive are an amiable gay couple in their mid-fifties, decked out in Crocs and sunhats. "This place speaks to our *Star Trek*-y tendencies, so we wanted to check it out."

As we stand there listlessly, waiting for an official person to show, the conversation turns more generally to the South: Florida State, memories of

Katrina. The woman from Stuart was living in New Orleans at the time of the disaster and regales us with several anecdotes that seem almost too bizarre to reproduce here with journalistic integrity, claiming that bands of kids with AK-47s occupied her alleyway, that the Secret Service was sent to the Superdome under the guise of relief workers.

"Seen any voodoo down there?" asks the man with the Jesus sandals.

"Not the legit stuff. But it was there, you could tell."

The older member of the Fort Lauderdale couple claims that when he was a boy growing up in Alabama his neighbor was a bona fide Vodouisant known for casting hexes on random townspeople. He was never supposed to tell his friends when he got sick because "Mom worried that if the Mambo found out, she might come over to the house and try to heal me with potions and chicken bones."

As though sensing my incredulity, he turns and asks me where I'm from.

"Wisconsin."

"Oh," he says, and the group momentarily falls silent. I try to conjure up some zany local folklore to impress these southerners, to prove that the Midwest is also a vector of weirdness and wonder, but nothing comes to mind. "It's pretty quiet," I say.

"So is the Northwest," says a college student from Seattle. "Someone gets a rock in their Earth Shoe and it's pandemonium."

The clouds part, and sunlight bursts through the serrated edges of the overhead palm trees, beaming down at schizoid angles. Geckos dash across the gravel and vanish into the shrubbery. Finally, one of Jacque's assistants fetches us from the driveway and leads us into the first building of the tour, a futuristic-looking structure made of white plaster and cement, shaped like a portabella cap. We approach a sliding glass door that reads THE VENUS PROJECT in creamy stenciled letters. Just around the corner is the man we're here to see.

—

I first heard about Jacque Fresco via a student of mine who chose to write his final paper about the Venus Project. The student was a hemp-clad kid, one who regularly derailed class discussions with elaborate conspiracy theories about the World Bank or the connections between the Bible and the Chinese zodiac. In his paper, he called Fresco "a modern-day Da Vinci" and "the twenty-first century's leading social architect of the future." A Google search soon led me to a *Larry King* interview from 1974 during which Fresco, a self-described industrial designer, detailed his plans for what he would eventually call a "resource-based economy," a neologism he minted to describe a system where all goods and services are available, free of charge, to everyone. As he told King:

> If you took all the gold and all the wealth of this country, all of the certificates of debt and all of the land ownership, all of the diamonds and rings, and dumped it off the coast of Japan, as long as you didn't touch the American way of thinking, our technology, and our resources, we would not be impoverished at all. America's wealth is not its gold, is not its banking institutions. These are false institutions. The entire money-structured and materialistic society is a false society. Ten or fifteen years from now, our society will go down in history as the lowest development in man. We have the brains, the know-how, the technology, and the feasibility to build an entirely new civilization.

This civilization would be created through "socio-cyberneering," a radical form of social engineering where automation and technology would bring about "a way of life worthy of man."

Throughout the interview, Fresco brandished full-color sketches of the future: white domes perched on the surface of the ocean and arranged in concentric circles so as to resemble the structure of an atom. Serving as the city's nucleus was a central computer, which would monitor the ecology of the region—measuring crop yields in farmlands, controlling irrigation, and overseeing hydroelectric power grids. Expanding outward were civic centers, museums, and universities, all of which would operate like public libraries in that any cultural artifact would be available for temporary loan. The next largest ring of the city consisted of a residential area, where denizens would dwell amid opulent gardens and manicured parks, in built-to-suit developments. These elliptical abodes would contain every amenity imaginable (at one point, Fresco predicts the invention of entertainment software that sounds breathtakingly similar to Netflix). The city's enclosure—the crust of the circle—would house a massive recycling center to which all trash would be ferried via underground conveyor belts. Once there, automated machines would sort the refuse for proper salvaging.

Fresco was gruff and humorless throughout the interview, wholly immune to King's attempts at playful banter. At one point, he pronounced, "Socio-cyberneering is an organization that is probably the boldest organization ever conceived of, and we're undertaking the most ambitious project in the history of mankind."

—

The Internet is teeming with lore about Jacque's origins, most of it adulatory and unnervingly detailed. He grew up in Brooklyn during the nascent days of the Great Depression, and at thirteen, he began sketching odd buildings, queer structures, visions of a better world. Perhaps as a coping mechanism to endure the deprivations of his hometown, he drew ritzy glass monoliths with finned roofs and curved walls, which recalled the slick architecture from Fritz Lang's *Metropolis*, a celluloid favorite of his at the time. So advanced were his sketches that his high school principal arranged for him to meet Buckminster Fuller, the neo-futurist known for inventing geodesic domes. When the two met, "Bucky" was seated in his self-designed Dymaxion car, with its odd teardrop contours, and the young Jacque wasted no time in pressing the famed inventor about "social things," asking if Fuller ever thought about redesigning the economy, such as giving laborers a greater share of the profits in order to incentivize production. Wise to systemic intransigence, Fuller explained it was hard enough to get a patent and produce a new car, let alone try to upend society. Jacque wasn't convinced.

Over the next decade, as the Dust Bowl smothered the Great Plains, Jacque hitchhiked across the continent, searching for examples of a more equitable social arrangement. His odyssey eventually led him to the tropics of Tahiti, where the "native sharing system" toppled his Western values. When a polygamous chieftain offered Jacque the "best" of his six wives for entertainment and sundry pleasures, Jacque bristled—until he realized that conjugal loyalty was nothing more than a social construct. But it was the tribe's allocation of resources that intrigued him most. Food wasn't divvied up based upon rank or status, nor was anyone denied sustenance because of financial lack. Instead, the bounty of the island was apportioned equally to all.

Such observations led Jacque to realize that humans weren't a bunch of slavering primates who sought to dominate one another, as Tennyson said, "red in tooth and claw." And despite the prevailing Hobbesian wisdom in the West, life on the island wasn't nasty, brutal, and short. Rather, Jacque saw that the tribe's egalitarian behavior was merely cultural, a reflection of its members' customs and mores, which led him to his signature idea: if we want the Western world to overcome war, avarice, and poverty, all we have to do is redesign the culture.

Despite these quixotic ideas, Jacque spent most of the post-war years engineering consumer products. He designed the first "Trend Home," a prefabricated residence that could be constructed in under eight hours, and established the Scientific Research Laboratories, where he dreamed up a trove of zany devices, such as an umbrella with an electrified disc that could repel rainwater through the polarity of its charge. Some of these designs were featured in *Popular Science*, *Variety*, and *Popular Mechanics*.

It wasn't until the 1960s that Jacque finally adumbrated his grand vision for the future. Concerned that most people would remain unmoved by such frothy proclamations, he decided to construct a life-sized model of his ideal city. In 1980, accompanied by Roxanne Meadows, his romantic partner and fellow architect, Jacque purchased twenty-two acres of land in Venus, Florida, a quaint hinterland just two hours north of Miami. Within a few years, the couple had built several concrete domes on the property, which itself was teeming with cypress trees, exotic birds, and a brood of alligators. Boasting lush vegetation and state-of-the-art design, the estate was meant to stand as the ultimate prototype, the consummate example of what life could look like when you marshaled science and technology toward building an efficient, peaceful society.

I found all of this exceedingly weird and fascinating. But what intrigued me most about the Venus Project was the extent to which the promises of social engineering, so uniformly disastrous when implemented during the twentieth century, were suddenly enjoying a revival. Jacque's ideas were particularly attractive to those Americans who had been left vulnerable by the fiscal tumult of the previous decade. Early in my research, I stumbled across a video of Jacque speaking at an Occupy Miami rally in 2011. Clad in vintage cabana wear—a canvas sunhat and an eyeblue t-shirt—he told the placard-bearing activists something that struck me as both candid and brave. "Protesting the stock market," he said, "isn't going to do anything. I hate to tell you this, but it's true." Such remarks led me to believe that the Venus Project might eschew simple transgressive gestures for a more substantial model of an alternative society. Perhaps it would go beyond the hazy objectives of Occupy Wall Street, a movement that did little, in the end, to diminish the brawn of financial capitalism. By the end of the video, I was flooded with questions: What *was* this resource-based economy, exactly? Could a community really operate without a monetary system? Was Jacque Fresco a genius or a loon, or both? I went to Venus to find out.

—

After filing into the small foyer of the dome, we fork over a two-hundred-dollar admission fee, a price that, in addition to the seminar and tour, apparently includes "one hundred dollars' worth of books and DVDs." We shuffle past a small sideboard table featuring a smorgasbord of nibbles and tidbits—carrots, fruit, and chips—as well as cups of pre-poured lemonade. I've been driving for two hours in a sweltering minivan and am perilously lightheaded, so I don't think twice about snagging a sweaty glass and guzzling down the syrupy beverage before I all of a sudden recall the old exhortation you're apt to hear whenever spending time around particularly charismatic figures: don't drink the Kool-Aid.

The dome is dark and surprisingly capacious, containing ten rows of chairs that face a tan leather sofa, which is surrounded by a forest of cameras and microphones. On the walls, laminated posters depict the buildings of the future: lozenge-shaped structures that float on pixelated oceans. And yet, despite Jacque's preoccupation with the world to come, the sad truth is that these printouts look decidedly outdated, on par with the video game graphics from the Sega CD era.

It's only after I take my seat that I spot the whiskered eminence himself. Jacque is seated up front on the couch, thronged by citrus-colored pillows, his face partially obscured by AV equipment. This is probably a good spot to mention that Jacque is ninety-nine years old and conspicuously senescent. Aside from his craggy face, he's garbed in winter clothes—a black leather jacket, dark jeans, matching orthopedic shoes—and sits on two supplementary cushions, presumably for sciatica support and general balance. While more visitors continue to file in and find their seats, Roxanne—Jacque's much younger inamorata, a brunette with librarian glasses—announces that we're about to get started.

After a second, Jacque, who has been sitting there silently observing us, blinking animatronically, finally speaks up. His voice is raspy and quavering: "I'm going to say a lot of things, and some things may bother you, but hear me out." What follows is difficult to describe. It isn't so much a sermon or address, but rather a fusillade of provocative statements, some of which sound like a George Carlin riff, while others resemble the CliffsNotes to Cultural Relativism 101. Here's Jacque on innate human talent: "Nobody has any gifts; you reflect your culture." On creativity: "There is no such thing as human creativity." Jacque Fresco on Christianity: "It's a wonderful idea; when are they going to put it into practice?" Jacque Fresco on the slipperiness of the English language: "Bullshit has nothing to do with the shit of a bull." On God: "They made God into the ultimate control device to tame stupid people." Jacque Fresco on the vagaries of human sexuality: "If a boy is raised by six women, he'll reflect the worldview of women and become a homosexual." On freedom: "You aren't free. You can't yell 'fire' in a theater, so how could you be free?" On beauty: "There is no such thing as a beautiful woman." On the Ku Klux Klan: "I dissolved the KKK in Miami." Jacque Fresco on the Western fetishization of female erogenous zones: "When you stroke the dog, you don't stop at the balls. You stroke the whole dog."

As far as I can tell, this speech is meant to recreate the lightning bolt moment he experienced while visiting the Tuamotus people in Tahiti—if you can recognize that your behavior is learned, your cultural customs are arbitrary, and your social structures are man-made, then you can begin to imagine alternatives. Like any good firebrand, he wants to shake up the Etch A Sketch of our worldview, erasing any trace of conventional wisdom. Throughout the disquisition, he speaks with a kind of revolutionary élan, gesturing broadly with a clenched hand. Many times, he will lean over to emphasize a certain point, and the precariousness of his pillowed arrangement will make me cringe.

After an hour of these free associations, Roxanne intervenes, reminding Jacque that he should probably explain the Venus Project's central ambitions. Quickly, he shifts into autopilot and delivers a scripted lecture on the pillars of the resource-based economy, a truncated version of the more sweeping utopic vision he put forth in his 2002 book, *The Best That Money Can't Buy: Beyond Politics, Poverty, and War.* "Simply stated, a Resource-Based Economy," he writes, "uses existing resources rather than money, and provides an equitable distribution of goods and services in a humane and efficient manner for the entire population." In this imagined world, the conditions of social and political life will not follow the erratic whims of the free market, but will be dictated by the irrefutable tenets of science. By using "cybernated sensors" to monitor the planet's resources, this society would supposedly bring an end to the toxic practices of scarcity and market speculation, thereby obviating the need for political institutions. All of the vital decisions about the direction of society would no longer be clouded by partisan fervor, but would instead be determined by a system of intelligent machines making passionless, algorithmic choices. "The fact that machines have no emotions," Jacque has written, "may in some ways make them superior to human systems."

Comments like these, for me anyway, serve to darken the sunny *building-a-better-tomorrow* aspect of the Venus Project's message. Beneath Jacque's airy ruminations about our post-capitalist future, there lurks a sniffy detestation for most human beings, whom he has regarded, both in print and in person, as irrational halfwits driven by greed and crass desire, an opinion that extends even to the members of his family. In a 2011 interview with *The Orlando Weekly*, Jacque described his parents as "normal," which is to say, "fucked-up by society . . . They knew nothing. I looked at them as children, pissants."

Because logic and reasoned argument cannot penetrate such minds, Fresco wants to re-engineer the social landscape so that individuals will be impelled to act rationally, even if they aren't aware of the degree to which they are being nudged. This underscores one of Jacque's central tenants: "building it into the design." The hope is that, by constructing a gadget, a building, or even a city in a certain way, you can elicit predictable social behaviors. For instance, instead of trying to convince people to monitor their water usage, you could design a bathroom where used shower water is automatically repurposed to fill the basin of a toilet. Likewise, exercise could be incorporated into the layout of public schools as a means of curbing childhood obesity. Rather than instituting sumptuary rules about vending machines or cafeteria menus, administrators could build schools on the crests of steep hills so students would have to perform gut-busting climbs each morning.

It's during the middle of this lecture that a lanky blond man wearing aviator shades enters the dome and saunters down the center aisle, holding the hand of a woman who is whispering, to no one in particular, repeated apologies for their tardiness. The couple beelines for the front row and takes a couple of seats directly in front of Jacque, who seems unfazed by the interruption. While I don't believe in auras or chakras or anything, I can't help but detect something gloomy and slightly unhinged about this blond guy, a fog of dread that hovers darkly around him. Sitting at the front of the room, he removes his sunglasses and begins to display an unsettling twitchiness—fidgeting in his seat, throwing an arm around his companion only to extract it and swiftly adopt the posture of Rodin's *Thinker*.

When Jacque grumbles something in passing about the inefficiency of the military, the blond man can no longer contain himself. "Can I say something real quick?" he asks in a thick Texan drawl. "Can I just tell you about how wars are run these days?"

To my surprise, Jacque nods, yielding the floor. The Texan explains that he's an Iraq War veteran and has witnessed firsthand the greed and truculence of our country. He suggests our protracted battle in the Middle East is nothing more than a self-fulfilling prophecy, where every enemy casualty only spawns a growing pool of combatants, since the kinfolk of these slain soldiers invariably respond by taking up arms and seeking vengeance. The soliloquy seems significantly inspired by Jeremy Scahill's 2013 documentary, *Dirty Wars*, which reported on the practice of clandestine assassination in Afghanistan and Iraq, arguing that this strategy did more to perpetuate violence and mayhem than it did to create lasting stability in the region. But something about the way the man describes it now makes the whole idea sound a little nutty, just another conspiracy theory.

Roxanne is the one to step in, interrupting the Texan's speech and opening up the floor for a Q&A. Jacque's hearing aids have been on the fritz, so she'll be "interpreting" our questions for him. Given the futuristic vibe here at the Venus Project, I assume this will involve a system of high-tech gizmos, but in the end, Roxanne just relays our queries by leaning over and shouting them into Jacque's ear at alarming decibel levels, with the frustration of a hospice nurse.

Journalistically speaking, there isn't much to say about this colloquium. Despite Jacque's repeated assurances that his plan for the future is comprehensive and practical, the project's underlying logic is revealed as decidedly muzzy when exposed to scrutiny. When one visitor wonders whether the Venus Project would ever form an army to protect the city from outside aggression, Jacque says the "people of the future" will be rational and therefore won't engage in such brute behavior. When she clarifies that she's referring to people who might see themselves as enemies of this society, Jacque replies that the dazzling wonders of the new cities would thwart any unwholesome invaders.

Other visitors stand up to introduce themselves. There is a twentysomething musician who incorporates Jacque's lectures into his songs, a Mexican documentarian who hitchhiked here just so he could videotape the seminar, which he hopes to screen for the citizens of his hometown. There is an Australian nurse who was drawn to the Venus Project after treating hundreds of people sick from contaminated well water.

A few of these visitors allude, in their questions, to the mysterious *Zeitgeist*, name-dropping it with a kind of insider familiarity. Later I'll discover that *Zeitgeist* is a trio of pseudo-anthropological documentaries that suggests, among other things, that the historical Jesus never existed, that the New World Order coordinates all global events, and that the attacks of 9/11 were orchestrated by the government in order to squash civil liberties and foment the War on Terror. The films are the handiwork of Peter Joseph, the raffish founder of the Zeitgeist Movement, a band of dissidents who want to replace capitalism with a resource-based economy. The first *Zeitgeist* film came out in 2007, and some critics have traced its popularity to the fact that its release coincided with the crash of the housing market, a time when many Americans were suffering, in very real ways, from the wanton excesses of capitalism. Late in the film, when discussing possible alternatives to the market, Joseph cites the Venus Project as an exemplar of a post-scarcity economy.

It's clear that the Venus Project has become a haven for disenfranchised individuals—veterans cast aside by the country they served; college graduates saddled with eye-popping debt; homeowners lured into toxic mortgages and eventually forced to foreclose. For those who've suffered the worst of this bleak fiscal landscape, the Venus Project presents itself as an escape hatch out of a system they feel powerless to change.

Many visitors are anxious to know what they can do to bring about the world promised by the Venus Project. What can they do on an individual level? How can they get their communities involved? On this point, Jacque and Roxanne are oddly blasé. They insist the new world will not come about until a majority of people are convinced of its necessity. It will take some kind of major disaster, natural or economic, to get everyone on board. "All we can do is spread the word," Roxanne says. She notes that anyone who wants to become an official Venus Project "ambassador" can sign up to receive more information.

Several folks are visibly disappointed by this tepid prescription, especially since a large bloc of them seem like pilgrims who've come here to receive a call to action from their beloved guru. Later, once we've migrated outside, I will notice the Texan smoking in the fulsome shade of a cypress tree, where he has donned a droopy safari hat. Pinching his cigarette in the three-fingered manner of someone sipping from a joint, he tells a crew of visitors that, despite what Jacque has said about waiting for the free market to collapse, he really wants to "get something started right now." He encourages the people around him to swap contact information.

Of course, not everyone here fits the mold of the disenfranchised pilgrim. There is also a brand of visitor who seems remarkably more cynical—the couple from Fort Lauderdale, for example, or a cluster of young people dressed fashionably in sundresses and fedoras who spent the entire lecture covertly snapping photographs of the eccentric décor. As far as I can tell, these are the two sides of the Venus Project's demographical coin: disillusioned citizens seeking political guidance and wealthy tourists hunting for kooky fun. As the Texan begins collecting information from people, the divide between novelty-hunter and true believer becomes painfully clear. The couple from Stuart shows enthusiasm, but the men from Fort Lauderdale swiftly turn their backs, barely suppressing their amusement.

—

It is easy to reject the Venus Project as nothing more than the doodles of a wizened crank, an impractical blueprint for an impossible way of life. To give into such skepticism, though, is to ignore the extent to which the concept of social engineering has served as the bedrock of our country. The founding fathers often relied on Arcadian language to describe the American experiment—"the city upon a hill," "the empire of liberty"—and many of the colonies were founded as planned utopian societies. Indeed, America presented itself as a tabula rasa for British Enlightenment thinkers who wanted to construct new social systems, which had been impossible to implement in their own country.

Georgia, for example, was established in 1733 by James Edward Oglethorpe, a member of British parliament who was inspired by the seminal utopian text *The Commonwealth of Oceana*. Oglethorpe designed Georgia as a system of concentric circles—with farmland on the outskirts, residential lots in the middle, and a commons in the center of town (a plan that bears a striking resemblance to Jacque's own proposals for the future). The colony was one of the first where social equality would be accomplished through comprehensive urban design. Profits that exceeded a certain figure would be recouped and invested in communal projects. Slavery was outlawed, as was alcohol. So ambitious was this plan that John Burton, a theologian and one of Oglethorpe's most trusted confidants, believed that Georgia would "seem in a literal sense to begin the world again."

Colonial America would ultimately host several other planned communities, but it wasn't until the Progressive Era that utopians would institute social engineering on a national scale. At the time, the United States was swept up in "an efficiency craze," where experts were counted upon to redress every social problem by eliminating waste and deficiency. Historian Samuel Haber has contended that, as the old haunts of God and spirituality were gradually exorcised by scientific reason, many Americans were in the midst of "a secular Great Awakening," replacing the Christian principle of "goodness" with the modern virtue of "efficiency."

Yet few people noticed the fascistic mindset lurking below the chirpy promises of social engineers. Blind deference to experts, after all, would inevitably give rise to authoritarian regimes like the Soviet Union, Mao Zedong's China, and the Khmer Rouge. Even the U.S. would flirt with more radical forms of social engineering. In the 1927 Supreme Court case *Buck v. Bell*, the justices ruled in favor of negative eugenics, which allowed states to carry out compulsory sterilization of "feeble-minded citizens." Perhaps swayed by the tides of the moment, the ruling was made in the name of efficiency. "It is better for all the world," wrote Justice Oliver Wendell Holmes, "if instead of waiting to execute degenerate offspring for crime, or to let them starve for their imbecility, society can prevent those who are manifestly unfit from continuing their kind."

This vexed history of social engineering meant that, for decades, the term carried these dark affiliations. Even Jacque and Roxanne are hesitant to use it, preferring instead "socio-cyberneering." In fact, when someone on the

Venus Project tour asks about "social engineering," Roxanne lets out an airy, pressurized laugh and looks suddenly flustered. "You know, that term makes a lot of people nervous, because we tend to associate it with communism." With the agility of a seasoned politician, she adroitly pivots into a discussion about how the Venus Project differs from Marxism, never really answering the question.

But the truth is that now, after decades in which social engineering was dismissed as undemocratic, many Americans are welcoming the idea. B. F. Skinner's theories on behavior modification, which were once deemed methods of brainwashing, are now enjoying a renascence among pop scientists and academics. Similarly, Daniel Kahneman's book on the psychology of judgment, *Thinking, Fast and Slow*, has become something of a vade mecum for policymakers interested in manipulating emotions to improve the electorate's mood. As technology and big data increasingly become part of the government's toolbox, it's easy to imagine a time when policy decisions will be determined not by consensus, but through the "objective" best-case scenarios generated by algorithms.

Some have even suggested that the U.S. follow the lead of countries like Singapore, which uses mass surveillance and predictive analytics to create a more harmonious society. Several U.S. officials have visited the island in recent years to study the country's "curious mix of democracy and authoritarianism," as Shane Harris has described it for *Foreign Policy*. More than anything else, these American diplomats are interested in Singapore's Risk Assessment and Horizon Scanning program, which helps avert terrorist attacks and other so-called "future shocks." The program also engages in social engineering—developing procurement cycles, making economic predictions, and building curricula for the nation's schools—and trawls the social media posts of ordinary citizens to measure the potential for popular unrest.

Most Singaporeans are remarkably unperturbed by this program, and perhaps it's easy to see why. The virtue of social engineering, after all, is its promise of moral relief. The citizen doesn't have to entertain those pesky questions of rightness or wrongness anymore, since the very armature of the social landscape nudges them toward the "right" choice. Questions about ethics once required an atmosphere of contemplation and debate, but in the eyes of social engineers like Jacque, such activities are frivolous and inefficient, just so much pointless theorizing. Now the moral realm is simply a matter of data and design. In the end, it's hard not to notice the resonance between this yen for greater social control and, say, the emergence of authoritarian leaders like Donald Trump. When so many Americans feel helpless against the volatility of the market and cannot compete with lobbyists for the attention of their elected officials, it's no wonder they are willing to surrender their liberties in exchange for the safety and certitude of social control.

—

Outside, the sun's molten glare makes the landscape seem blanched and depthless. It's 90 degrees, and the air is sodden and hot, not unlike the innards of a just-removed mitten. Eventually, Roxanne appears and leads us on a tour. Speaking with the enthusiasm of docents everywhere, she chronicles the early history of the Venus Project, dispensing nuggets of information at every turn. Initially, she and Jacque considered buying one of the Exuma Islands in the Caribbean, which were too expensive, so they decided on the land in Venus for only ten thousand dollars. Since then, they have occasionally completed freelance architectural gigs to cover the cost of new renovations.

As we walk around the grounds, it quickly becomes clear that the campus is in a gradual state of decay. The lawns are withered and yellow. The pool, which on the website appeared to be a limpid sapphire, is actually a scummy green, fetid with vegetative rot. Earlier, when Roxanne spoke of the Venus Project's dire financial straits, I assumed this was a fundraising ploy, a subtle form of busking. Now, though, it's obvious that they've fallen on hard times or, at the very least, have had to cut back on horticultural upkeep.

Approaching the first dome of the tour, which is a model home, Roxanne confirms my suspicions, saying that, while she and Jacque wanted to expand the Venus Project, all of their plans have been stymied by the miserable fiscal climate, a comment that inspires the Texan to unleash yet another full-volume tirade, this one about the evils of the debt economy.

"They've got our hands tied around our backs and we don't even know it!" he yells. He holds his arms out, wrists together, miming a man in chains.

Roxanne nods with the cheeriness of a preschool teacher, waiting until he's finished, then calmly echoes his general sentiment, explaining that anyone who needs to remind you that you're free has probably already abridged your freedom.

The Texan silently repeats this to himself. As we walk into the dome, I overhear him ask his girlfriend for a pen, presumably so that he can write down the adage for posterity.

Inside, the dome is furnished with retro-looking sofas and kitchen stools built into the wall. It's a vision of the future conceived in the 1970s—*The Jetsons* meets Soviet futurism. A kidney-shaped breakfast island demarcates the start of an efficiency kitchen, and huge portholes let in mote-ridden tunnels of lemony sunlight. Roxanne tells us the dome is meant to approximate what most residences would look like in the future, noting that the white concrete exterior helps keep the home well-insulated and cool.

Despite these reassurances, the inside of the dome feels every bit as humid and sweltering as the swampland outside. Mosquitoes blitzkrieg us in dark swarms, and everyone starts swatting frantically until little asterisks of squashed bugs constellate our t-shirts. Roxanne apologizes for the pests but explains that we're in swamp country, so there's little she can do. While I would normally accept this brand of fatalism, I find myself more than a little irked. If the whole point of the Venus Project is to marshal science and technology toward optimizing human life, can't somebody around here cook up a simple bug zapper?

Already, the Venus Project has proven to be a mighty disappointment. To my mind, the success of any alternative vision for society rests in its ability to instantiate those utopian aspirations expressed so elegantly in its pamphlets and propaganda. While Jacque may have constructed a sleek and neatly appointed estate, none of the buildings on campus actually conduct the operations of a resource-based economy. There's no farmland generating edible crop. There's no omniscient central computer monitoring the ecosystem of the region. Even Jacque's bathroom appears to be your standard, run-of-the-mill lavatory with conventional plumbing, failing to incorporate the central tenet of his own architectural approach: building it into the design. The Venus Project thus stands as nothing more than an overpriced museum, a collection of relics from the career of an inventor who once harbored idealistic ambitions but has now retreated into the outskirts of Florida, living out his days in gruff dismissal of the system.

—

As we're returning to the Venus Project's headquarters, I notice another visitor's backpack, the front pocket of which reads FACEBOOK in stitched white letters. The man wears a Hawaiian shirt *and* Hawaiian shorts, although the bottoms have a different motif and color scheme than the top, which makes him look like a parody of tourism. But it's the backpack that throws me off. Perhaps he's just an ordinary guy, a big fan of social media who shills for the company whenever he has things to tote? But does Facebook really have its own line of apparel? What gives? I pick up the pace and, upon approaching him, ask whether he works for the social network, if he's a congregant in the House of Zuckerberg.

"Yes," he says, with great formality and evident pride. "I work for Facebook." In this moment, I'm too distracted by his German accent, full of glottal diphthongs and abrasive consonants, to analyze his curious choice of preposition—he works *for* Facebook, not *at* Facebook.

He says that he and a friend came all the way from California just to visit the Venus Project. They flew into Miami last night and are leaving later this evening. We commiserate about the Texan's disruptive outbursts and swap comments about Fresco's myriad innovations. "You know," he says, after a long silence, "it's funny, Facebook is actually doing a lot of the things Jacque talks about."

He explains that the company has started providing Wi-Fi access to developing countries through its Free Basics program, which connects people to the Internet in places like Africa and southern Asia. Facebook has also been developing drones that could eventually beam Wi-Fi to rural areas. The way he presents it, the project sounds like an act of corporate philanthropy, one that will improve the lives of millions—perhaps even billions—of people. There's a triumphant pitch to his voice, a barely repressible giddiness at the fact that Facebook can so speedily address the digital divide with a simple automated solution.

I happen to know something about this project, and what he doesn't mention is that some critics have pilloried this endeavor for violating net neutrality, seeing it as one more instantiation of the company's effort to harvest data and secure their global hegemony. The program was initially designed so citizens of these impoverished countries could only browse the Internet through a Facebook-controlled portal, conveniently allowing the company to expand its data market while limiting access to other sites. Zuckerberg has argued, somewhat petulantly, that these criticisms are idealistic and unfair: "We have collections of free basic books. They're called libraries," he wrote in *The Times of India*. "They don't contain every book, but they still provide a world of good." Facebook has since expanded the program to websites that meet its technical criteria, though the service remains something of a walled garden.

Projects like these are, of course, a more immediate and realistic glimpse into the future: one in which the latest technology is harnessed not in the service of utopian communalism, but rather for profit. If anything, Facebook's presence here at the Venus Project draws into clarity something that has been bugging me all day. It may well be that Jacque's brand of technological solutionism—to borrow Evgeny Morozov's term—sounds so familiar because it recalls the dogged optimism of Silicon Valley, an unwavering belief that we can code our way toward wealth and ethical perfection. Just listen to Marc Andreessen, a Menlo Park venture capitalist, wax grandiosely on the Valley's vision for the future:

> Posit a world in which all material needs are provided free, by robots and material synthesizers . . . Imagine six, or ten, billion people doing nothing but arts and sciences, culture and exploring and learning. What a world that would be.

Historically, social engineering has been the preferred strategy of utopians looking to overthrow capitalism. But Silicon Valley presents a rare case where private corporations have taken up the mantle of designing a better tomorrow—albeit not for its citizens, but for its customers. Scads of smart technologies have been released over the last decade—fridges, cars, and thermostats—promising to nudge customers toward more ethical behavior. In his book *To Save Everything, Click Here*, Morozov, a strident critic of Silicon Valley, examines one such research project called BinCam. This invention outfits an ordinary trashcan with a smartphone that takes pictures of the bin's contents whenever the lid is closed. Workers for Amazon's Mechanical Turk program then review each photo, determining whether any of the discarded items could have been recycled. This info is then automatically posted to the person's Facebook page and given a conservationist score, allowing users to compete with each other.

On the surface, BinCam seems like an ingeniously playful solution to the problem of shoddy recycling. But embedded within the product are a whole host of dubious ethical assumptions, which Morozov proceeds to usefully interrogate: "Should we get one set of citizens to do the right thing by getting another set of citizens to spy on them? Should we introduce game incentives into a process that has previously worked through appeals to one's duties and obligations? . . . Will participants stop doing the right thing if their Facebook friends are no longer watching?" What Morozov doesn't mention, of course, is that the real motivation behind these products isn't conservation or social justice. It's profit. Beyond whatever minor conservation efforts BinCam might foster, the gadget's chief function is to allow Facebook to dig through your trash and determine which products you buy and at what frequency, thus enabling it to more effectively sell your information to advertisers.

In other words, Facebook operates as a classic example of the ways in which Silicon Valley cloaks its economic motivations beneath the jargon of altruism. The company bills its features as convenient ways of staying more intimately "connected," but seldom mentions that Timeline tracks consumer habits across a lifetime or that Open Graph stalks users around the Internet even when they're not on Facebook.

From the podiums of tech conferences, luminaries from Silicon Valley often adopt the rhetoric of revolutionary utopians, insisting that the doctrine of disruption can guide us toward moral betterment, that social ills are actually just "engineering problems." Several Menlo Park investors have even taken a page from Jacque Fresco, specifically his designs for nautical cities. Back in 2008, Patri Friedman—grandson of Milton Friedman—established the Seasteading Institute, an ocean-based community that wants to experiment with alternative social and political systems. According to *The New Yorker*, the project received a $1.25 million investment from Peter Thiel, the outspoken libertarian and former PayPal CEO, who hoped, along with Friedman, to capitalize on the UN's lax maritime laws and explore new governmental frameworks, including those of pure, unregulated capitalism. One potential model was something Friedman called "Appletopia," which he told *Details* would allow a corporation like Apple to found its own country. And they aren't the only tech folks with this idea. In 2013, the entrepreneur Balaji Srinivasan called for Silicon Valley to secede from the union. This "Ultimate Exit," as he termed it, would require programmers and venture capitalists of the West Coast to "build an opt-in society, ultimately outside the U.S., run by technology."

Of course, the relevant difference between the Venus Project and Silicon Valley is that the latter group actually has the money to carry off such a project and thus has little incentive to abolish the free market system. Utopian rhetoric aside, these tycoons are not about to endorse a resource-based economy. In such a climate, to think that technology and good design are the last bastions against the bruising effects of financial capitalism would be a grievous misapprehension. If anything, these moguls want an even freer exchange of capital and ideas, untrammeled by oversight or regulation. And as the election of 2016 made clear, when Facebook failed to police misinformation that was driving activity on its site, the company is far more interested in the bottom line than it is in preserving the democratic rudiments of truth and justice.

—

Our tour ends where it started. When we return to the dark dome—the Venus Project's headquarters—Jacque is waiting for us, still positioned atop his cathedra of pillows. Everyone is glazed with perspiration, and the heat has spawned a sudden camaraderie, prompting all of us to help out in the common cause of cooling off. One Venus Project staff member arranges a fan to oscillate across the first few rows of chairs, and a few female pilgrims help Roxanne fetch more glasses of lemonade. For a minute, you can almost imagine what it would be like to live here, with everyone cooperating like a motley Von Trapp family, a cheery symbiosis worthy of song.

Many of the visitors want to have their pictures taken with Jacque, so they queue up like congregants waiting to receive communion. The rest of us settle into our chairs. A few of the fashionable kids brandish their smartphones and begin flipping through the selfies they've taken while on the tour, posting the most flattering ones to Facebook and Instagram. Tendrils of sweaty hair are plastered darkly to one visitor's forehead. Another's cheeks are sun-scorched and crimson. After six hours here at the Venus Project, all of us are beginning to display the sleepy lassitude of the heavily medicated.

I take a final look at the people around me. Here is the poor musician who incorporates Jacque's lectures into his songs. Here is the Mexican documentarian—wearing a Stetson hat over long raven-colored hair—who hitchhiked here just so he could videotape Jacque's seminar. Here is the Australian nurse, her arm thrown over Jacque's shoulder, smiling plastically into the flash of a smartphone camera. And here is the Texan, gesticulating wildly, telling another visitor about the resource-based community he wants to establish in Nicaragua. These pilgrims—each forsaken by our system, each longing for a brighter future—have come to the backwater fringe of South Florida, searching for a vision of society where their grievances will be addressed, where the injustices they've faced will be acknowledged and treated with swift remedy. And yet, as dusk falls over Venus, Florida, I can't help but wonder who, in the end, will profit from this spirit of discontent.

CALLING AUDIBLES

The limits of my language mean the limits of my world.

—LUDWIG WITTGENSTEIN

On the afternoon of September 11th, 2001, I was at football practice. Unlike Americans who lived in cities and thus feared their own buildings might be attacked, residents of Brookfield, the suburb of Milwaukee where I grew up, harbored no such immediate concerns. While folks in New York hunkered down with loved ones or attended mass vigils, my teammates and I were suiting up. Our locker room was a chamber of institutional gray, rife with damp tile and cold metal benches, muggy with odors that only teenaged boys can manufacture. I'm sure there was some talk of what happened, but all I remember is the weird reverential silence, which was disturbed only by the susurrus of practice jerseys getting pulled over shoulder pads and the blunt staccato of cleats on the hallway tile as we trotted out of school, toward the practice fields.

Our coaches probably had some elaborate pedagogical justification for their decision to hold practice, one that had little to do with preparing for Friday's game against West Allis (a team with a scrawny offensive line and an anemic defense) and more to do with distracting us from the nonstop montage of blazing skyscrapers and people jumping to their deaths that we all watched on classroom TVs that morning.

Our varsity coach was an old leathery man with a newscaster's coiffure of dime-colored hair. As he patrolled the practice field and surveyed our efforts, his default expression was that of someone who has just eaten a gas station hot dog and now regrets it. Suffice it to say that he took absolutely zero in the way of shit. Unlike the passel of assistant coaches who tried to buddy up with us by shit-shooting and cracking-wise, Coach never ingratiated himself with his players, preferring instead to hang back and win our respect with his frosty disposition. But halfway through drills that day, Coach tweeted his whistle and sent us for a water break, which was the only time during practice when we were allowed to remove our helmets and take a knee. Such was a jarring moment. For two hours, you regarded your teammates through bulky gladiatorial masks, which gave their appearances a dark predacious aspect, but during water breaks, the helmets would come off and out came these doughy innocent faces—an album of big kind eyes, zit-greased miens, cheeks that sprouted sporadic facial hair. It was like you all of a sudden remembered that these guys had moms at home who kissed them goodnight and laundered their underwear.

I remember kneeling there and swilling water in the end zone—the ground torn up and cratered from our cleats—when Coach corralled all of his assistants over to the goal post, saying "Com'ere, boys."

Wearing ballcaps and beer guts, the coaches tottered over, their brows furrowed with curiosity. Reluctantly, they congregated near him, like disciples around a lesser prophet. He pointed up at the limpid blue sky. "Boys, there's not a single plane in that sky tonight."

I followed Coach's finger, the significance of his statement kindling my spine. It was true: the sky was empty, showed nothing, seemed endless. It was as if the national tragedy had somehow reversed our course and sent the heavens back to its antediluvian status, bare of contrails, emptied of planes. It was a scene Norman Rockwell might have painted: *Tableau of American Football Coaches Contemplating Sky with Boyish Wonder.* I stayed there for a long time, kneeling on the green provident grass, gawking up at the high blue quiet, preoccupied to the point where I missed the second whistle and didn't notice the other guys jogging back toward the practice field for wind-sprints and a team breakdown, until all of sudden Donaldson trotted over and jolted me out of this trance by smacking me on the ass with harnessed momentum and apparent feeling, saying, "Come on, Swany. Look alive, brother."

That Friday, before our game, our coaches decided to set aside the bitter rivalry and have both teams walk onto the field together, with each team's captain up front and clutching one end of the American flag: It was meant to serve as an eye-watering moment of patriotism, a purely American scene—corn-fed Midwestern boys sticking it to the terrorists by playing America's game only three days after what happened. Our school's drumline escorted us into the floodlit stadium, the curt patter of their snares lending our pageant the attitude of a funeral. In our snazzy uniforms and glinting helmets, we marched through the end zone, heading for the fifty-yard line, passing a trio of referees who were stationed on the sideline and whose eyes went crystalline as we approached, their mouths squiggled with some queer mixture of pride and grief. Squadrons of cheerleaders waited for us at the fifty-yard line, their eye shadow lurid and abundant, their hairdos lacquered and complex. The stadium was otherwise silent. Fans stood in the bleachers, a hushed tribute to our arrival. A photograph of this moment made the city papers. I'm three players back from the front, and you can just barely make out my face over one of my teammate's shoulder pads. My eyes are cast side-long and have little black hyphens drawn underneath them, and my face is terribly boyish despite the feeling I had at the time, which was that I was a man who could grasp every hue and nuance of what happened.

It's difficult to overstate the effect this moment had on me. On some level, I was aware that we boys were supposed to stand as riveting symbol of the American idea, a reassurance to a shaken community that life as we knew it could—and would—return to normal. Of course, this was theater, a sleight, a distraction. Nothing about teenaged boys (some of whom were old enough for military service) playing a child's game on a temperate September night would rinse the fans' minds of those harrowing pictures we all saw only a few days earlier. In our plasticine suburb, far from the smoldering ruins of Ground Zero and the stark silhouette of the New York firefighter, we served as unprepared understudies for the role of an American hero. Standing there on the dew-glittered field during the national anthem, holding the calloused hands of my teammates, watching the big lamp-lit flag flutter in the south end zone, I felt that our small town had channeled all its grief into the game, as if what were being enacted here wasn't the age-old pastime of boys at play but the early stirrings of battle.

———

Toward the end of that month, while firefighters, police officers, and volunteers were still clearing away rubble from the ash-confected streets of Manhattan, the NFL began a quiet campaign to purge the language of war from its broadcast commentary. Within days of the attack, seasoned sportscasters like John Madden and Al Michaels were already making public vows to avoid militaristic diction in their play-by-play:

> You'd never want to stray into an analogy like a "hijacking." But I'm not concerned we'll fall into that trap. (Michaels)

> The first thing I thought about, seeing people run out and the firefighters and police go in, was, I'll never use the word "tough" again to describe football players. (Madden)

One hopes that on-air semantic choices wasn't actually the *first thing* Madden thought about—one hopes he reflected on the victims' families or the geopolitical ramifications for our country, anything but the narrow imperatives of his professional life. Still, despite their baffling inelegance, what these pledges underscored was the extent to which we relied on the lexicon of combat to describe our nation's game. Consider, for instance, that most defensive schemes include a "blitz," which is a truncation of the German word *blitzkrieg*, meaning "lightning war." Or that West Coast offenses typically line up in "shotgun" formations in order to execute "aerial assaults." Receivers snag "bullets" in the red zone while linebackers "blow up" draw-plays. Quarterbacks are often extolled as "field generals" who can "marshal" their teammates toward victory. And linemen are said to battle in the "trenches."

These are obvious examples; how about more insidious ones? A "huddle" was initially meant to resemble the German military's *Leitungsbesprechung*, a method of coordination developed in the nineteenth century by Prussian war theorist Carl von Clausewitz, whose book *On War* has influenced leaders of all political stripes—everyone from Mao Zedong to President Eisenhower—and allegedly sat on Vince Lombardi's bookshelf. Interestingly, the huddle wasn't incorporated into the game of football until the 1890s, when Paul Hubbard—the quarterback for Gallaudet College, a deaf school in Washington, D.C.—instructed his teammates to encircle him before calling plays so the defense couldn't read what he was signing. In other words, the huddle was meant to facilitate communication.

It's easy to see why, in the fevered weeks after 9/11, the NFL decided to recalibrate its vernacular. News networks were humid with forecasts about the coming war, and hordes of young Americans were filing into recruitment offices and pledging their lives to the inevitable revenge effort. Soon, these men and women would be dispatched to perilous frontlines, and for the league to continue comparing football to these sacrifices would have been grossly inappropriate. "It's a matter of common sense," said commissioner Roger Goodell.

Such linguistic upheavals didn't trickle down to the youth level. During the late 1990s and early 2000s, the years I played middle school and high school football, the barbed nomenclature of war continued to pervade our semantic imagination, even after the Towers fell. Our team t-shirts were emblazoned with phrases from gangster rap, heavy metal, and, of course, the argot of war—expressions like "Seek and Destroy," "Band of Brothers," and "Let the Bodies Hit the Floor." We wore this apparel at practice, around town, until it was yellowed at the armpits. Even now, I can recall walking down the hallways of my high school after the last-hour bell and hearing the squelched reverb of electric guitars emanate from the weight room, where bands like Rage Against the Machine, Alice in Chains, and Marilyn Manson played on steady rotation. Invoking scenes of anarchy and mayhem, this music was belligerent and fuming, supplying us with anthems for our years of gridiron glory.

It's difficult to deny the longstanding romance between football and war. As Steve Almond notes in his trenchant manifesto, *Against Football*, the game was first spawned by college students on the East Coast during the 1820s, although, at that time, it was known by a variety of names. Harvard students called their version "Bloody Monday," which functioned as a form of hazing that sophomores inflicted upon their freshmen classmates (a much harsher initiation rite than what was practiced in my own glory days—namely, the porcelain swirly or the atomic wedgie). Princeton termed it "ballown" while Dartmouth played "old division football." In these various incarnations, the game was invariably gory and enfeebling, a mongrel of rugby and wrestling, with offenses marching downfield by standing side-by-side, fastening their elbows, and ramming their unhelmeted heads into a similarly postured defense. Collegiate coaches—including Yale's Walter Camp and Harvard's Percy Haughton—scoured military texts for strategies on spurring men toward such martyrous action. Injuries were so rampant and the violence so ghastly that, by the early 1860s, Yale and Harvard banned the game, though the prohibition wouldn't last long. By the end of the decade, the sport would return to college campuses revamped and somewhat tempered, having evolved to include kicking, running, and lateral passing plays. Yet despite these amendments, football continued to be treacherous, oftentimes yielding gouged eyes and snapped necks, as was the case in the 1894 contest between Harvard and Yale—dubbed the "Hampden Park Blood Bath"—during which four players suffered paralyzing injuries. During the 1905 season, 19 players died and over 150 others were critically injured.

News of these events eventually drew the attention of the White House. Theodore Roosevelt—whose son played for Harvard—convened coaches and administrators from sixty schools for a symposium on eliminating the game's "brutal features." A self-professed fan of the sport, the president was responding to critics who wanted the game outlawed after the grisly 1905 season. As John J. Miller reports in his book, *The Big Scrum: How Teddy Roosevelt Saved Football*, "There's this social and political movement that rises up to outlaw the sport. It's led by the president of Harvard and a number of other well-known figures. They equate football with homicide and think it has no place in civilized society and they just want to get rid of it." While the fatal consequences of the game may have been incontrovertible, they did little to dampen the enthusiasm of its fans. Even though the sport was new to many Americans, stadiums were routinely crammed with upwards of fifty thousand people and oftentimes resembled, in both volume and ardor, Roman coliseums bewitched by Nero's amusements. In the 1890s, riots would occasionally break out on days when tickets to collegiate championship games went on sale, since students could hawk them for five times the original cost. The sport wasn't just lucrative for enterprising undergraduates, though. College administrations soon took advantage of the game's jaw-slackening profitability, as when, in 1903, Yale's football team netted almost $110,000 in revenue, a value roughly equivalent to the combined income of the university's law, medical, and divinity schools.

Aware of the sport's popularity and its economic potential, Roosevelt had little incentive to abolish the game (plus, his son's involvement in the sport made him a partisan, not to mention the fact he did not have legal authority to forbid play). Instead, Roosevelt called for new rules that would decrease potential dangers while ensuring the game not be played "on too ladylike a basis." Roosevelt, a champion of the outdoors and an avid big game hunter, was no prancing ninny or foppish wimp, going on to say, "I believe in outdoor games, and I do not mind in the least that they are rough games, or that those who take part in them are occasionally injured." The burly machismo of Roosevelt's statements reflects the prevailing cultural ethos at the time, which was that football could be a venue for men to parade their brawn in a post-frontier America that offered few opportunities for such displays. As many sports historians have noted, the new industrial economy forced men to toil inside dimly lit factories, denying them the chance to complete the manhood-confirming demands of agriculture. As a result, they sought out gladiatorial sports like football as a way of quenching their id-based urges.

Among the 1905 changes was the eradication of "flying wedges" that often resulted in player deaths. The committee also instituted a neutral zone, a series of downs, and the use of a forward pass, all of which would lift the game out of its terrestrial chaos, spreading out offenses and dispersing players who once used the turmoil of scrums to conceal illegal, injury-inducing tactics. Now, teams would be arranged across a larger swath of the field and forced to execute coordinated plays, which would supposedly make the sport less violent, adding agility, grace, and beauty to a game that had formerly been the province of teeth-clenching mammoths. As Almond notes, "A game heretofore restricted to one thudding plane was suddenly, miraculously, bestowed a z-axis." In the intervening century, we've seen the sport take ever more precautions to reduce the dangers of play—the use of helmets and shoulder pads, penalties for unnecessary roughness, plus new rules meant to reduce the number of concussions and career-ending injuries.

And yet war has continued to serve as the prevailing metaphor for the sport throughout the twentieth century. Here's Jim Otto, who played for the Oakland Raiders during the 1960s and early '70s, explaining the costs of his career, "I know that I went to war and I came out of the battle with what I got, and you know, that's the way it is . . . we battled in there, and this is the result of it, sitting right here, looking at you." Vintage NFL Films from the 1970s are overdubbed with gravel-voiced narrators who explain that "the meek will never inherit this turf, because every play is hand-to-hand and body-to-body combat . . . in the pit, there is more violence per square foot than anywhere else in sport." Other titles from the NFL Films oeuvre include *Linebackers: Search and Destroy*. In 1987, the University of Miami football team arrived in Phoenix for the Fiesta Bowl dressed in military fatigues. And during the 1990s, the NFL advertised its contests with bellicose semiotics, as evidenced by the opening sequence of Monday Night Football, which culminated in two helmets colliding and shattering into little incandescent bits. (Note: head-to-head tackles are now illegal tactics.)

In the end, the post-9/11 attempts to reconstitute the language of football were short-lived. After the Towers fell, sportswriters continued to draft paeans to players who supposedly embodied a kind of front-lines valor. Here's a snippet from Frank Deford's elegiac tribute to Johnny Unitas in a 2002 *Sports Illustrated* article entitled "The Best There Ever Was":

They didn't have coaches with headphones and Polaroids and fax machines then, sitting on high, telling quarterbacks what plays to call. In those halcyon days, quarterbacks were field generals, not field lieutenants. And there was Unitas after he called a play (and probably checked off another play when he saw what the ruffians across the line were up to), shuffling back into the pocket, unfazed by the violent turbulence all around him, standing there in his hightops, waiting, looking, poised. I never saw war, so that is still my vision of manhood: Unitas standing courageously in the pocket, his left arm flung out in a diagonal to the upper deck, his right cocked for the business of passing, down amidst the mortals. Lock and load.

Journalists aren't the only custodians of this indecent cliché. Even now, NFL players call upon the tropes of combat when describing their own careers. Recall the 2003 season, when Kellen Winslow, the tight end for the University of Miami, explained why he loomed defiantly over an injured opponent by saying, "I'm a fucking soldier." As recently as 2010, New York Giants safety Antrel Rolle compared fans heckling NFL players to citizens booing U.S. soldiers returning home from war. "When soldiers come home from Iraq, you don't boo them. I look at it the same way. I take my job seriously."

Such statements invite fans of the sport to consider a few pertinent questions: Are football players fundamentally dumb? Are they oafish and insensitive? Do they mean to trivialize the service of our uniformed men and women, what Lincoln called "the last full measure of devotion," or do they just suffer from a stuttering ineptitude when it comes to dealing with the press? I'm inclined to think that these are facile conclusions, and there's perhaps something deeper and far more disturbing about this language than we might care to realize. Maybe when NFL players compare themselves to soldiers, they are actually revealing their knowledge of a fact the NFL has worked hard to keep football fans from learning: like our uniformed men and women, who risk their lives on the battlefield, these athletes know they could potentially die from their involvement in this sport—either from an injury incurred while on field or from the long-term effects of concussive and sub-concussive hits, which the average pro will endure roughly 130,000 times during his career. While there's obviously much to be said about the differences between dying for the sovereignty of your country and dying for the entertainment of its citizens, the effects of such violence can be distressingly similar. So much so, in fact, that the NFL is now using military-grade helmet sensors to monitor the neurological status of players who suffer big hits on Sundays. The Army created such devices to measure the brain trauma sustained by our soldiers, either from roadside IEDs or rocket-propelled grenades.

Autopsies of former NFL, college, and high school players' brains reveal that simply participating in the sport can cause chronic traumatic encephalopathy (CTE), a form of permanent neurological damage that stipples the brain with clusters of the tau protein, which increases the incidence of dementia-like symptoms, such as depression, memory loss, aggression, and suicidal ideation. For nearly fifteen years, the NFL has whitewashed this research, fearful that public knowledge of the link between football and CTE could imperil the future of the sport. In the PBS Frontline documentary, *League of Denial*, Dr. Bennet Omalu—the Nigerian-born neuropathologist who first discovered CTE in former Pittsburgh Steeler Mike Webster's brain—recalls a league representative explaining to him the implications of this research. "[The representative] said if 10 percent of mothers in this country would begin to perceive football as a dangerous sport, that is the end of football."

Or maybe not. It's breathtakingly naive to think that a few neurological studies will effect much of a chink in the NFL's shield, especially when it's fortified by profits of $8 billion a year, when the ethos of the sport so thoroughly decorates the American psyche. This is a country where the Super Bowl functions like an official holiday, where congregants schedule Sunday church around kickoffs. Like 1905, the game needs to redress the brain-shriveling dangers of the game, but such amendments will not be made unless we forge a new way to describe the sport, with metaphors no longer rooted in war imagery and violence.

Language shapes thought, which then molds behavior. In the ambit of linguistic philosophy, this is known as the Sapir–Whorf hypothesis, which contends that the language we use and the linguistic habits we practice not only demarcate the boundaries of our cognitive functions but also shape our perception of the world and our actions within it. Developed by the

American linguist Benjamin Lee Whorf and his mentor Edward Sapir, this theory holds that

> human beings do not live in the objective world alone, nor alone in the world of social activity as ordinarily understood, but are very much at the mercy of the particular language which has become the medium of expression for their society. It is quite an illusion to imagine that one adjusts to reality essentially without the use of language and that language is merely an incidental means of solving specific problems of communication or reflection . . . Even comparatively simple acts of perception are very much more at the mercy of the social patterns called words than we might suppose . . . We see and hear and otherwise experience very largely as we do because the language habits of our community predispose certain choices of interpretation.

My point, then, is that the language we use to describe the game actually ends up shaping both its public perception and its course of play. If we exalt its brutality, if we extol its players in militaristic terms, then we as fans become ever more willing to condone crippling, career-ending violence as nothing more than the tragic but unavoidable byproducts of a savage sport in which informed athletes voluntarily participate. The truth is that, despite all the war metaphors and brothers-in-arms camaraderie that colored my adolescent experience with football, the most compelling aspect of the game— and what still fascinates me about it today—is a more tenuous transaction that takes place between players: not brutality, but communication.

—

Like most accomplished prep athletes, my career was monitored by my dad. I'm aware of the stereotype: the sullen patriarch barking admonitions from the stands. You've probably seen this type before. These small disgruntled men in Nike tracksuits who haunt gyms and practice fields. Who range up and down the sidelines with crossed arms, chewing gum and shouting rebukes at their sweaty, downcast children. Dad wasn't like this. He had been a standout athlete in his youth, which meant that he didn't need me to live out any of his own unconsummated dreams. His athletic élan flourished most conspicuously on the basketball court and would ultimately take him to Marquette University, where he played under Al McGuire. (Part of the reason why I never excelled at basketball was that Dad was so much better at it than I ever could be. As a boy, I once encountered a sneaker ad in *Sports Illustrated*, or maybe *ESPN: The Magazine*, that listed goals every aspiring basketball player must accomplish on his rise toward stardom—things like: *learn to shoot; learn to layup; beat your brother in one-on-one; beat your dad in horse; make JV; make varsity; win state; get recruited* . . . etc. Of course, if your dad played D-1 basketball and could stand in the driveway and drain nineteen three-pointers in a row while you and your brother stood there watching with popped eyes and slackened jaws, the prospect of ever beating him in H.O.R.S.E. was like nil. His jump shot was so formidable that our special family sobriquet for him was "The Machine." I don't think I ever aced him. During the eighteen years that we shared a hoop in the driveway, I maybe got a game of P.I.G. on him. Maybe.) All of which is to say that Dad's athletic shadow was long and broad, and though he would never force sports upon me, I would always detect an ambient pressure to live up to his reputation.

Though sports was the mortar that held us together, Dad and I never quite figured out how to talk to one another. We never went on camping trips where we might have a Folgers moment around a fire. Nor was he the type to regale me with stories about the good old days while quaffing cold foamers.

So instead of talking, what Dad and I would do is go out in the yard after dinner and work on my mechanics. There was something spiritually nourishing about playing catch with my father, and those evenings still live on my nerve endings with impeccable fidelity: the fresh loam odor of the yard; the pebbled leather against my fingers; the thin whistle of the ball as it zipped between us. Dad and I would spend hours out there. He'd scrutinize my throwing motion with forensic care, making sure I hoisted the ball to my shoulder after the snap, monitoring my little tap dance of three- and five-step drops. To ensure that I kept my eyes downfield during rollouts, he'd stand twenty yards away and flash random numbers with his hands, which I was supposed to call out before chucking him the ball. I'm sure there were retributions if I bellowed the wrong number, but I don't remember them—pushups, probably.

We hardly talked during these études but would adopt a coded shorthand for the things I needed to work on. "Eyes up." "Plant and release." "Follow through." If my father and I shared a language—a diction and syntax that could approximate our feelings—it was this patois of quarterbacking. After a shitty day at school, still wounded by some girl's rejection or a friend's betrayal, I would throw sharp darts at my father's chest, stamping his ribs with watercolor bruises he'd show me the next day. If I spent the afternoon listening to Nirvana on my Walkman and was thus clouded with ennui, my throws would be sluggish and uninspired, slow torpid lobs that would gull against the wind and flutter. Somehow the trajectory of the ball authored sentiments that would have otherwise gone unexpressed between us. Every pass was a physical manifestation of the connection I hoped to establish with him but that our paucity of words chronically denied.

And yet when I entered high school, this makeshift language of ours began to erode and break down. Like most Americans who grew up in the late 1990s and early 2000s, most of my social interactions took place online, guised by screen names meant either to obscure one's identity (sportsfan18) or glorify it (bigpimping69). Now, given the frequency with which we communicate via Facebook and Twitter, this distance is a commonplace, part of our dialogical landscape. But at the time, as a fifteen-year-old boy, the detachment offered by digital interaction was a revelation. Instant Messenger functioned like alcohol, lowering my shame quotient to like nil. It was as if AIM had suddenly become the dank basement party at which I'd had too much to drink. I was abruptly garrulous. I'd strike up conversations with screen names that signified individuals whom I'd never actually talk to in real life, and like any good barfly, I'd spew nonsense about current events and recent gossip, maundering on and on with a haughtiness and verbosity I wouldn't dare display at the cafeteria table or during passing hours.

In hindsight, it's easy to see how this type of communication was adolescent—the other person here hadn't manifested as a vivid, living being with a nervous system as complex and sensitive as my own. On AIM, the other person was just a soundboard, a literal screen onto which I could impress my thoughts and feelings. Whereas I was alive, animate, and incarnate, other people seemed two-dimensional, flat, an encoding of 1s and 0s, an audience to my oratory, a witness to my construction of a self. I wasn't speaking *to* someone else. I was talking *at* her.

This ultimately carried over to the ways in which I started to interact with my dad. After a while, I began to reject his help, preferring to practice my throws in solitude, which, for a quarterback, given the nature of the enterprise (i.e., throwing a ball to a moving receiver), is a kind of insane strategy to get better. To compensate for the absence of a receiver, I spray-painted an X on the crenellated bark of a tree at the far end of our lawn. I would stand twenty or thirty yards from it, crouch down, call hike, and drop back to pass, firing a spiral across the gathering dusk, watching the ball carom off the tree in wild directions, clipping off a confetti of bark with its explosive force. I would do this for hours. The ball's brailled leather was soon scuffed and scratched, like the hide of an abused whale. In hindsight, it saddens me to think about how many hours I devoted to this activity. I imagine my frumpy septuagenarian neighbor inside her living room, trying to read *TV Guide* or *Ladies' Home Journal*, but constantly getting interrupted by the crack-prone adolescent tones of a boy calling audibles to no one in the dark. I imagine her pulling back a drape to watch the fifteen-year-old version of me, attired in sweatpants and cleats, roll out on the flush vernal lawn, throwing a ball against a maple tree as hard I could. I must have looked deranged or lonely—maybe both.

But it wasn't until Christmas that year that I truly betrayed my father. With one swift consumer purchase, I denied him the only expressive activity we shared. Topping my Christmas list was a piece of sports equipment called a Dual-Sport Canvas Catcher, a contraption that consisted of a blue canvas sheet stretched across a large metal frame. Painted white on the navy tarp was a semion of a football player, a cartoony approximation of a wide receiver, but instead of a stomach, it had a mesh net into which I would deposit my passes. During the remaining years of my football career, I used this thing all the time, hauling it out to our backyard and positioning it at different distances and angles to resemble the various routes a receiver might run during a game—a corner fade, a fifteen-yard out, a streak. Hour after hour, I'd stand in the yard, chucking the ball at this flat, two-dimensional object—a crude mockery of a receiver—when only a few feet away Dad was inside the house, languishing in front of the television after a long day at work, more than willing to play catch with me. It pains me now to think of him sprawled on the lumpy couch, tie loosened, holding a postprandial Diet Coke poured into a small tumbler, a mist of carbonation sizzling above the glass, and hearing through the window the dull metronomic thud of my passes hitting the tarp. *Thump. Thump.*

Perhaps it was a stroke of cosmic irony that the more I practiced with the Dual-Sport Canvas Catcher, the more my accuracy suffered. Because I was working with a stationary object, my throws during games were always errant, landing a little behind my receivers, tempting cornerbacks and safeties to jump the route and intercept the pass, which occurred during my junior year with a frequency that still makes me cringe. Later, at home, while icing my knees or scrubbing paint from under my eyes, my parents treated these on-field flops with euphemistic caution—graciously dubbing them "struggles" or "tough games"—when the truth was that I had played like total shit. By the end of that year, Dad realized the sunken resentments between us were now burbling up to the surface and blighting my progress as a quarterback. What he did next strikes me now as a breathtakingly generous act of fatherhood, but at the time I just thought it was downright bizarre.

During the summer leading into my senior year, Dad outsourced his role as trainer/confidant to another man, enlisting his close friend, Dean—a cheery guy who coached youth football and who was flat-out gregarious compared to Dad—to take me to parks and fields near our house where we'd work on mechanics and rap about life. Dean was a convivial, widely berthed Greek man who maintained the solar disposition of a talk-show host. It was hard not to like him. He had a jaw-dropping story, too. Apparently, during his early twenties, he woke one morning to discover he was paralyzed from the neck down. There was no triggering event, no seismic crash or gruesome injury to explain this abrupt stultification. Doctors were flummoxed. There wasn't even a word for what happened to him, he said. He was in the hospital for months. Days were spent meditating on missed opportunities. As he lay there, immobile as stone, his mind audited his every regret: not crossing the room at a raucous college party to talk to a girl; not taking a gamble in his professional life that might have yielded a swift windfall; not believing in himself when he was an athlete in high school. Eventually, after a couple months, he regained mobility and, with the help of physical therapy, his body returned to full functionality. Now, he said, he wasted no time worrying about the past or what might happen in the future. He simply tried to do right by the present moment. Eckhart Tolle he wasn't, but these bright pontifications helped me. It was a plangent lamentation of *what might have been*, except I didn't hear it as a ballad of a scarred middle-aged man. I took it as an injunction to get better as a quarterback. Rarely had an adult male talked to me about my feelings, whereas Dean would drive me to McDonald's before our workouts, treating me to soggy egg sandwiches and asking about my non-football interests—the girl I liked, the status of my friendships, what I wanted to study in college—topics that would have fallen squarely within a father's jurisdiction.

By all accounts, Dean was a standup guy. I don't know whether Dad paid him for these training sessions, whether they worked out some handshake arrangement, or if Dean was simply drawing from a quarry of intrinsic kindness. I suspect he was like a lot of grown men who can no longer play and thus enter into coaching for the vicarious pleasure of being around a young man who still can. Such middle-aged men trail behind the young athlete, like vassals behind a prince, and monitor his trajectory with the hope that he will later praise them in interviews with ESPN. They're "difference-makers." They want to contribute. They want to be listed in the acknowledgments of some best-selling sports memoir.

The following autumn, my senior year, I became the starting quarterback for Waukesha Catholic Memorial. The school was a few birch-lined blocks away from Carroll College, which is where, in 1906, Bradbury Robinson—the quarterback for St. Louis University—threw the first legal forward pass in the history of the game. Our team finished the season with a winning record, but we were knocked out of playoff contention during our last game, after which I shed genuine tears in a locker room where displays of fraternal love were both rugged and abundant.

But there were moments during that season when I completed passes that would have been impossible a year earlier, when the full scope of my repertoire consisted of chucking darts at fixed, inanimate objects. It is difficult to describe the peculiar beauty of a completed pass. Let's first acknowledge that, during the course of any given passing play, a quarterback is rushed by colossal linemen, whose sole telos it is to knock him down. The second he calls hike, he invites the prospect of his demise. Let's also acknowledge that football is not a game of stasis but of variables in constant flux—wind/rain/snow, physical balance, the swift diminishment of throwing lanes, the discordant patterns of defensive backs, the snarling aggressions of linebackers, etc. All of which means that the QB can't simply stand in a vacuum and toss the ball at some inert object. No. The magic of a truly great pass is that, amid the turmoil of the pocket, the quarterback must anticipate where his receiver will be, which requires him to send the ball toward empty space. The leather projectile revolves at dangerous rates toward a space unoccupied by anyone at all. There is blind trust, a brittle faith, in this action. It's the little divinity of the game that only a quarterback ever experiences. This is the sadness of your position. For that single dark instant when you throw a pass, before the receiver makes his cut, you seem to be alone, throwing to absolutely no one. But this is a necessary deception, the game's intrinsic feint and dodge, because soon the receiver finishes his route and emerges from behind the linebacker or cornerback, and sprints into green open field, snagging the ball out of the air with a practiced deftness, a nifty grace.

There's something utterly gorgeous about this exchange. If a prayer is nothing more than an earnest transmission directed at someone whom you can only hope will be there, then I submit that leading a receiver into empty space is a kind of prayer. In down after down, with marmoreal goliaths hurtling toward you, you cannot pay attention to where your receiver is, but must devote all your imagination to where he'll be. Forget the raw data, the ugly unyielding material of the moment. Step outside the exigencies of the self and enter your receiver's head. See what the receiver sees. It's only then that the ball can enact the connection its trajectory describes—linking one player to another. Despite the bloody chaos all around, you have connected, understood each other, somehow.

It wasn't until after I stopped playing football that I learned to describe the game in such fumy metaphysical terms. In college, like an alcoholic who swaps booze for ice cream, I replaced my addiction to the game with a compulsion for studying. Instead of spending hour upon hour in the weight room or on the field, I became one of those blanched, misanthropic-looking guys you were apt to see scuttling out of the college library on Friday nights while shoals of other undergrads were migrating to the next house party.

College is an opportunity for self-invention, and after giving up on athletics, I decided to let myself explore some of the intellectual concerns that had preoccupied me during my adolescence but that I had suppressed for the sake of becoming a top-flight athlete. Such were the circumstances under which one spring day I found myself lounging on the manicured plaid of the Union lawn, reading a text for my philosophy class, a book by Martin Buber called *I and Thou*. It was an odd, slender volume, chocked with aphoristic prose that sometimes sounded more like poetry than continental philosophy. Here's a random example:

> I consider a tree.

> I can look on it as a picture: stiff column in a shock of light, or a splash of green shot with the delicate blue and silver of the background.

> I can perceive it as movement: flowing veins on a clinging, pressing pith, suck of the roots, breathing of the leaves, ceaseless commerce with earth and air—and the obscure growth itself.

Surely such verse crinkled my brow, at least initially. But over the course of the book, it became clear to me that Buber wasn't simply bombarding his readers with abstruse balladry. Instead, he was attempting to describe our relationship to the world, providing us with a glossary of terms for a category of perceptions that, to me anyway, had always seemed ineffable and therefore invisible. Central to his thesis is a distinction between what he calls "I-It" and "I-Thou" relationships. When we take part in "I-It" relationships, we regard other people as detached things—predictable objects that can be manipulated for our whims and predilections. In such cases, other people exist only in our experience of them. By way of example, imagine an unctuous womanizer telling a female that she's pretty, not to proffer an objective claim or make the woman feel good about herself, but to inveigle her into giving this Lothario something that he wants, which in this case is probably some form of sexual gratification.

By contrast, "I-Thou" relationships occur when we enter a state of mind where the material illusions that separate us from other people—namely, our bodies, our selfishness, our in-born habit of seeing ourselves as the center of the world—dissipate and where we begin to regard the Other as another "I." In such mental states, the borders between us become porous and we are drawn speedily into a system of spiritual relation where difference evaporates and outliers diminish, where, like Emerson says, "contrary and remote things cohere and flower out from one stem."

Such frothy concepts may seem impertinent to football, but as I lay on the university lawn that day, with young people swiveling down the sidewalks and hemp-clad hippie-types playing hacky sack under auburn elms, I discovered in Buber's weird gnomic prose a comprehensive description for what it felt like to play quarterback. When you drop back to pass, you suspend the limited itineraries of the self. You must regard your receiver as another "I," someone who accompanies you into a world of play where every movement is connected, contingent, consequential. If this aspect of the game feels spiritual to me—and can at times assume the metaphysical frequencies of art—it's because it enacts and seems to solve one of the most basic problems of existence itself: How do I minimize the window of the self and see the world from someone else's eyes? How do I escape my inborn subjectivity? For Buber, such a task involves practicing habits of perception that force you to remember that the interior lives of other people are as complex and sensitive as your own. And for me, the sport was a way to do that. It's not for nothing that Buber refers to "I-Thou" relationships as "dialogical." Nor is it an accident that when a quarterback misfires and overthrows his receiver, broadcasters are apt to call these flubs "miscommunications."

One would be hard pressed to claim that every facet of the game perpetuates this brand of thinking. Certainly one cannot find it in the chest-thumping hubris of post-game interviews nor in the rash of noodly touchdown dances. But I've been trying to suggest that certain aspects of the game ascend to a spiritual register precisely because they ask its participants to aim for communion. Anticipating the movements of your receiver, laboring to see what he sees, and trusting him enough that you can throw the ball to a spot on the field before he has even made a gesture toward heading there—the perceptual habits of making a pass train the mind for other-directed thinking.

Buber's *I and Thou* anticipated some of the main communicational questions we as a culture face right now, when our most ubiquitous form of interaction happens via digitized screen. At a moment when our culture is fixated on narcissism and the breakdown of communication, when the ease and frequency of "connectivity" is often privileged over the more hard-won skills of empathy, perhaps the most potent metaphor for our national sport is one that calls attention to that rare miracle of connection between two individuals.

Make no mistake: I'm not suggesting that football is the panacea for our impoverished perceptual habits, nor am I saying that the game is a treasury of sensitive, other-directed messages. I'm merely trying to describe why the game is gorgeous to me and why the language of communication—of true connection, of love—might be applicable to a sport so often associated with grisly violence, gross egos, and oozing machismo.

—

As an NFL fan, it's been interesting to watch the evolution of broadcasting language since 9/11. Commentators have mostly abandoned the brutish vernacular of war only to adopt the starchy jargon of capitalism. No longer do we have quarterbacks as field generals who marshal their platoons into enemy territory. Now, we have "game managers" who understand the "costs" of risky throws, who eek their offenses out of "point deficits." Recently, New Orleans head coach Sean Payton, when asked to describe what he looks for in the consummate NFL quarterback, said, "I mean, you gotta be able to sit down with these players after watching production on tape and feel like you're talking with the CEO, and if you don't feel like you're talking with the CEO, or someone that potentially could be, then uh, it's tough."

Does this symbolize a shift in the game? Perhaps football, which once served as a metaphor for manhood, is now nothing more than a brass-tacks venture, where valor and victory lose precedence to the bulk of one's paycheck? Can this account for our wolfish interest in trade deals, salary cap adjustments, and other fiscal concerns?

Still, old habits die hard, and war metaphors have slowly encroached back into our vocabulary. In September 2014, *ESPN: The Magazine* ran a feature-length profile of Belhaven University coach Hal Mumme, who pioneered the "Air Raid Offensive" that many college and most pro teams deploy. The article was accompanied by a portrait of the coach wearing a cheap imitation of a military helmet, a plastic green shell blotched with camouflage. Bridled to Mumme's head by a loose nylon strap, the contraption looked ridiculous, as if it had been swiped from the novelty aisle of a children's toy store. It seemed especially odd that ESPN was celebrating the godfather of the "air-raid attack" only a week after the White House announced coordinated air strikes to foil the advance of ISIS in the Middle East.

We end up mobilizing this terminology only to invoke the old American verities—courage and grit and indefatigable spirit. This sort of language glorifies the game's violence, encouraging fans to cheer for an opera of collisions, cracks, whumps, and crashes. So perhaps we need a new vocabulary to describe football, a language that asks us to appreciate aspects of the game unrelated to the molar-loosening hits and the pugilistic combat.

The other option is obsolescence. We might readily imagine a time when the NFL will collapse under the weight of evidence that links the sport's violence to neurological damage, when enough concerned American parents will direct their children away from the hashmarked gridiron between goal posts and steer them instead toward the less perilous turf of the soccer field; when the sport will become a bloody novelty, an activity future generations will regard with the same nail-biting apprehension most of us now reserve for ultimate fighting. However naive it may be, my hope is that the game will undergo a 1905-like revolution and the powers that be will amend the game to ensure players' neurological safety.

Whatever shape such reforms take, I hope they preserve moments like this: Christmas morning of 2013 when, after coffee and homemade breakfast and all the grandkids opening presents, my dad and I step out to the driveway under Californian sunshine and find my nephew's Nerf football lodged behind the lawnmower. We trade a wordless glance, and it's in this moment I realize that my father has become much older than I ever thought he could be—his mortality has finally assumed discernible qualities: craggy face, silvered pate, hobbled posture (though he's still quite handsome). He ambles out to the end of the yard on achy hinges, stopping under the fronds of an efflorescent palm tree. I'm twenty-eight years old, and my father is almost seventy, and we're going to play catch with a neon foam football. The sun is out, and the grass is a lurid, flashing green, and Dad brings a hand over his eyes, almost like he's saluting me as he waits to receive my pass. He's been living in California for a couple years now, helping my brother raise his kids, so the two of us don't talk much, except for the occasional catch-up call or laconic text, the types of interactions where our expressions are scrubbed of any real feeling. And as the distance between each phone call grows longer and as the rhythms of our conversations get more deeply entrenched, it becomes harder and harder for me to talk to my dad, to somehow overcome whatever barriers the plight of being father and son has been erected between us. It is difficult to swallow the cliché and tell him before time runs out that everything I've done in my life has been in some way an effort to make him proud of me. Even here, like this—with this fickle, crumbly language—it feels almost impossible to say it.

It's maybe been a year since I've thrown a pass, and the Nerf football is squishy, foam, and light. Unconcerned about the silliness of this performance, I crouch down and bark out in sonorous baritone an old Crusader cadence, "Blue 18, Blue 18," raising my leg swiftly as if to send some phantom fullback in motion, just to make Dad laugh. But when I drop the charade and glance across the lawn, I see that Dad has broken into a run. It's a slow, lumbering route, though he still displays a great athlete's eternal coordination and native grace. He's headed across the street, weaving through parked cars, trotting through long pools of tree-shade, but somehow he starts moving through decades, shedding wrinkles and paunch and gray hair, speeding up as time reverses, his legs gaining virility and youth as he gets farther and farther away from me. Soon, we're back in that drab Wisconsin yard, the one with uneven footing and the rampant patches of dandelions and crabgrass, the lawn of my boyhood, and Dad is going long. He's nearing the edge of our property, a distance that requires a degree of strength I'm not sure my young arm can summon. But I hear him calling out to me across the partial dark. It is a voice that the distance between us has rendered deserted-sounding, somewhat desperate, bereaved, seemingly, and fearful that I might lose him, I raise the ball to my shoulder and try one more time to lead him out into the open.

FLOOD MYTHS

The vacation was a professional recommendation. After two years of pursuing academic tenure at a small university in Wisconsin, an interval during which I had served on department committees and advised undergrads, composed new essays and taught sixteen classes, I had finally reached a point in my life of near-catatonic exhaustion. Granted, I did my best to keep up appearances on campus. Each day I donned a happy pedagogical mask of good cheer and scholastic rectitude, enthusiastically responding to every last student email (*Of course I'll write you another rec letter! Of course I'll read seventeen chapters of your unfinished fantasy novel!*). My use of exclamation points in work emails became worryingly frequent and was perhaps my lone sign of psychic unraveling. At home, however, I wore my darkness on my sleeve. Evenings I would brood stoically beside the fire, muttering to myself recombinant strings of my most frequent comments on student papers: *Wrong word, comma splice, fallacy, abstraction. Wrong word, comma splice, fallacy, abstraction.* This eerie anthem, whispered under my breath, was enough for my spouse to ask, "Is everything OK?" It wasn't. Not really.

At work, the mask started to slip. One student remarked that I looked so dejected before class, but when the morning bell rang, I seemed to "come remarkably to life." And in my second-year review, one colleague noted that while I had been steadily publishing in Tier 1 journals and earning high marks on my student evaluations, his lone concern for me was one of stamina and endurance. Was it possible for me—for anyone, really—to keep up this pace across the duration of one's career? Perhaps I would appreciate the unburdening of leisure, the more tranquil activity of apple-picking, say, or a recuperative binge of Netflix? What this colleague neglected to observe, however, was that his very injunction to relax was now a professional fiat, thereby making the prospect of leisure yet another requirement for securing tenure. It was maddening, this paradox—a grim joke. A dark dream. And yet maybe he was right. Maybe I needed to ease off the throttle and cool down a bit. Maybe I needed some good old psychic untethering.

Then, all at once, it hit me: I would summer, rendering the whole season into a verb. The pastimes of June and July—redolent of chlorine and sunshine—would become my lone nutrients, my sole preoccupation. Think: tilt-a-whirls and funnel cakes. Think: roadside attractions and state fairs. I would become a connoisseur of all this forgotten Americana, all this kitsch and treacle of the season.

Which was how I found myself standing in front of my wife one Saturday morning in May, talking very rapidly, with a Clark-Griswold-ish gleam in my eye. I was brandishing a Groupon for Noah's Ark, America's Largest Waterpark, which was only a scant hour from where we lived. On my head was a jaunty Gilligan's cap, and my nose was a sad white diamond of SPF cream. "Do they have a lazy river?" my wife asked. "They have *two* lazy rivers," I said. "I'll only go," she said, "if I can read Hannah Arendt on my raft."

Only upon approaching the entrance gate did my enthusiasm begin to wane. Only then did I remember some crucial facts about myself—namely, I hadn't been to an amusement park since 1996. When I was eleven years old, a friend had invited me to Six Flags with his family, and after going on what I was later told was a fairly tame ride called "The Whizzer," I nevertheless erupted into tears and refused to go on any more coasters. This prompted my friend's mother to ask, unkindly but not unfairly, "Well, why did you even come then?" To which I rather histrionically replied, "Because I wanted your son to like me!"

Spread out before me now was a garish metropolis of death, brightly colored tubes that corkscrewed menacingly through the air, plummeting at such sheer grades that, I saw now, one had to climb woozy towers of wooden stairs just to even reach their entryways. As we tromped across the parking lot, the ear-rattling shrieks of children—birdlike, evocative of pterodactyl—were already becoming the dominant soundscape. Soon we hurdled through the turnstiles, joining the throngs of near-nude Midwesterners, our procession a timpani of footsoles and aqua socks.

—

For whom is the waterpark fun? Perhaps for lovers? On the "Adventure River," one of the two lazy rivers on campus, I watched an octogenarian married couple sit face-to-face on a see-through raft, smiling at one another and barely moving, looking very much like waxwork sculptures. Actually, for a while, I began to wonder whether they might be some kind of themed animatronic exhibit, until the man said, "Are you having fun, darling?" And the woman replied, "Oh, yes, father. And you?" Teen couples giggled brightly on the speckled deck, chasing steeper thrills, such as "The Black Thunder" or "Congo Bongo." Soon the lazy river careened around a contoured rock wall, out of which spurted geysers of water at random intervals, and along the berm of the river, a mob of young lifeguards stood sentry, bandoliered with life preservers, looking tight-lipped and very serious. Roundly they ignored my queries about rescue ratios, and one boy merely shrugged when I asked him how many gallons of water the park goes through per annum.

As its name makes clear, Noah's Ark is aggressively themed after the biblical flood myth, which is weird because even though this is supposed to be a haven of rest and relaxation, it casually introduces to the parkgoer's mind scenes of mass genocide and global annihilation. The dissonance starts right away. Entering the park, you are immediately bombarded with a mockup of the Old Testament watercraft—in this case, a climbing tower for children—from whose contours hang a whole phylum of molded plastic animals, no doubt intended to signify the passengers that Noah brought onto his ship. "And of every living thing of flesh," sayeth the Lord, "you shall bring two of every kind into the ark, to keep them alive with you." Every few minutes, a massive carafe gets overturned and dumps a pond's worth of water onto the children's heads, presumably in simulation of Yahweh's wrath, at which point all the little ones scamper madly through the eyeblue shallows, a storm of floaties and diapers, whereupon all the parents laugh and say things like, "Are you having fun, sweetheart?" And the children nod psychotically and enter, once more, into the deep.

The standard critical reading of a waterpark—of all amusement parks, really—is that they embody the quintessential American yearning for unattainable "Reality." Because the thrills and splendors of nature are fickle and unpredictable, an amusement park can furnish us with reliable simulations of those natural experiences that we so desperately crave. Why tempt fate with a whale-watching expedition when you can scoot on over to SeaWorld? Why traipse up a mountain when you can glimpse a waterfall at Noah's Ark? The postmodernists went a step further with this line of thinking and wondered whether Americans need ersatz re-creations of the real world in order to believe that life outside the amusement park was still, somehow, authentic. Thanks to the homogenizing impulses of commercialization, every last sector of American life, from Main Street to Madison Avenue, had been so thoroughly Disneyfied that there was nothing left in our country that wasn't already synthetic. And so if the hokey replicas of the amusement park could serve some nobler purpose, it was to make the world outside the admission gates seem real by comparison.

Through the scrim of 2019, however, it would be difficult for the average parkgoer to labor under this delusion. After all, just consider our Reality TV president. Consider our Boris and Natasha geopolitics. Think about Incels and butt implants and Sophia the AI. Is anyone still so canny to suggest that America hasn't become the funhouse version of itself, the Janus twin of the founders' ideal? All of which leads me to wonder whether the standard postmodern formula has been decisively reversed. What does it mean when the world outside the amusement park is more zany and plasticine than our previous zones of amusement? Does it suggest that themed evocations of primeval floods or magical kingdoms can actually serve as more faithful indices of reality? That they can show us who we are?

After a spell of self-exhortation, I commenced to go on some slides. At first, I applauded myself on overcoming my fear of heights and trying out some real arrhythmia-producers, but then I realized that I was the tallest person in line by a foot—and the oldest by several decades. Queuing up for something called "Monkey Rapids," I saw that it was just me among maybe a dozen fifth-graders. In fear of sounding stranger-danger alarms, I hightailed it over to a more adult-level stomach-churner called "The Black Thunder," a large, dark esophagus of plastic on whose second bump I went airborne and yelped, a sound that one patron from rural Michigan later informed me "sounded like a terrier getting stepped on." Later I partook of "Congo Bongo," a dizzying plummet which I rode with a cohort of chiseled frat boys who kept bellowing things like "Dudes, whoa!" I won't spend much time on my experience with "The Flying Gecko," except to note that its name turns out to be thoroughly descriptive of what one's body looks like as one goes down "The Flying Gecko."

—

I walked a lap around the park's digressive footpaths and thought aimlessly about my family. Perhaps in sharing public space with so many joyful, laughing clans, I had grown lonesome, in an unutterable way, for those bygone days of childhood. Because we couldn't afford the standard Florida vacation when I was growing up, there are no Epcot relics or Mickey Mouse ears in my family scrapbooks, sadly. Instead, we ventured every summer to a bucolic outpost called "The Heidel House." Often I think of the Heidel House. What a weird idea for a getaway. In its old-world majesty and sweeping, gilt-tinged lobby, it recalled that one lodge from *The Shining*, although as a kid I lacked this cinematic reference point and could only intuit something vaguely off about the place. The disco lounge featured a band called The House Cats, and its ponytailed lead singer did croaking renditions of "Footloose" and "The Piano Man." Hardly would I say that these sojourns were momentous or enchanting, and yet what I remember most vividly about those weekends was the weird, existential thawing, a sense that whatever acrimony lingered back home could be momentarily suspended here, amid the freshly laundered sheets of the hotel room, amid the sundrenched ebullience of the courtyard. It was as if, by virtue of geographical displacement, we could inhabit the hotel's idea of serene domesticity and forget the sadness and disgruntlement that plagued us back home. Of course, the cataclysm was unavoidable. Eventually, my parents divorced, and our family, wounded in that cliché way of all legally ruptured families, never quite recovered. Like a nation, like an amusement park, a family requires the fulfillment of a certain kind of story, an enchantment whose endurance depends on a willful suspension of disbelief. I remember one night at the hotel we were watching The House Cats, and my father leaned across the table to reach for my mother's hand. A child is uniquely attuned to such gestures, having become, by the age of ten, a connoisseur of his parents' emotions. But my mom let my father's hand rest there on the table. She looked at him for a long time. The moment seemed to elongate and distend, a terrible postponement. My brother was bobbing his head to the music, and my sister was half-asleep in her chair, and even though the undercurrent of my mom's reluctance was lost on me, the gist of its meaning remained.

—

By mid-afternoon, I found myself in the "Big Kahuna Wave Pool." It was a football-field-sized body of water whose Prussian blue surface was haphazardly dotted with several hundred tubes and rafts. All of these were populated with cheerful, undulant families, who themselves were trying to survive the gradually worsening tempest. Every ten minutes, the subaquatic turbines were activated, sending Poseidon-type waves across the pool and making everyone go bananas. In all the tussle and mayhem, we seemed to resemble the fatal jetsam of a recent shipwreck. Actually, what we looked like was the latest pictures of flooding in the Midwest. Car-sized chunks of ice, having detached from a nearby river, careened into one family's barn, putting an end to their generations-old steer business. I remember reading one article about a Nebraskan cattle rancher who lost three hundred calves in the flooding, who spent several weeks extracting their bodies from debris and carrying them back to his property. "It's probably over for us," he told the reporter, sounding far more like Job than Noah.

As a mammoth wave capsized the family next to me, I couldn't help but wonder whether attending a waterpark in 2019 now requires a willful self-blindness, whereby all fun and thrill-seeking depends upon blinkering oneself to the fearsome changes in our climate. Because who can enjoy the "Congo Bongo" in light of mudslides in the Pacific Northwest? Who can enjoy "The Flying Gecko" when you have species-wide devastation in the Amazon? Actually, the sheer insanity of a waterpark in the age of the Anthropocene won't hit me fully until I coax a young staffer into revealing that the park goes through two million gallons of water per day, a cruel parody of our country's dwindling natural resources. It was in the context of this thought that the Big Kahuna Wave Pool began to strike me as a dress rehearsal for our coming disaster, a nightmarish burlesque of a live-action drill. I watched then as a stern-faced boy, no older than ten, got violently thrown from his raft, and a rogue wave pulled his family a terrible distance away from him. When he emerged, red-eyed and frightened, exhaling a mist of water, the family, still swept up in the amusements, chuckled brightly and said, "Come on, Dmitri! Save yourself!" The moment was so upsetting that I left and immediately purchased a funnel cake, which I ate distractedly and tried to calm down, moseying for some time on the park's vast, labyrinthine walkways.

I must have taken a wrong turn. Soon I found myself lumbering up a flight of creaky wooden steps, climbing higher and higher into the sky. There came a point in my ascent where I had an unimpeded view of the whole park below. That's odd, I thought, but maybe this was just a hike to some scenic promontory? The wind was stronger here, and the trees were bubbles of green, like those found in a Grant Wood painting. And threading through it all was a lurid vasculature of color—the other water slides— which I was petrified to realize were impossibly far beneath me. Somehow I was in line for the park's tallest ride, a free-fall they called "The Point of No Return." People were ahead of and behind me in the line, and so, unless I wanted to reveal certain deficiencies of spirit, I plainly saw that I had no choice, that there was no other exit. Every few minutes, a person received instructions from the ride's attendants, and filtered through my morbid imagination, they sounded like last rites or funeral preparations. "Okay, just lie flat!" they said. "Stay down and don't move! Are you ready?" Then came a scream—thin, metallic—a sound that shrank rapidly as the person fell. The line dwindled in front of me, and now I could see into the mouth of the plummet. I could see its large, dark throat gape menacingly at me as it swallowed another parkgoer. One after another, the people fell, until soon I found myself trudging toward its entrance. The drop was so precipitous that I saw in just a few short seconds I would go abruptly verti-cal, vanishing briskly down a long dark well. It was the point of no return, a waterpark in 2019. And for reasons I struggled to explain, I desperately missed my family. Look how far the fathoms have taken us. Look how far we've strayed.

LETTER FROM A TARGET-RICH ENVIORNMENT

I t's a bright day in early August, and the semester hasn't yet started. There are twelve of us altogether—new hires at the university—and we've been summoned to a classroom on the sixth floor of the Humanities Building for yet another seminar in professional development. For the last week, we've been subjected to a dull march of policies and protocols, reviewing instructor manuals clotted with indemnifying legalese. So far the gist of orientation can be summarized with two brainless provisos: *don't sleep with your students* and *don't buy them beer.*

This session is an active shooter training. In the designated classroom, twelve rows of desks face a projection screen up front, and the ceiling's ancient fluorescents give off a wan, spectral glare. I find a seat among my colleagues, and though we have come to this university from places as varied as Togo, Korea, and New York, we are all in our late twenties or early thirties, and thus share a common history. At cocktail parties and departmental mixers throughout the week, we bond over the usual adolescent touchstones, regaling each other with stories about where we were on 9/11 and marveling at the fact that, even though we were children, our parents still let us watch the O. J. Simpson trial on TV. As people who came of age during this epoch of hysteria, all of us are naturally a bit jittery about the seminar. After all, we have no trouble recalling a time when newspapers were glutted with articles about razor blades in aspirin bottles, when people in matching Reeboks quaffed mugs of arsenic-laced Kool-Aid. What was the name of that cult again? No one can remember. Then someone brandishes a smartphone and tells us it was Heaven's Gate.

The seminar is conducted by two plainclothes officers, both of whom have guns holstered to their hips. Pacing at the front of the classroom with a grim, prosecutorial air, one of the cops clears his throat and says, "Before we dive in here, let me ask you all a question. Where are you right now?" What follows is a long beat of claustrophobic silence, perhaps because, as academics, we resent the use of cute pedagogical tactics. "You mean where we are, like, existentially?" one colleague quips, but the cop remains wholly unfazed. Finally, another colleague responds in a dutiful tone that we're on the sixth floor of the Humanities Building. "Good," the cop says, pointing at her. "But better yet, does anyone know what room we're in?" There are a few mumbled guesses, but the exact location eludes us. This causes the cop to shake his head, as if our ignorance were a matter of a great personal umbrage. "Why do I ask you this? Why do I make such a fuss? Here's why: because when it comes down to it, in the heat of an emergency, you're going to need to tell us where you are and what's going on, so we can respond swiftly and effectively to the particulars of your situation. And please excuse my language here, but as instructors, when the shit hits the fan, it'll be your responsibility to keep those kids safe."

The silence is chastened, and we straighten up in our chairs. Our sheepish expressions seem to reflect the solemnity of this charge—or perhaps simply the absurdity of the premise: that we have been entrusted with something so tenuous and elusive as the maintenance of anyone's safety.

—

When I was young, the specter of violence was always loitering around the corner or visiting neighbors up the street. In third grade, a close friend of mine slipped and fell while scrabbling up a tree in his backyard, and his neck got snagged on a lattice of rope that had been tangled in the tree's lower branches. At his funeral, which was an open casket, all of his friends wore starch-coarsened Boy Scout uniforms, and while sitting in the drafty pews of that Gothic church, I overheard another parent tell my mom that it had been the boy's grandmother who found him and who apparently fell to her knees at the sight of him swaying. Then there was the dour-eyed girl I knew from middle school choir, a girl with a welter of brown curls and a wardrobe of Nirvana t-shirts. She shot herself with her father's gun on the pink carpet of her childhood bedroom, her mother fixing supper only two rooms away.

In the weeks after each of these tragedies, something inside me broke open, and it was not uncommon for certain kinds of thoughts to colonize my head. It could happen anywhere. After school, while trundling up the driveway, I would imagine the garage door scrolling back to reveal my family hanging from the rafters, strung up with orange extension cords and arranged in order of diminishing height—*dad, mom, brother, sister*—each of their heads cocked brokenly to the right. Or whenever I went for evening jogs, I would trot beside a pond hemmed with cottontails and think, *This is where I will be abducted. In those shallows is where I'll be found.*

As isolated and parochial as this thinking may have been, it was no doubt exacerbated by the many public traumas of that era, those that were couriered into our homes in the alarmed cadences of newscasters: the aerial-shot mayhem at Columbine or the footage of the Twin Towers collapsing in flames. I found a strange comfort in these images, a sense of vindication, if only because they seemed to confirm my burgeoning suspicion that horror was commonplace, perhaps even inevitable. It would be naive to think there were more large-scale catastrophes in the late 1990s and early 2000s than at any other moment in history, but the steady faucet of twenty-four-hour news and the grainy intimacy of cellphone cameras ensured that this violence became the psychic backdrop for my Little League games and family trips to the beach.

When incidents of such grievous violence intrude upon the happy kingdom of your childhood, you fall prey rather quickly to two countervailing ideas. The first takes the form of wholesale generalization. Humanity, at its roots, is wicked and depraved. No matter what the optimists say, you hold fast to the notion that the history of our species is nothing more than a colonnade of disaster, punctuated by spells of butchery and ruin. The second idea is whimsical and untrue. The child who is burdened with heightened sensitivities nevertheless believes that he can insulate himself from the world's misfortunes. That he can erect a fortress impenetrable to the schemes of would-be assailants. That he can protect himself and his loved ones. That he can be safe.

—

After a rundown of the standard evacuation procedures—what route to take in the event of a fire, where to find shelter if there's a tornado—the cops begin reviewing the active shooter protocol. For the next fifteen minutes, we are made to endure a slideshow of various scenarios, which we're supposed to identify as either "suspicious" or "not suspicious." The first image depicts a pudgy man with diabolical eyebrows who dawdles beside a file cabinet and furtively snaps photos of a folder marked CONFIDENTIAL. Educated in public schools, all of us know to respond in unison, and for some reason we transform the word into a cheerful multi-toned song. *Sus-pi-cious*, we sing. The next photo presents a bedraggled homeless man using a Styrofoam cup to mooch for spare change. Almost uniformly Democrats, we uphold our good liberal bona fides and intone, again musically: *not sus-pi-cious*.

Finally, we are confronted with an image of a North Face backpack sitting desolately at the end of a dormitory hallway, against a carpet that is the color of industrial exhaust. I know I'm supposed to regard this rucksack as some murderous instrument, but for some reason I am given to entertain alternate possibilities. Perhaps the bag contains a bunch of dildos and was left here by some puckish undergrad bent on scandalizing his priggish Christian roommate? Or maybe the backpack was chucked by an overachieving millennial exasperated because he got a B? I suppose it strikes me as a deficit of imagination to assume that an object out of context necessarily warrants a dose of suspicion.

One would think we'd have greater respect for the element of surprise. How many times have we heard the neighbors of serial killers describe the person in question as "unassuming" or "approachable"? Such offbeat descriptions only underscore the extent to which these tragedies are unpredictable, full of red herrings and false alarms. But in the cops' view of the world, danger is obvious and readily identifiable—the only thing that would cause someone to overlook it is a dearth of vigilance, or lack of proper training.

—

A year before Dylan Klebold and Eric Harris stormed into Columbine High School and gunned down their classmates, they were arrested for breaking into a minivan. Though they filched several hundred dollars' worth of the owner's belongings, the boys' parents, as well as the local authorities who arrested them, ultimately saw the act as nothing more than a blip of childish malfeasance, hardly a precursor to bloodshed. When the boys stood trial for these burglaries, the presiding judge was struck by their unswerving deference in the courtroom. They peppered their statements with honorifics; their eyes glistened with regret. That such actions could so effectively conceal the bellwethers of psychosis probably says more about the credulity of the judge than it does the guile of the two boys, but perhaps that is a cruel opinion, one that can only be leveled in hindsight. It's possible the boys' guilt did seem genuine at the time.

As part of their sentence, the boys were asked to write a letter of apology to the van's owner. But what they ended up producing was more like an opera of remorse. At its climax, Eric Harris spoke in plaintive tones about the degree of violation the owner must have felt, suggesting that if the van had been his, he would have trouble even driving it again, so fearful would he be of another invasion.

But shortly after delivering the letter, Harris was clacking away at his keyboard and spewing venom on his website:

> Isnt America supposed to be the land of the free? how come if im free, I cant deprive a stupid fucking dumbshit from his possessions. If he leaves them sitting in the front seat of his fucking van out in plain sight and in the middle of fucking nowhere on a Frifucking day night. NATURAL SELECTION. Fucker should be shot.

A year later, in the wake of the bloody rampage, the judge who tried the boys for burglary was not insensible to his mistake. "What's mind-boggling is the amount of deception," he said. "The ease of their deception. The coolness of their deception." What was mind-boggling, in other words, was the degree to which the boys could appear, simultaneously, as ordinary kids engaging in run-of-the-mill hijinks and unremorseful psychopaths gearing up for slaughter—the holographic way their actions appeared harmless from one angle and, from another, full of murderous intent.

—

"Take a minute to look around you," the cop instructs us now. "I want you to think about what objects in the room could be used as weapons in the unlikely event of an attack." My colleagues begin scanning the area, and although I expect smirks and weary glances, the opposite encounters me. In a voice of utmost seriousness, one colleague suggests knuckling your car keys and jabbing the assailant's head. "Good!" the cop says. "What else?" Perhaps another person's water bottle could be repurposed as a bludgeon? "Absolutely. With enough force, you could do some serious damage with this thing." As I watch my colleagues scour the classroom, their eyes alighting on each object with palpable alarm, I can tell that for many of them it is unnerving to filter this immediate reality through the lens of its violent potential. But for me these dark torsions of mind are familiar—the type of precautionary thinking that mollifies me whenever I'm at airports or shopping malls, or even when I'm teaching my classes. I raise my hand. "What about the heating ducts in the ceiling? Couldn't you remove the metal vent and use its corner as a blunt edge?" I'm hoping for an *atta-boy* commendation, but the cop crumples his face and shoots a meaningful glance in my boss's direction. "OK," he says. "Not sure I would've thought of that, but sure."

I'll admit my mind has a conspiratorial bent, but it seems hard not to notice that I've raised the cop's suspicions, that my name has probably been added to the annals of some mental watch list. Things get worse when the cop asks if anyone can remember when Columbine happened, and I supply not only the year of the massacre, but also its month and calendar date. At this point, hoping to uncork some of the accumulating tension, the cop swivels around to face my boss and says, with cartoonish insistence, "You guys run background checks for these fellowships, right?"

Everyone is laughing. Even I am laughing. But there's no point in trying to explain why this knowledge is wedded indelibly to the events of my own life. If I have excelled at these exercises, it is because I've spent a lifetime in thrall to vigilance, running down the same kinds of facile checklists this training is meant to inculcate. Yet the irony is not lost on me: filtered through the dumb binaries of today's lesson, it is my own behavior that has been classified as sketchy, suspicious.

—

One morning, when I was in the seventh grade, a hit list was discovered on the mirror of the boys' bathroom. In total there were eleven names, each scrawled in livid red marker. For a little while, at least until the school administrators took action, my fellow students regarded the list as an object of general hilarity, something your classmates exhorted you to check out during those interstitial moments between classes. To their pubescent minds, it was another gag, no more serious than the caricature of fellatio rendered in Sharpie above the toilet.

That my name was included among the targets came as something of a shock. My interactions with the list's author were few and far between, and the two of us probably traded as many glances as we did words. It was true we shared a math class, and a history class, but I don't think we ever engaged in a real conversation.

To stand at a mirror with the bulletin of your own murder superimposed across your face was a heady experience for a twelve-year-old. But the gravity of the situation was swiftly dispelled by a trio of my close friends, who told me not to worry, that it was all a bunch of bullshit. Their names were also on the list, and so, for the time being, I let myself be persuaded by their outlook of raffish calm.

That night, my parents and I watched the evening news, and the screen flashed with a live shot of my school, where a female anchor was feigning consternation. Apparently, investigators were still trying to determine the seriousness of the boy's intentions, and local parents were already attempting to explain the dark swerve in his behavior. In their haste, they trotted out a roster of ludicrous abettors: everything from the desensitization of video games, to the moral corrosion of MTV, to Bill Clinton's dalliances in the West Wing. In retrospect, it's difficult not to feel the desperation of these sweeping narratives. Scarcely could we imagine what lowdown thoughts or grim circumstances would lead a boy to such lethal urges. But against the threat of our own culpability and a needling sense of fear, we labored to control the story, grasping at hypotheses, drawing makeshift lines between cause and effect.

In the end, I don't remember what happened to the author of the list. His being shipped off to juvenile detention seems as likely as the prospect that he reappeared in school at some point that semester, tempered by lithium and the emollients of professional therapy. The only thing I can recall with any reliable measure of certainty is that, shortly after this incident, I started behaving in ways that caused my parents no small degree of distress. Before bed each night, I began checking the locks on the doors dozens, if not hundreds, of times. And on many occasions, in the wee hours before dawn, my parents woke to find me standing at the brink of their bed, hovering over their faces, trying to verify whether their hearts had stopped beating in the night.

—

One little discussed anecdote from the horrors of 9/11 is that, in the weeks after the attack, dozens of teenaged girls arrived at various Manhattan hospitals with a set of common symptoms. Each had trouble swallowing and every utterance was an exertion. Though they arrived separately, the girls nonetheless came to the same conclusion about their ailment. During the chaos of that morning, while sprinting through clouds of rubble and dust, the girls probably inhaled chunks of debris, which must have gotten lodged in the pith of their throats. But two of the girls entertained other, more unsettling explanations. Perhaps the obstruction was a human limb—a dismembered finger, a dollop of bone.

Very quickly the incident was interpreted as a metaphor for our national crisis. "[These girls] expressed hysterically what many of us feel," one commentator wrote, "that the information is too difficult to swallow." Others consulted Freud and suggested the condition was a form of visceral displacement, an incarnation of the ways in which we were unable to express ourselves in the wake of horrendous trauma. 9/11, in other words, was "a story in search of a voice."

188 | LOST IN SUMMERLAND

In her book *The Terror Dream*, Susan Faludi finds such metaphors woefully insufficient. She contends that, in the fevered days after 9/11, our media outlets simulated the construction of a meaningful narrative, prattling on endlessly about "the death of irony" and "the end of post-modernism," but never once offering a true account of our situation. "The cacophony of chanted verities," Faludi writes, "induced a kind of cultural hypnosis." It is easy to recall the palliative bromides from that era: *Never Forget. Axis of Evil. Everything Has Changed.* Such catchphrases were often paired with footage from the disaster, which served unwittingly as a kind of twisted mnemonic device. How could anyone worry about forgetting the minutiae of the attacks when one was constantly bombarded with pixelated reenactments, with clips of the south tower engulfed in flames, or images of people coated in ash trudging zombie-like through the ruins? Such reruns, Faludi notes, did little "to plumb what the trauma meant for our national psyche." We ran our hands over the scars but could not fathom the depth of our injuries.

Fifteen years later, it seems we are no closer to comprehending our losses. In lieu of meditation or genuine comprehension, we still observe the easy rituals of bereavement, uttering solemnities whenever someone mentions the events of that morning, as though recurrence were a conduit to understanding. But like the ash that blanketed Manhattan, the ash inhaled by legions of New Yorkers, the aftereffects of the horror still loiter in the body, still infect the inner spaces, a contagion that expresses itself in oblique and myriad ways. It can be seen in the scores of Trump supporters who address their fellow countrymen with vile slurs and naked bigotry. And it can be found in the precautions of Williamsburg mothers who micromanage their toddlers' diets and disinfect the playpen with clockwork regularity. What joins these individuals, what still unites the states of our republic, is the vantage of total fear.

For those of us who came of age in the eighties and nineties, merely mentioning places like Columbine, Aurora, and Virginia Tech can evoke as much splintering pathos as once did battlefields like Normandy or Hanoi.

Now, however, when our wars are carried out with the impersonality of un-manned drones, when our leaders make no meaningful distinction between civilians and soldiers, the new theaters of that more intimate historical vio-lence are our shopping malls, our movie theaters, our classrooms. Which is to say: the landscape of violence is coterminous with the landscape of youth.

Here the average American confronts the prospect of horror once imag-inable only to a soldier of a foreign war. In the blink of an eye, a food court or museum can transmogrify into the acreage of a warzone, which is why, in such venues, I have begun to approximate the uneasy vigilance of combat: darting glances at the doors, inspecting the faces of passersby for some tell-tale hint of malevolent objectives. Whenever I'm at the cinema and someone leaves to use the restroom or visit concessions, invariably I will monitor the length of that person's absence, wondering if they've gone to their car to retrieve a stockpile of weapons, or if in a few minutes they'll come bursting through the doors to begin firing at will. With my feet adhered to the soda-confected floors, I make plans and develop contingencies. I make myself aware of the exits.

—

A college campus is, empirically speaking, one of the safest places on the continent. On this fastidiously groomed, well-lit estate, the greatest threat I face is also the most unlikely one. And yet I cannot help thinking that vio-lence in a place like this would catch us completely off guard, interrupting a game of Frisbee or a lecture on Plato's cave. These visions of carnage seem always to visit me on days when the sky is clearest and the quad lawn is tenanted by students lounging on blankets, insouciantly engrossed in their textbooks, their frozen yogurts, their phones.

Which is not to say the students are exempt from these anxieties. Whenever there's an unscheduled fire drill or a disturbance in the hallway, they revert to autopilot, brandishing their cellphones by reflex and casting stricken glances in my direction. It seems we have primed them for every taxonomy of disaster. I suppose it is in such moments that I glimpse the frontier of trigger warnings and safe spaces, for as much as we might try to protect them from needless disruption and preserve their serenity of mind, I suspect that, deep down, the students know as much as I do: that no space can ever truly be safe, that there's no end to the chute of trauma through which ordinary objects can become the correlatives of our worst disasters.

A few days after the safety seminar, my colleagues and I return to campus for a catered lunch, and while we poke at our salads, the director of our program solicits our opinions. Notwithstanding the huffy machismo of the trainers, was the seminar worthwhile—anything to recommend it?

A gust of silence enters the room, and I glance at the far wall, where a window overlooks a sunless lake. Over the gunmetal water, a mob of starlings has begun to unfurl, widening and then contracting in pursuit of unseen prey.

"I guess you could say I found it triggering," one of the poets says, "for lack of a better word."

Several colleagues hum in agreement.

"That's what I told my therapist," a fiction writer says. "I told her, *We've got a whole new batch of issues to talk about.*"

For those tenured faculty who did not attend the seminar, our advisor rattles off a few morbid highlights: the suspicious/not suspicious game, the discussion on makeshift weapons, the memorization of the safety motto— RUN, HIDE, FIGHT.

"My feeling is there's nothing I can do," one of the fiction writers says. She is in her sixties, with a pelt of hair that is gray and hatchling-soft. "If they're coming for me, they're coming for me," she says. "At my age, it's not like running is gonna help."

A few colleagues chuckle experimentally, as if trying to gauge her tone, and for a moment the table seems to crackle with tension.

"I mean it," she says. "Better to just line us up in the corner and get it over with. Guy comes into the classroom with a gun, and without hesitation I'll say, *Just tell me where to stand, kind sir.*"

Now almost everyone is laughing—a monstrous, cathartic laugh. It is the sound of grief corroding, a knot of fear slowly coming undone. How free we feel in the wake of this vulgar confession. It is a fantasy of deferred obligations, in which we will not be held responsible for anyone's safety; in which our mettle, shallow and unpredictable, will not be tested. Here, at this moment, we could lie down and die, and no one would blame us. To live under the tyranny of constant vigilance is, after all, its own kind of violence, and in the clutches of this wearisome existence, it has become easy to mistake fatalism for relief.

STARVING

Every semester I make the mistake of teaching Franz Kafka's "The Hunger Artist" in my Intro to Literature class. It's an error not owing to the story's inscrutable meaning, nor because its tropes are alien to millennials. It is rather that, during those few weeks that we devote to Kafka's corpus, the story comes to reside within me with such potency and force that I can hardly think of anything else. When I should be grading papers or prepping for another lecture, I'm deep in the thickets of JSTOR, wading through yet another exegesis of the tale. My wife calls it the month of my metamorphosis.

I should mention that the students who take this introductory seminar are rarely English majors. None of them brandish their knowledge of Jameson or make snappy allusions to late-career Foucault. Instead, most of them are business majors or nurses in training—the two most prominent courses of study on campus—and select literature as an elective because it satisfies so many "General Education" requirements (that grim, unserviceable term). But it seems the motifs of Kafka's masterpiece appeal, however indirectly, to the ambitions of these students. Perhaps the freshman in the starched polo and cotton Dockers recognizes in his pursuit of profit and suburban comfort a kindred craving to that of the hunger artist. And those nursing majors, who arrive in my classroom garbed in white unbesmirched scrubs, like a fleet of new cherubs, know well the gross degradations of the body, its slow and graceless struggle. They know, too, how some corner of the mind still glows despite these attenuations. Some profess to have observed in the eyes of terminal patients a scintillating presence, the mark of a ghost.

These associations are not made without struggle. On the first day of lecture, when I ask for their initial impressions of the story, they groan—a bit animalistically, I'm afraid. This makes me smile. Their slumped postures and drooped expressions, conveying both boredom and disrespect, fill me with a strange delight. This is what a litigator must feel before opening statements to the jury, the odd delicious joy of knowing the case before it's made.

—

Set in a nameless country at an undisclosed time in history, "The Hunger Artist" concerns a man who starves himself not *for his art*—as the old adage goes—but as a *form of art* itself. His abstinence becomes fodder for public consumption. In the opening pages, we're told that the hunger artist travels to little hamlets and villages across the country, where he puts on performances in town squares. For forty days at a time, he sits inside a barred metal cage whose floor has been padded with straw, and sips from a thimble of water, not as a form of nourishment but rather to "moisten his lips." Hordes of eager spectators peer into his kennel and gawk at his deprivation—the protuberant ribcage, the twiggy limbs, the gaunt and phlegmatic expression. But as the days wear on and tastes change, the crowds thin. Enthusiasm wanes. Soon, out of financial desperation and artistic despair, the hunger artist parts ways with his loyal publicist and joins a circus, the last venue where he can procure a stage for himself, however shabby and undignified it may be. "In order to spare his own sensitive feelings, he didn't even look at the terms of his contract."

Upon his arrival at the circus, he's stationed at the far end of the grounds, amidst a menagerie of loud, squawking animals that prove to be more compelling to the guests than the sight of a rail-thin man sitting immobile in worsted vestments. From his vantage inside the cage, he can observe a collection of garishly painted signs advertising other exhibits, which contrast starkly with the drab interior of his own dwelling—the iron bars, the coarse straw, the pale skin. Eventually, people forget about him, even neglecting to change the number on the tablet outside his cage that denotes the duration of his fast.

One day a supervisor totters past the exhibit, seeing only a mound of hay, and asks a nearby attendant why a perfectly good cage is going to waste. Eventually, one member of the grounds crew recalls the presence of the professional faster, prompting everyone to start jabbing at the straw with poles until they locate the skimpy frame of the hunger artist, who rouses slowly. The conversation that ensues is the coda of the story:

> "Forgive me everything," whispered the hunger artist. Only the supervisor, who was pressing his ear up against the cage, understood him. "Certainly," said the supervisor, tapping his forehead with his finger in order to indicate to the staff the state the hunger artist was in, "we forgive you." "I always wanted you to admire my fasting," said the hunger artist. "But we do admire it," said the supervisor obligingly. "But you shouldn't admire it," said the hunger artist. "Well then, we don't admire it," said the supervisor, "but why shouldn't we admire it?" "Because I have to fast. I can't do anything else," said the hunger artist. "Just look at you," said the supervisor, "why can't you do anything else?" "Because," said the hunger artist, lifting his head a little and, with his lips pursed as if for a kiss, speaking right into the supervisor's ear so that he wouldn't miss anything, "because I couldn't find a food that tasted good to me. If I had found that, believe

me, I would not have made a spectacle of myself and would have eaten to my heart's content, like you and everyone else."

These are his last words. Upon his death, the cage is promptly evacuated, and he is replaced by a young panther, a lithe creature who prowls the confines of his tenement and has no trouble enjoying the food the guards bring him.

In the century since its publication, the story has spawned any number of interpretations. Numerous critics have pointed out its obvious Christian allusions. Because the hunger artist's fasts transpire over a period of forty days, they situate him beside other biblical figures, whose own crucibles of faith spanned the same length of time—Moses at Sinai waiting for the commandments; Jesus in the desert, brushing off the devil. And yet, ideologically, Kafka was anything but an apostle. Clearly, he didn't intend for the hunger artist to stand as a simple Christlike symbol. Nowhere is this more apparent than when the impresario calls the hunger artist an "unfortunate martyr," which Kafka qualifies with a telling parenthetical: "something the hunger artist certainly was, only in a completely different sense."

There are, of course, two senses in which one can be a martyr: when one is killed for one's religious beliefs or when one embellishes their suffering in order to garner the condolence or commendation of others. Throughout the story, the hunger artist professes no article of faith, no strident political position. Instead, he's monomaniacally preoccupied with being respected and adored, which gives us good reason to believe that Kafka wants us to regard him in the second, more pejorative sense of the term. The hunger artist's claim at the end of the story that he "couldn't find a food that tasted good" to him is hard to take literally. Instead, it seems to signal that his only nourishment—the only sustenance he hungered for—was approval and veneration. The fickleness of the public proved to be a meager diet, though, and since he had nothing else to live on, he wasted away to a husk of skin and bones. He was, quite literally, starved for attention.

—

It can be counted on that at some point during the discussion of Kafka, one of my students will mention the Kardashian family. The first time the conversation veered in this direction, I was somewhat baffled. But it turns out that for a particular segment of young people, the most immediate contemporary analogue to the hunger artist are celebrities who have made a career not from any particular talent or ability, but rather on their identity alone—the kind of celebrities who have transcended the realm of personalities—and perhaps personhood itself.

In 2015, Kim Kardashian—whose nude callipygous figure was said to have "broken the Internet"—published a collection of photography under the title *Selfish*. For research purposes, I bought this volume at my local bookstore, hiding it under copies of *Bookforum* and *The Paris Review* as I wandered the aisles, then arranging my face into an expression that I hoped would tell the cashier, *No big deal, nothing to see here!*

Despite her evident self-obsession, Kardashian supposedly harbors other-directed intentions for the book. The jacket copy includes this note from the author:

> The pictures in this book bring back so many memories. Spanning almost a decade, [the pictures] are only a small fraction of the thousands of selfies we considered for publication. From digital camera, to Polaroids, to Blackberries, and smartphones, these photos document the evolution of my selfies. And as I printed them out and laid them on the floor to make a final edit, I reflected on my very public journey as a daughter, sister, friend, wife and mother. This book is a candid tribute to all my fans, who were with me the entire time.

Across the book's 445 pages, all of which are selfies, Kardashian is depicted in various states of undress. In some photos, she's playfully razzing the camera, sticking out her tongue or screwing up her face into a loony glower. In others, her face is molded into a smoky, Zoolander-esque expression, a pouty mien with her eyes either gazing at the viewer or drifting off into some luxurious middle-distance ("luxurious" because most of the selfies are taken at resorts, in her mansion, or on the set of a photo shoot). Dozens of selfies are taken in the bathroom of her house, a capacious powder room with gilded faucets and marble sinks. In terms of motif, there is little variance. At a certain point, while flipping through this endless parade of glamour and pulchritude, the mind enters a blank, trancelike state, and one's hand proceeds to turn the pages robotically, much as one might peruse the *SkyMall* on an airplane.

When looking at these photos, I try to imagine why a celebrity—after a long day of eluding paparazzi, shooting her reality show, and doing interviews with *Variety* and *E!*—would feel compelled to spend these precious few moments of privacy making herself yet another object for the camera's gaze. But perhaps for someone so accustomed to living in the public eye, to be alone without a beholder is to suffer a kind of death. Without the record of a selfie, such a person may begin to question the existence of her "self" at all.

—

I never lasted long on social media—there were a few weeks back in 2004 when I used Facebook, a dark period during which I also wore an eyebrow ring and still had hair—so its operations invariably feel exotic to me. Whenever my friends log on, I always jump at the chance to look over their shoulders and read their newsfeeds, trying to get a sense of its interpersonal flavor. But even though its codes and mores strike me as queer and foreign, I don't bring to these investigations the bigoted attitude of a xenophobe nor the unalterable nostalgia of a Luddite. I'm genuinely curious about the potential benefits of expressing myself and curating my own life online. Surely, there are social advantages. And for a writer there are professional ones, too.

By now, the fact that social media conventions mirror the undertak-ings of celebrities—the meticulously curated profiles, the group-tested posts written in press-release diction, the endless photos of our friends' meals, their leisure activities, their dogs (it's true, "the stars are just like us"—in fact, they are us)—is usually acknowledged with sheepish embarrassment. We cop to our self-promotion and blush upon admit-ting that, yes, okay, it's true: we do in fact take down Facebook posts or Instagram pics that don't garner enough likes or favorites. We do sometimes, when polling our "friends," address them this way: "Dear Facebook" or "Dear Hivemind." But we defend against these minor humiliations of personhood by suggesting that they're required by our neoliberal landscape. Perhaps the wisdom of *Citizens United* can be ap-plied in reverse: yes, corporations are individuals, but individuals are corporations, too.

But when we regard our "selves" this way—as a product to be marketed, a message to be promulgated, a brand to be "liked"—something strange happens. We begin to feel the gathering pangs of a clenched inauthenticity, which accrues ever more quickly under the pressure to keep up appearances, to apply yet another coat of varnish to the surface of our brand. We may feel lonely or "unknown" in ways we could never admit. Of course, all so-cial roles are inescapably performative, and it would be naive to think that we can totally avoid the dramaturgy of self-presentation simply by staying offline. But in the age of wearable technology, push notifications, and selfie sticks, it has become difficult to adequately distinguish between our virtual and visceral selves, to know when exactly the curtain closes and the back-stage begins. Kafka notes that toward the end of his life, malnourished by a thankless audience, the hunger artist never leaves the circus. It is perhaps no accident that the site of his exhibit, the very proscenium of his performance, is also a cage.

—

It's usually this line of thinking that gets my students to sit up in their chairs. With widened eyes and hands shooting up from their desks, they offer a torrent of confessions. One student tells me about the two-and-a-half hours she spent photoshopping her profile picture. Another confesses that whenever she posts something to Facebook or Instagram, she will sit there at her desk, in the feeble blue wash of her glowing screen, until a friend or follower "likes" it. I watch as her peers nod in fervid agreement. At a certain point, the lecture comes undone and assumes the parameters of a counselor's office. One meek boy with a quiet, soulful voice—a photography major— recounts his trial with anorexia during high school, something he claims to have documented on Instagram. Hoping to contain this wellspring of emotion and keep the conversation at least passably academic, I cite a note from David Foster Wallace's essay on Kafka and tell them that the etymological root of *anorexia* happens to be the Greek word for longing.

In a spirit of connection, I confess to them a certain constitutional inclination, as a writer, a teacher, and a citizen, to please others and win their approval: in this way I feel the stains of my generation, those consummate millennials raised to harvest gold stars. No matter the social context, I yearn to be liked. This is why, during a recent trip to Florida for my brother-in-law's wedding, I spent the majority of the rehearsal dinner ingratiating myself with the bride's family, a conversation that featured her uncles and me trading ripostes and nimble one-liners until our end of the table was erupting with laughter. At the end of the weekend, the father of the bride presented me with a hulking, gourmet cigar, and for reasons not entirely clear to me, pumped my hand with great vigor and said, "I really hope to see you again, my friend."

My wife calls these episodes my "Golden Boy" moments. She presumably means to compliment my social graces, but I can't help sensing a darker edge to her remark. The very fact that these episodes warrant their own designation signals the extent to which my longing to be accepted is transparent—that while I'm merely trying to get along with others, my behavior actually comes off as canned, scripted, as if someone had just pulled my drawstring. "The tricks that work on others," Joan Didion writes, "count for nothing in that very well-lit back alley where one keeps assignations with oneself." This back alley is a necessary refuge, a corridor of silence where the task of self-inventory is unavoidable.

Getting along with others is, of course, a natural impulse. All of us calibrate our personalities to our social setting—it is the kernel of good manners. But it is also a high-wire act. The risk is that you might not be able to distinguish your sense of self from your longing to be admired. One of the reasons I have avoided Facebook is that I can sense the software has been coded to nurture precisely these sorts of anxieties. For someone with my appetites, it would offer an all-you-can-eat buffet of potential social approval, each one, though momentarily satisfying, inexorably giving rise to some other, more desperate hunger.

"You have to be somebody," Jaron Lanier writes in *You Are Not a Gadget*, "before you can share yourself." A fine sentiment, but I prefer Marilynne Robinson's formulation in which she speaks of a not-so-ancient era when we prized the gorgeous difficulty of becoming a person. "Truly and ideally," she writes, "a biography was the passage of a soul through the vale of its making, or its destruction, and that the business of the world was a parable or test or temptation or distraction and therefore engrossing, and full of the highest order of meaning . . ." In our era, our souls do not pass through a vale but ascend to a different Valhalla, one built in binary code, where those albums of selfies will surely outlast us. I shudder to think of myself eternally marooned in that afterlife, squished between ads for diet pills and a poorly lit pic of a meal recently consumed by a "friend." If anything, such documents will speak to those old enduring hungers. But like so many other fixations, just because we crave it doesn't mean it will nourish us.

POLITICAL FICTIONS

n times of chaos, we turn to narrative. Throughout the tumult of the George W. Bush years, the preferred palliative for the demoralized left was Aaron Sorkin's *The West Wing*—a political drama about the lives of White House staffers in the administration of Josiah Bartlet, a fictional Democratic president played by Martin Sheen. The show, which originally aired in the late 1990s and early 2000s, depicted a world in which government could serve as an engine of good, an instrument of change. Across the series, the staff brokered peace in the Middle East, dreamt up free college education, and unraveled the Gordian knot of entitlements like Medicare and Social Security. In the wake of 9/11, as the U.S. was contending with the specter of domestic terror and gearing up for an unpopular war in Iraq, the show's viewership tilted toward seventeen million.

The storyline I found most compelling as a young, aspiring author was the thread about the presidential speechwriters. Throughout the show, Toby Ziegler (Richard Schiff) and Sam Seaborn (Rob Lowe) sequestered themselves in the darkened catacombs of the White House, armed with nothing more than legal pads and Bic pens, testing out snatches of oratory on each other as they sought to draft a comprehensive narrative about America. "To-night, what began in the commons of Concord, Massachusetts," President Bartlet intones in a campaign speech, "as an alliance of farmers and workers, of cobblers and tinsmiths, of statesmen and students, of mothers and wives, of men and boys, lives two centuries later." It was this heady idealism—the notion that America itself was merely a story, a fragile narrative continually authored by each administration—that led me to see politics as a noble call-ing, a redoubtable vocation. The depth of my fandom revealed itself in ways that were oblique but no less shameful. Throughout college, I festooned the walls of my bedroom with the same framed "Don't Tread on Me" flag that Seaborn keeps in his office and, on weekends, recreationally performed critical exegeses on the rhetoric of presidential inaugurals. After watching the 2004 Democratic National Convention, during which Barack Obama delivered a speech whose elegance rivaled anything Aaron Sorkin had writ-ten, I wrote an effusive fan letter and shipped it off to his senate office in Chicago. A few weeks later, a staffer called and suggested that I apply for an internship, which led, somehow, to me spending the next several years in Illinois, toiling first in Obama's senate office and later in the headquarters of his presidential campaign. An intern in the correspondence department, I was fairly low on the totem pole and had exactly zero sway in shaping the candidate's agenda. Instead, my job involved wading through thousands of letters from ordinary voters, an epistolary scramble out of which I could sense a national longing for a different kind of leader, one who could con-nect the bloody doldrums of the nation's past to the more hopeful arc of its future. After long train rides home to my garden apartment on the north side of Chicago, I binge-watched episodes of *The West Wing*, often falling asleep to the DVD menu's soaring orchestral theme.

Now, in 2018, that time of my life seems lacquered with the same gauzy-edged cinematography as Sorkin's televisual fantasia. Eventually, I abandoned my aspirations to be a presidential speechwriter and enrolled in an MFA program in creative writing. In retrospect, it seems a slender mercy to have escaped the political arena before the American presidency devolved into the blustering Twitter volleys of our current mogul-in-chief. But over the past several years, *The West Wing* has made a swift and surprising comeback. Owing in part to the convenience of Netflix, the show has been enjoying a resurgence among younger viewers, who weren't yet born when the series first aired. *The West Wing Weekly*, a podcast devoted to rehashing episodes, has garnered some fifty-five million downloads and over eighty thousand followers on Facebook and Instagram. So seismic was this revival that earlier this year rumors began circulating about NBC possibly rebooting *The West Wing*, with Aaron Sorkin wrangling his old crew to serve as a foil to the Trump White House.

Last summer, I learned that these new *West Wing* fans, or self-described "Wingnuts," along with the original Aaron Sorkin faithful, were planning to commemorate the show with its first ever fan convention in Bethesda. There would be panel discussions about public policy, a *West Wing* Trivial Pursuit night, plus a mock state dinner. When I showed my wife the event's Kickstarter page, which was soundtracked by the show's triumphant-sounding theme, she said, with no small amount of grief in her voice, "Please tell me you're not thinking about going."

—

Wood-paneled and fern-studded, the Marriott Hotel & Conference Center in Bethesda, Maryland, is thronged with excited Wingnuts. Retrieving welcome packets and plastic lanyards from the lobby desk, the fans trade introductions with the restive energy of long-lost friends and peruse the daily schedule with palpable elation. Eventually, a bovine line forms outside the White Flynn Amphitheater, where the welcome session will soon start. It is difficult to describe why a cadre of policy wonks would strike anyone as an alluring premise for a fan convention. *Hey, guys, let's cosplay a senior staff meeting*, is something no one says on Reddit. My older brother, who

204 | LOST IN SUMMERLAND

prefers action-based entertainments, likes to disdainfully point out that *The West Wing* is nothing more than "just a bunch of old guys walking around in suits." But in the Kickstarter promotion for the West Wing Weekend, Elisa Birdseye, its programming director, underscored the event's fundamental appeal, "Don't we all want to go somewhere where Jed Bartlet is our president?"

The lure of escapism is echoed by Clay Dockery, the head organizer for the West Wing Weekend, who hustles to the front of the amphitheater wearing a suit and a red tie, one that has been snipped with a scissors just below the solar plexus. The maimed Windsor is an homage to episode 6 from season 4 (entitled "Game On") in which the first lady amputates the president's necktie as a prank just before he goes on stage for a reelection debate. I can't say what's more embarrassing—that someone would actually do this or that I, a supposed journalist and thus an innocent bystander, can immediately spot the reference.

Slouching at a chestnut lectern, Dockery looks like a sullen, middle-aged version of Harry Potter—squat, portly, nervously adjusting his owl-eyed glasses—and explains that the West Wing Weekend should be an occasion to revel in Sorkin's genius and make friends with likeminded people. Then, almost as an afterthought, he says the conference will also "send people home with tools for organizing," which is why, in addition to the fan programming, there will be panels hosted by NGOs like Emerge America, Wolf-PAC, and Emily's List. (Ultimately, this will prove perfunctory. Such events will be woefully under-attended, with the Wingnuts proving far more keen about press secretary cosplay or "*West Wing* Speed Dating" than they are about lectures on civic engagement.) Once the introductions are over, Dockery looks momentarily flummoxed, unsure of how to close out the session. "Should we sing the theme?" one audience member yells. There's a wave of sheepish laughter until one bold attendee starts humming, quite tunefully, the opening bars of the anthem. One by one, the Wingnuts join in until eventually the entire auditorium resounds with their song.

It is difficult to summarize my first day at the convention. Should I tell you about the episode-watching session where a coterie of Wingnuts discussed season 1, episode 19 ("Let Bartlet Be Bartlet") with the exegetical rigor of a grad seminar? Would you like to hear about the table read I attended, where your fellow citizens sat on folding chairs and paged through *West Wing* scripts, delivering Sorkin's breakneck dialogue with enviable thespian élan? Should I tell you about the *West-Wing*-themed punk band called "Steph Anderson and the Two Bartlets," whose pink-haired lead singer abused a maroon Stratocaster and screamed into the microphone lyrics like "I serve at the pleasure of the president"? Because, sadly, I could, friends. I was there, your humble correspondent.

Again and again throughout the first day of the convention, the Wingnuts keep rhapsodizing about the analgesic properties of the show, a much-needed tonic for our current political turmoil. I meet a white-haired man named Lou, who owns a Sparkle Car Wash in suburban Pennsylvania and who has been a diehard fan of *The West Wing* ever since it first aired. These days, he likes to stream episodes on repeat, which has allowed him to watch the entire series "probably fifty or sixty times." "My daughter recently got married," he tells me, "and she used *The West Wing* theme song for the father-daughter dance." In a hotel corridor, a bearded and ponytailed landscaper named Greg, who traveled here from Cleveland, tells me that he watches two episodes of the show every night, the televisual equivalent of an Ambien. "I can't go to bed without a little bit of it. And I just keep going through the seasons. For me, *The West Wing* isn't just an entertainment anymore. It's the way we wish it were, and the way we hope it will be the next morning."

To my mind, this desperation for an alternative political narrative reveals something crucial about the governing styles of the last three presidents. If *The West Wing* snagged Emmys and garnered large audiences during the Bush years, and if the show witnessed a resurgence during the scandal-laden first term of the Trump administration, it seems to suggest something peculiar about Obama, apart from his status as a liberal democrat. Perhaps it owes something to the fact that Obama was himself a gifted narrator—who, before running for office, penned a *New York Times* best-selling memoir, *Dreams from My Father*, and who arguably won the election for his ability to tell Americans a particular kind of story. Not only did this narrative flatter the yearnings of the Left, but it also had the power to loosen Republican strongholds throughout middle America. In the last days of the Obama administration, when asked whether he and the president had tried to manufacture a new American narrative about politics and public service, Jon Favreau, the president's head speechwriter, said, "We saw that as our entire job."

—

"Governments require make-believe," the historian Edmund S. Morgan writes in *Inventing the People*, a trenchant monograph on the origins of democracy. "Make believe that the people have a voice or make believe that the representatives of the people *are* the people . . . Make believe that all men are equal or make believe that they are not." In other words, nations are nothing more than fickle acts of imagination—America itself, a story written across three centuries. We rarely acknowledge the fictitious underpinnings of our nation's founding, but the self-evident truths that Jefferson inscribed in the Declaration were not actually axiomatic but depended instead upon a willful suspension of disbelief. (After all, this putative equality extended only to the rights of white male landowners.)

It is not at all coincidental that the most venerated presidents throughout history were fluent in certain literary tropes and thus operated as cunning dramatic narrators: Reagan, with his tinsel-town charm and his grandfatherly locutions; Kennedy, with his rousing calls to national service; Roosevelt, with his palliative fireside chats, the oratorical approximation of a bedtime story. What these stewards of the American ideal understood better than their blundering counterparts was that in order to govern effectively, one needed to remain cognizant of the motifs and themes that animate the American fable—optimism, progress, hard work, and inclusivity—a narrative expansive enough to hold together the disparate factions of the nation.

For vast swaths of the electorate, part of the comfort we took in the Obama presidency was knowing that we were in the hands of an adept storyteller—one who admired the poetry of Derek Walcott, one who understood the rhetorical valence of singing "Amazing Grace." No matter the national turmoil or geopolitical crisis, we felt confident that, with Obama at the helm, the plot would invariably swerve toward a denouement of decency and justice. Such soliloquies, it must be acknowledged, didn't always have wholesome intentions and often went some way toward obscuring Obama's more unsightly policies—the ramping usage of drone warfare, the cozying up to Wall Street. Still, it was a "dramatic," televisual narrative about America—a Hegelian unfolding of hope and change. By contrast, Donald Trump, Steve Bannon, and Kellyanne Conway proved dexterous postmodernists, deconstructing not just the narrative about America that Obama and his speechwriters had spent the previous eight years fashioning, but also the rudiments of narrative itself—plot, coherence, truth, and meaning. Whereas Obama followed the rules of Aristotelian drama and thus resembled a president from Aaron Sorkin's imagination, Trump obeyed the anti-narratives of reality television, where what matters most is not coherence or logical progression, but chaos and titillation.

—

On the night of the mock State Dinner and Presidential Ball, the Wingnuts stroll into the conference center, looking stuffy and uncomfortable in tuxedos and ball gowns. Before dinner, we're treated to a concert by a Croatian cellist named Dorotea Rácz, who opens her set with Bach's Suite in G Major. The song is an allusion to a *West Wing* episode called "Noel," in which deputy chief of staff Josh Lyman (Bradley Whitford) attends a state dinner featuring Yo-Yo Ma and has a PTSD-grade flashback of getting shot during an assassination attempt on the president. As the song enters its second movement, it becomes difficult for me not to sense a slippage in the meridians, an imbrication between the real and the imagined. After all, sitting beside me in this Bethesda ballroom are a half dozen former *West Wing* cast members, whose job required them to portray White House staffers and who doubtlessly recall filming this episode on a mock set in Los Angeles. But also in the audience are former White House staffers—real ones, like Stephen Goodin, who was Bill Clinton's presidential aide, and Bob Lehrman, who was chief speechwriter for Al Gore—men who doubtlessly attended *real* state dinners. That I'm also rubbing shoulders with hundreds of ordinary Americans who are gussied up like White House officials sends me into a vertigo of epistemological uncertainty, where the differences between reality and its simulacrum are so dizzying and complex that even Baudrillard would've blanched. It occurs to me that as much as the West Wing Weekend has promised an escape from the grisly realities of our political moment, the ontological blurriness at the mock State Dinner actually feels like a faithful reenactment of the last election, where the reins of the nation were given over to someone whom we knew mostly from television.

—

At the State Dinner, I sit next to David Kusnet, President Clinton's chief speechwriter from 1992 to 1995. It seems important to stress that this is the real David Kusnet—not someone cosplaying him. He'd been invited to be on a panel called "Real Life in the West Wing" and had decided to stay for the gratis dinner. As he takes a seat, several of my tuxedoed dinner companions drop their forks and start stage-whispering amongst themselves, saying, "Oh my God! Do you know who that is?" To his credit, Kusnet pretends not to hear them. As he and I gobble down our salads, one of the Wingnuts says,

"OK, here's a subject for a panel: How would *Game of Thrones* be different if Aaron Sorkin had written it?"

Wearing tortoiseshell glasses and gray wisps of Einstein hair, Kusnet has the rumpled appearance of a longsuffering professor. We trade potted biographies and discuss the midterm elections, then I ask him what he makes of the West Wing Weekend. This causes him to smile, a bit ruefully. "Well," he says, "like so much else in America, it's nostalgia for a time that never really existed." Kusnet then launches into an impromptu colloquium on the political semantics of the last three decades, something he's uniquely equipped to do, since this is the guy who literally wrote the book on twentieth-century political discourse. His manifesto, *Speaking American: How Democrats Can Win in the Nineties*, was, at one time, the vade mecum for leftists and was so rife with crackling rhetorical advice that Clinton hired him after its publication. Kusnet tells me that the American narrative reached poetic heights with Obama, who mixed the argot of progressivism with the homiletics of the Civil Rights Movement and, as a result, became an incarnation of American progress. Merely by casting a vote for Obama, he says, Americans felt themselves pushing the national story from injustice toward tolerance. Over and again, Obama reminded us that electing "a skinny guy with big ears and a funny name" was proof enough of our national betterment.

However effective this rhetoric proved to be at the ballot box, it ultimately obscured the unresolved economic and social issues that Clinton had confronted in the early nineties, when Fukuyama proclaimed the end of history and small towns across America were ravaged by deindustrialization. For a Democrat running in such a climate, the linguistic task became one of convincing the rural quadrants of America—places like Little Rock, Arkansas—that re-education and job training were exigent and necessary. "So Clinton couldn't talk like a character from *The West Wing*," Kusnet says. Instead, Clinton's orations were steeped in the idioms of southern moderates, like the midcentury North Carolina senator Frank Porter Graham, a downhome vernacular with which Kusnet had to familiarize himself. "Clinton used to give speeches to high school classes in Arkansas," Kusnet says, "where he'd say, 'Do you know that kids in Korea do two hours of math homework a night? Now, why the hell do you think you're going to make more money than they are when an employer can hire them or hire you?' So, that's how he'd talk to people, but he'd do it like he was on their side . . . So that's a complicated narrative . . . I mean, he really believed that you couldn't get New Deal liberalism in a globalized economy and a fractured society. That sounds like a point you'd make in a seminar at the Kennedy School or something. But to explain that as someone whose rhetoric came out of the folksiest politics of Arkansas and not scare people off, that was impressive. But he could do it. I mean, he could really do it."

Doubtless we could categorize this as one staffer's rosy-tinged hagiography, as we haven't yet talked about his boss's centrist compromises (NAFTA) or his queasy philandering (not to mention his equivocations about what the definition of the word "is" is, etc.). Still, it could be argued that Clinton was the last politician to place the grim realities of globalization at the forefront of his campaign, as evidenced by James Carville's twangy, exasperated dictum, immortalized in the classic 1993 political documentary *The War Room*: "It's the economy, stupid." Kusnet tells me that whatever happens after Trump, the narrative will inexorably return to the difficulties Clinton faced in the nineties. "We might not get Clinton's solutions, but we will face his problems."

As I loosen the knot of my Windsor and toss an arm over the back of a nearby chair, I realize that the tenor of our confab is not at all dissimilar from the big-think strategy sessions that Toby Ziegler and Sam Seaborn used to have on episodes of *The West Wing*. It must be admitted that, for all my cynicism about the conference, if anyone could be accused of succumbing to the escapist appeal of cosplay, it was me.

It grows late, and most of the Wingnuts have repaired to the dance floor, boogieing with the halfhearted enthusiasm of middle schoolers at a sock hop. As "Blame It on the Bossa Nova" pours through the speakers, I ask Kusnet what he's been up to these days, and he tells me that while he's spent the last few years writing for a PR firm, he's recently returned to his own writing, a transition that has been bumpy to say the least. "It's strange to say for a man in his sixties, but I suppose I'm trying to find my voice."

It's only when we stand to leave that I recognize the metaphorical weight of his confession. After all, here is a man who once served as America's voice and who is now struggling to find his narrative persona at an hour of national disarray. It is a literary predicament that seems to embody our own existential crisis: Is America's story one of tolerance and progress? Or is it a scrambled, fragmentary tale whose meaning is uncertain? I suppose I'd been hoping that Kusnet would offer me a soothing interpretation, a new way of stitching together the plot twists of the last few years, but sadly he seems just as boggled and lost as I am.

We shake hands and part ways, with me wandering toward the dance floor and him making a beeline directly for the exits. A phalanx of Wingnuts are socializing in the hallway, talking passionately about squandered storylines, and, suddenly, I feel like a fraud in my blue suit and press pass. It's easy to sneer at the escapism at the West Wing Weekend, but I can't help thinking these citizens understand something crucial about the American experiment. At a time when the country seems incurably divided, when the news chyrons have become a grim pageant of scandals and Twitter rants, when the president has picked schoolyard fights with political opponents, the fervor for Sorkin's feel-good chimera reveals the degree to which American optimism relies, in part, on the sustainment of certain narratives, ones that have the power to flip rural Midwestern districts and elect unlikely candidates. Whether anyone has the skill or gumption to write this story is still unclear, but it feels like we're heading toward the final chapter, and the hero's destiny is uncertain.

LOST IN SUMMERLAND

As best we can tell, the hauntings began after Andy's traumatic brain injury. On Christmas Eve, 2005, outside a scuzzy bar on the East Side of Milwaukee, a drunk man sucker-punched my elder brother, bashing his head against the wall of a brick alcove and leaving him splayed on the snow-confected sidewalk, unconscious with seven brain contusions. For several days, my family sat vigil around Andy's bed in the ICU, whispering prayers into clasped palms, wincing at the doctors' ambiguous status updates. At first the prognosis was fatal. So extensive was the bleeding, the hospital felt sure it was only a matter of time before Andy slipped irrevocably into a coma. But he woke fortuitously on the morning of the 30th, wide-eyed and cogent, requesting of all things a meal from Boston Market.

After a nine-month-long odyssey of dizzy spells and aphasic episodes, my brother salvaged most of his memory and, as we liked to joke, the better parts of his personality. He bought his own apartment and finished a bachelor's degree, got married and took a corporate sales position. But something strange started to happen over the next couple years. At night, he began hearing creaky footsteps in the hallway or stray voices in the closet. Initially, we feared the worst and believed the head injury had jostled his brain into psychosis—a grim but not altogether unreasonable conclusion. Almost immediately my dad flew out from Milwaukee to visit him at his new house in Houston, and when he arrived, he found my brother sitting meditatively cross-legged on the kitchen floor, with the lights of the chandelier above him flickering of their own accord. Without even the most cursory acknowledgment of my father's arrival, Andy said, with a kind of holy calm, "There's someone in the room with us."

In time, my brother began to insist that he could speak to the dead and receive dispatches from the spiritual realm. Whenever I visited him on the West Coast, where he had eventually taken a job in the tech industry, his friends would pull me aside at bars to confide that Andy had "summoned" their dead relatives, battering me with questions about what it was like to grow up with him. Most of my family grew convinced of his paranormal talents. (Bear in mind that up until that point my parents had been lapsed Catholics and flinty-eyed Midwesterners, with little tolerance for the supernatural.) My father once gawked at water glasses that slid across the breakfast island—presumably the work of spirits—while Andy stood transfixed at the kitchen's threshold. When my grandmother passed away, my sister-in-law reported seeing a green orb floating over Andy's bedside, and upon shaking him awake, they both watched dumbfounded as the glinting emerald sphere drifted toward the ceiling and vanished. "Your brother," my mother once said to me, in a solemn whisper, "has powers." Things reached some sort of apogee when Andy was stopped for a traffic violation, and just as the cop began scribbling a ticket, Andy summoned the ghost of the officer's mother, who had recently died from congestive heart failure. The cop let Andy off with a warning.

Naturally, I tended to regard these stories with smirks and sidelong glances. Andy, who is three years older than me, has long had a weakness for parlor tricks—his coworkers nicknamed him "The Bull" for his ability to BS his way through corporate presentations—and to those who know him well, it wouldn't be inaccurate to suggest that he has coasted through life on the wind of his own charisma. I have seen him make barrooms come to life with karaoke renditions of "November Rain." I have seen him dicker with car salesmen, performing such adroit campaigns of ingratiation that he invariably rolls out of the lot in a vehicle for which he has paid several thousand dollars below sticker. I once joined, very briefly, a rave at a club in Milwaukee, a victim of my brother's coaxing. And so it was precisely this capacity for stagecraft and sweet talk that made me doubtful of—and amused by—his claims of paranormal élan.

But soon, these "visitations," as Andy likes to call them, began happening with a fervor and frequency that made his wife scared. Whenever he went on business trips to Amsterdam or Beijing, she'd receive odd transcontinental phone calls during the wee hours, with Andy sounding rattled and nonplussed, muttering darkly about spirits in the bathroom or unattributed thuddings on the hotel room walls. Hoping to leaven the issue when I later learned of it, I waggishly ventured that perhaps the noises were merely the clamor of some netherworldly tryst, lost souls reuniting in the honeymoon suite. But he dodged my attempt at humor and said, with absolute zero irony, "You know, you might be right about that."

I worry my tone might seem to gainsay what I said before about maintaining a dose of utmost skepticism. But if you could only hear the earnestness of my brother's testimony, then you too might entertain a squirm of doubt. You too might suspend your disbelief. Could it be that my brother, by fluke of grievous brain injury, had somehow become a maître d' to the underworld, summoning wraiths to ease suffering and evade misdemeanor tickets? Was he some kind of a modern-day Charon, straddling the river between the living and the dead?

Last spring, he called out of the blue and asked whether I'd ever heard of a place called Lily Dale, a quaint hamlet an hour south of Buffalo. It was home to 275 residents, many of them registered psychics and mediums. Each year, some twenty-two thousand tourists descend upon the assembly for séances and drum circles, hoping to reunite with departed loved ones. "Imagine *Wet Hot American Summer*," Andy said. "But with dead people."

Initially, I begged off, claiming a busy summer of yard work and academic committees.

"Oh, come on. It could be a bros' trip," he said. "Plus, you could watch me do my thing. By the end of the week, I guarantee you won't think I'm full of shit."

"I don't think you're full of shit," I said.

A silence came over the line. Truth be told, I knew this bluster was Andy's cover, that perhaps he was trekking to Lily Dale because he had grown frightened by what was happening to him and was now desperate for an explanation.

Cursory groundwork on the Internet yielded several reports of marquee Spiritualists who'd be heading to the camp that summer. There was the feral-eyed Michelle Whitedove, a fiftysomething "angelic channeler" and "forensic medium" with a mane of autumn-colored hair, a woman who had been named "America's #1 Psychic" by a reality TV show in 2007. On You-Tube, I found a clip of the show, called *America's Psychic Challenge*, where Whitedove roams a ten-acre swath of desert and augurs the exact location of a man buried six feet underground, lest he die of asphyxiation. Also in attendance would be Reverend Anne Gehman, a pearl-wearing, lid-fluttering medium who taught classes on bending spoons and whose clairvoyant abilities apparently helped investigators catch the serial killer Ted Bundy.

"Well, what do you think," Andy said, "do you want to come with me?"

———

Over the next few months, whenever I mentioned my impending trip to "Silly Dale," as online wags have rechristened it, colleagues at various universities would barrage me with paranormal tales. In the interest of leaving their academic records unbesmirched, I will refrain from uttering their names in print, but rest assured: these were highly credentialed members of their fields. In hushed tones, they told of dalliances with clairvoyance, about sourceless bumps in the night. One colleague, a poetry professor, regularly consulted psychics and mediums; another put her faith in the portents of tarot card readings. All this seemed of a piece with the broader resurgence of heterodox traditions, for in the days leading up to our trip, it seemed like I couldn't hop on the Internet without stumbling across stories about millennials turning to astrology, or CEOs embracing Eastern religion, or covens of young witches casting spells in New York City. Even the renewed interest in psychedelics—see Michael Pollan's *How to Change Your Mind* or Tao Lin's *Trip*—seemed a quest to open up the doors of perception.

Perhaps it's telling that Spiritualism was born in the middle of the nineteenth century, a time when many Americans were suffering, in similar ways, from a welter of epistemological disruptions—the Civil War and Darwinian theory, the death of God and the birth of capitalism. Its nativity scene took place in Upstate New York in the 1840s, when a trio of precocious sisters—Leah, Kate, and Margaret Fox—reportedly heard mysterious rappings on the walls of their parents' house. Once news spread of their ethereal abilities, the girls launched a whirlwind tour of New England and the Midwest, holding séances in town halls and hotel parlors, drawing audiences of all classes and backgrounds. What emerged over the next four years was a national craze for spirit communication, with "spirit circles"—clubs for channeling the dead—forming in almost every city that the girls had visited. One newspaperman in Cincinnati claimed that some twelve hundred local mediums came out of the woodwork in the wake of the Fox sisters' performance.

The notion that spirits could intervene in worldly affairs was, of course, not new, but there had never been a formal religion based exclusively on the premise that humans could receive communiqués from the dead, particularly their dead loved ones. While the movement's various sects quibbled over doctrinal differences, Spiritualists were united in the belief that a brigade of so-called spirit guides helped each individual find their way toward "Summerland," a term that eventually became the religion's sobriquet for heaven. And while we might expect modern science to have rinsed such thinking from the American imagination, the movement has remained surprisingly durable, as evidenced by the political tumult of the 1960s—another period of narrative breakdown—when many citizens turned to New Ageism for balmy existential comfort.

Once again, the center was not holding. By 2018, the country lacked a workable epistemology, and even our most cherished pieties were wobbling or already lay in smithereens. I'm not sure how many examples I should provide. Need I mention that our nuclear codes were in the hands of a buffoonish real estate mogul? Would it suffice to say that *The New York Times* was running page-one stories about the existence of UFOs? Meanwhile scientists alleged, in peer-reviewed journals, that octopuses were aliens, that particles could be altered through perception, that reality was nothing more than a pixelated shell game. Perhaps this is why members of the commentariat began sounding the death knell, contending that, with the 2016 election, America had at last fulfilled John Adams's 1814 disclaimer about the fate of any democracy. "It soon wastes, exhausts, and murders itself," he wrote in a letter. "There never was a democracy yet, that did not commit suicide." It seemed we had now passed onto some bleak, dusky afterlife, a mist-swarmed purgatory of facts and alternative facts, out of which emerged such fearsome ghouls as Stormy Daniels, InfoWars, and Space Force. Given that our lives had essentially become posthumous, could you really blame me for wondering if my brother could summon ghosts?

—

The route to Lily Dale wound through parts of Upstate New York that once served as the fertile crescent of American utopian thinking—John Humphrey Noyes's Oneida community, Frederick Douglass's abolitionist newspaper—and yet the scenery itself was hardly so auspicious. Much of this area was waylaid by the 2008 recession, and husks of mills and factories still dotted the adjacent landscape. As Andy and I drove, we glimpsed remnants of the old Bethlehem Steel plant, and the Concord grape vineyards south of Buffalo looked like a postapocalyptic Napa Valley. So godforsaken was this neck of the country that Donald Trump, in the waning days of the 2016 election, had condemned it, not unfairly, as "a death zone."

Hunched at the wheel, I snuck glances at my brother, whose face was sallow and draggy with fatigue. Most days he resembles a bald and musclebound Elijah Wood, but his flight the previous night was delayed by several hours, so both of us were running on no sleep and looked a bit like revenants.

"Here are just a few of the workshops on deck this summer," Andy said, thumbing his smartphone and scanning the agenda from the Lily Dale website. "There's *Fairyology: Finding Fairies 101.* There's *Orb Phenom—Orbs Are Among Us!* Or we could check out *Getting to Know Your Spirit Guides.* Plus, there's a drum circle on Friday, and a séance tomorrow night."

"You sure you're up for this?" I asked.

"Yeah, man," he said. "Let's get weird."

Mercifully, things brightened as we veered toward the encampment. A sign read LILY DALE 1 MILE ahead. We flew past three lakes rimmed with cottages, and when the clouds parted, the sky unleashed a bucolic, life-affirming blue. Nevertheless, I felt a burgeoning unease about our whole larkish adventure. Not only was this the first trip I'd ever taken with my brother, but I also wasn't sure if I was prepared—emotionally, spiritually— for the week ahead. What if our cavortings with mediums caused Andy to have a psychotic break and I had to commit him to some remote Upstate hospital? There were historical precedents for such crackups. In 1852, some ninety individuals from around the country were said to lose their minds and enter asylums after partaking in spirit-rappings. Or what if I discovered he'd been lying about his abilities and this effected some irrevocable schism in our relationship, sundering our bond for all time? Then there was the possibility that he'd prove himself a bona fide medium, which would mean what, exactly, I had no idea. Yet for reasons I struggled to explain, I secretly hoped that my brother was the real deal, that he'd prove me wrong by the end of our voyage. Something lodged deep in our past—a moment long banished and left unspoken—seemed crucially to depend on it.

At the end of a secluded road, Lily Dale came into view.

"Look at my forearms," Andy said. His skin was brailled with goosebumps. "The energy here is ridiculous."

Threading through a warren of elm-studded streets lined with pastel Victorians, we saw a battalion of stone angels guarding the porch of one gothic-looking home and, a couple blocks later, a bay window had been plastered campily with a decal of Casper the Ghost. Was it possible that I heard, from somewhere far off, a group of people singing Bob Dylan's "Blowin' in the Wind"? Soon we passed a hillock near the main auditorium where a scrum of aging tourists was performing the languorous waltz of tai chi. Near the Pet Cemetery, we made a wrong turn and had to swerve past an open field, which was already filling up with tents and RVs. My first thought was that the campus looked like an old-fashioned summer camp, except that instead of trust falls and archery classes, there were astrology walks and confabs with ghosts.

When it was our turn at the gate, the attendant met our eyes, then pressed his fingers to his temples, as though receiving a radio dispatch via dental fillings. "Welcome, welcome," he said, with an impish grin. "We've been expecting you two."

—

Our first day on the grounds was a derby of occult activities. After meditating in something called the Healing Temple, we met a septuagenarian Reiki instructor named Pilar who had tufts of peacock feathers superglued to her spectacles. She called them her "eyeglasses" and explained that she was slowly transforming into a blackbird. On the patio of a coffee shop, Andy befriended an affable blond man named Jayson, who professed to be a medium-in-training from Brooklyn and whose first coup as a psychic came when he divined the future spouse for one of his clients. (The couple's subsequent gratitude was noted in the "Vows" section of *The New York Times*.) He and Andy hit it off by making fun of my skepticism—*God, he's so emotionally closed off, isn't he?*—at which point Jayson scrolled through his phone, showing me grainy nocturnal photos of Lily Dale's enchanted Leolyn Woods, an apparent hotspot for nymphs and orbs.

"OK, so these you could argue are bugs or whatever. But, this," he said, pointing to the relevant photo, in which a cricket was frozen wing-spread in the flash of a smartphone camera. "I mean, come on. That's a fucking fairy."

Throughout the day, people kept showing us their photos. A gray-haired pilgrim named Susan accosted us on a veranda. "Can I show you guys something?" she asked. Before we could answer, she rifled through her purse and unearthed a dozen photos, each of which she laid on the surface of a wicker end table. "I have a lot of activity in my house," she said. One image depicted a mishmash of Scrabble letters in which I slowly perceived the relavant message. MOTHER LOVES SUSAN, it said, WHO IS MY DAUGHTER.

"Automatic Drawing with Miss Bonnie" took place at 9:30 a.m. in the Octagon Building, not far from the Lily Dale museum. After a short prayer and some guided breathing, we were paired off and asked to close our eyes before "surrendering to spirit." From across the room, I watched Andy blindly sketch a tableau of what looked, frankly, like a thicket of penises, which I was worried would offend his partner, a medium-in-training from Pennsylvania. When time was up, Andy relayed his message. "I know it's strange," he said, "but I keep seeing the name 'Tom' among all these phallic symbols."

The woman gasped. "Tom is my husband's name," she said. "And that's just his issue. I'm going through menopause right now, so let's just say that he's been frustrated with certain aspects of our marriage."

I watched as she and Andy erupted with guffaws, whereupon Andy turned to me and raised his eyebrows, simpering triumphantly. Yet it was hard for me to take this as ironclad evidence. Show anyone a hodgepodge of random images, and if they've thrown off the tethers of logic and coherence, doubtless they'll be able to conjure associations to their own interpersonal dilemmas. Still, that Andy had intuited the husband's name did leave me somewhat dazzled.

Things on my side of the classroom were hardly so jovial. I was partnered with a rawboned blonde woman named Ashley who looked to be in her late thirties and who had come to Lily Dale with her parents. Gravel-voiced and sullen, she worked full-time in a Walgreens warehouse, and while there was an Amazon distribution center down the road, it was hard to land a gig there. So far at Lily Dale, the messages she'd received "from spirit" had been spot-on and uplifting—exhortations to stop stressing. I asked what sorts of things she fretted about.

"Sometimes I wish I had gone to college and actually done something with my life," she said. "The problem was, I never knew what I wanted to do. So I never ended up doing anything."

In the face of her weary candor, I couldn't seem to muster the journalistic moxie needed to ask a follow-up question. But what I discovered over the coming days was that Ashley's story chimed with many testimonies of Lily Dale's pilgrims. Hailing from beleaguered rural towns across New England and the Midwest, they were suffering from all manner of emotional or financial disaster and were desperate for a more hopeful story—that their lives were being guided by cadres of benevolent spirits, that though present circumstances were bleak, they shouldn't give up the ghost.

—

That evening at the Maplewood Hotel, I unpacked my suitcase while Andy lounged on the bed, swiping languidly at his smartphone. Between responding to what appeared to be a deluge of work emails, he told me, with a baffling nonchalance, that he'd been having a recurring vision about a kidnapped Midwestern girl whose face had colonized network news that summer. He was vague about what exactly these visions entailed, though the images he disclosed were not especially promising (cornfield, head injury). Then, without prompting, he said, "Whenever you travel, it's always important to unpack. That's what makes it feel like home." I wasn't quite sure how to respond to any of this—the visions, the unsolicited travel advice—and so our conversation was full of awkward lapses and long moments of silence.

Not since childhood had Andy and I shared such close quarters, and even then, the propinquity usually resulted in a verbal skirmish or an all-out fracas. I suppose our relationship in those days could be best described as Cain-and-Abel-ish. This was owing, more than anything else, to our wildly divergent temperaments. Whereas he spent most nights hunkered in the basement and pummeling a Stratocaster, I would toil under the glow of the desk lamp, trying to make Honor Roll for another semester. Whereas he wore earrings and leather jackets, I jogged across town in ankle weights, hoping to make varsity as a freshman. Our mother often explained the variance in our personalities this way: "Aren't genes amazing?"

Still, as adults, we somehow managed to construct a passable relationship as brothers, even if, at times, it could feel performative and falsely nostalgic. Whenever our family got together for birthdays or Christmas celebrations, a manic one-upmanship tended to infuse our interactions such that within minutes of him picking me up from the airport, we'd be quoting lines from old movies, doing our bad Al Pacino impressions, or making fun of each other's hairlines, all of it delivered with the snappy banter of brothers on a network sitcom. Rarely did we spend much time alone, however. And while we had joked over the years about his psychic abilities, we had never once hazarded an earnest discussion about them.

Which was why it was so unsettling to find ourselves inside the cramped precinct of our hotel room, brushing our teeth or changing clothes only a few feet away from each other. Almost by reflex I found myself curious about his habits of being—his shaving techniques, his pre-bed calisthenics—rather the same way I would creep into his room as a child to marvel at his possessions. I'd flip through his CDs—Nine Inch Nails, Spiritualized—or try on his flannels, occasionally summoning the courage to pluck out a few notes on his Fender. And so, even though I was a man in his early thirties—a husband, a university professor—I somehow found myself becoming again my brother's little brother.

Perhaps this was why I found it so gratifying that the merry denizens of Lily Dale kept referring to us as a unit. As we shuffled from one psychic appointment to another, or traversed campus on our way to a séance, they'd bellow at us from across the road, "Hey, hey, it's the brothers!" One medium traipsed over while Andy and I were eating dinner at a picnic table, and said, "Well, are we making any progress with this guy?" I assumed he was referring to my glacial incredulity, and I was curious to hear what my brother might say. "I think he's weakening," Andy said. "But I'm not sure he buys it."

"Bah," the medium said, waving his hand at me, like a Dickens character. Then he slapped Andy's back with affectionate gusto and stomped off toward the Healing Temple. We chewed for some time in silence. Then Andy gave me a styptic look. "I know you think this place is nutty," he said.

I reminded him that we'd just seen a man barf up jewels that he claimed were relics from the spirit world. This was at a demonstration of something called "apportations," which is where a medium will brusquely produce supernatural objects through a transdimensional portico (in this case, his mouth).

"It's just, I was really hoping to get some answers here," he said. He explained his wife had grown increasingly worried about him. Before he left for Lily Dale, there'd been a scene. They feuded in the car outside the airport, with finger-pointing and furrowed brows. Perhaps she doubted him, called him crazy, something like that. His prognostications had grown darker over the years, more unsettling, and she didn't want to believe what he had to say. "It's not like she gave me an ultimatum or anything. But I know she wants me to get it under control," he said.

———

In the mid-nineteenth century, Spiritualism's earliest practitioners were inclined to believe that technological advances like electrical wires could be divine portals to the spiritual realm. It was for this reason that Benjamin Franklin became the movement's patron saint and that its flagship periodical was dubbed *The Spiritual Telegraph*. One early adherent believed that electricity was "the vehicle of divine mentality," which could be harnessed to communicate with "all parts and particles of the universe." At a distance of two centuries, it's easy to malign these Americans for their braindead naiveté, but we must remember that, within the span of two decades, they'd gone from waiting months to get a letter in the mail to somehow receiving a cross-country dispatch by telegraph within minutes. From there, it was only a short leap of logic before supposing you could commune with ghosts.

Part of me wondered whether my brother's job in the tech industry had made him susceptible to precisely this delusion. An evangelist for cloud software, he had decked out his house over the years with a whole flotilla of smart technologies: thermostats that respond to voice commands, a refrigerator that alerts him whenever the eggs are running low. Even Amazon's Alexa had become a frequent interlocutor at family dinners, telling knock-knock jokes to his children or dispensing Jeopardy-grade trivia to him and his spouse. To be ensconced in such an environment—one so seamlessly attuned to your whims and predilections—perhaps it was only a matter of time before you regarded yourself as similarly omniscient.

The reigning consensus at Lily Dale, however, suggested otherwise, because virtually all the mediums to whom I spoke suggested that my brother's premonitions were likely caused by cerebral hemorrhage. "That, or a high fever can trigger it," said fifth-generation Spiritualist Gretchen Clark. Lauren Thibodeau, a Lily Dale medium with a PhD in counseling, explained that it's not uncommon with near-death experiences. "Depending on the study," she said, "you find that between three-quarters to one hundred percent of people who almost died will tell you that they became psychic, they became healers, they became mediumistic."

This supposition is more or less in keeping with the findings of Dr. Diane Hennacy Powell, a neuroscientist trained at the Johns Hopkins School of Medicine. Powell has written a book called *The ESP Enigma: The Scientific Case for Psychic Phenomena*, which I brought with me to Lily Dale and had been reading surreptitiously by lantern-light whenever Andy went on jogs or bedded down for the evening. Though derided by critics as wholesale bunkum, the book is interesting in places, particularly when it conjectures a direct correlation between brain trauma and clairvoyant prowess. While some mediums are genetically predisposed to their gifts, she writes, "There are also cases where people haven't had psychic abilities until they've suffered head traumas. What's common is that these people who've had this head trauma, the structure and function of their brain has changed."

Ordinarily, I would not be willing to lend these theories much credence. After all, as a dutiful child of poststructuralism, I'm well aware that science suffers from a dastardly case of confirmation bias and one needn't wander far to locate rigged experiments or cherry-picked data. But it turns out that modern researchers *can* replicate the results of parapsychological studies— those that supposedly prove the existence of clairvoyance and telepathy. Shortly before our expedition, I dredged up an article from the *American Psychologist* by Lund University professor Etzel Cardeña, who suggests that the most cogent and persuasive explanations for these phenomena involve fringe physics and quantum entanglement, which view objects not as isolated and entropic, but threaded together in a vast tapestry, where every movement is connected via gorgeously reticulated spindles, even across time and space. It gets weirder. The Princeton physics philosopher Hans Halvorson has determined that this "superentanglement" explains why an individual can sense, even across unfathomable distances, the abrupt death of a loved one. It was this theory, in particular, that I kept returning to in the days and weeks that followed. Was it possible that family members could be quantumly entangled?

About a year before our trip to Lily Dale, in the midst of an unremitting depression, I began to contemplate suicide. I will resist the sentimentality of describing its causes. Enough to say that I had been plagued by a neurochemical glitch since childhood, and some periods of my life were worse than others. I had tried everything: Prozac and CrossFit, yoga and therapy. Routine occurrences prickled my thoughts like wind against a burn scar, and most days were less endured than climbed. For the first time in two decades, I found myself down on my knees, my hands threaded in unstudied prayer, whispering pleas and apologies to the God-shaped hole in my mind. I told no one—not even my wife—of my plans, that the escape offered by leather belts and ceiling beams had begun to strike me as inordinately appealing.

Then I awoke one morning to a voicemail from my mom, telling me to call her as soon as I got up. Naturally, I worried that someone had died, that our family had been visited by yet another disaster. But it turned out my brother had called her in the middle of the night, terrified and inconsolable. There'd been tears in his voice. Back on the West Coast, he'd been out barhopping with friends when he got the most unnerving presentiment. "What did he say?" I asked. "He—" my mom started, her voice wounded with concern. "Oh," she said. "He just drank too much. I'll tell him you're fine, honey."

—

On our second afternoon at Lily Dale, Andy and I wandered to the Forest Temple for one of two daily "message" services. Each featured a round-robin of seven or eight mediums standing at the front of an outdoor amphitheater and haphazardly beckoning spirits. We sat below a sun-dappled canopy of hemlock and elm, amid roughly two hundred other tourists, and watched as, one by one, the mediums did their thing.

Like all niche communities, the Spiritualists at Lily Dale have evolved their own extensive lingua franca, rife with daffy euphemisms for the brute facts of life, the most representative of which are their various phrases for death. These include "passing over," "in spirit," "going from the earth plane," and "departing for Summerland." So much of the ethereal argot is gooey and granola-crunching, but at times its poetics attain a distinctly erotic mood, especially when a medium approaches one member of the audience and asks, "May I come to you?" Other idiomatic expressions amplify the carnal entendres with shades of penetration. "May I step into your vibrations?" or "May I touch in with you, my friend?"

This consent seeking seems proper. After all, the communiqués can get fairly intense. Toward the end of the service, one of the mediums brought forth a message for a shaggy-haired twentysomething named Bobby, who was sitting in the back pews with his friends, a cluster of raffish-looking bohemians. The medium described the spirit of a gaunt, pallid man who'd been pacing across his apartment in the moments before he died and over whom "a river of tears had been shed." After the service, Andy caught up with Bobby and asked whether the medium's description had meant something to him. "Yeah, man, that's my cousin, who ODed on heroin," Bobby said. "The last couple days, he's been following me around."

That evening, we met up with these kids under the gazebo of Lily Dale's dock, which jutted into the moon-glazed shallows of Cassadaga Lake and offered us shelter from a pinprick drizzle. Soon cans of Budweisers were slugged, and packs of American Spirits were torn open. There were seven of them altogether, wearing prototypical hempen fibers and various configurations of tie-dye. One got the sense that their Birkenstocks had treaded the grounds of many outdoor music festivals. Each introduced themselves with one fun fact and their astrological sign, as was their special custom whenever meeting new people. Bobby was a Taurus who was slogging through a master's degree, penning a thesis on agricultural reform movements in postcolonial West Africa. His girlfriend, Erica, was a grad student with a pixie haircut whose fun fact was that she was a rabid fan of the Red Hot Chili Peppers. But the obvious ringleader of the group was MeKenna, a big-eyed, fast-talking hairstylist in her mid-twenties. A Pisces, naturally, she said, and everyone laughed.

It turned out that MeKenna, T. C., and Meredith were all seventh-generation Spiritualists whose distant ancestors helped found Lily Dale at the crack of the twentieth century. They grew up coming here every summer, studying the Fox sisters, attending the Lyceum, and playing tag among the crystal-clutching tourists who thronged the streets from June to August. MeKenna's grandmother is a longtime Lily Dale resident, and her mom is a practicing medium in Milwaukee. For a moment, I tried to imagine a childhood where your parents routinely nattered with spirits—where nightly prayers might involve the ectoplasmic manifestation of your dead grandpa. Reckoning with such phenomena as a digital native must have been a trip. Consider the impulse to live-tweet family séances as a sullen, irascible teen: *FML, Mom is channeling grandpa again. He says I'm too boy-crazy for my age. LOLZ.* But growing up, MeKenna and Meredith kept their theology under wraps. Turned out their peers weren't exactly inclusive. Often recess featured a hail of vicious schoolyard epithets: *Demon! Satanist!*

Of course, now that nearly every strain of American occultism has experienced a sudden renascence, the kids don't much witness this kind of opprobrium anymore. If anything, they said, there's been a mushrooming tolerance for all things esoteric: jade stones for Kegel exercises, crystals for off-kilter chakras; even a mainstream lifestyle brand like Goop can get rich by peddling New Age curios. It was enough for me to wonder why occultism had become so voguish again.

"Look at what's going on in the planetary alignment. That would help explain things," Meredith said. "The outer planets are generational, so when we think about big movements or certain decades as having unique characteristics, it's probably because Pluto was in Libra then." Pluto in Libra turns out to be a quintessential astrological formation among stargazers and is believed to be responsible for the upswell of divorce throughout the 1970s. Despite whatever coldhearted materialism I professed to endorse before our trip, I nevertheless found myself enthralled by a worldview that could so neatly explain massive social disruptions. Part of me worried the group would think I was baiting them, but I asked anyway: "So why is Trump happening?"

The gazebo resounded with their collective groans. But Meredith had an answer at the ready. "So, last year's solar eclipse lined up with his chart exactly, in countless ways."

"But astrology is not determinist, so it didn't make Trump happen," Bobby cut in. "There's plenty of socio-political underpinnings to our societal problems." Unlike Meredith, MeKenna, and T. C., who were raised in the cradle of Spiritualism, Bobby came to this theology as an adult, and I got the sense that he was worried I might see them as witless yahoos, clutching maladaptively to backward explanations.

Again Meredith countered, looking toward the stars. "You can do charts of countries or events—anything that has a time and place—and the birth chart of America is like very, *very* Cancer," she said. "So why is the United States so concerned about defense? Why are we about protecting the homeland?"

"Well," Bobby said, "whomever we elect is a symptom of a larger disease—that being our economic system of capitalistic exploitation. Obama was a symptom of this larger disease as well. He came at his particular time and his particular place. And we didn't get a whole lot different from Obama." He quickly sketched the last decade of geopolitical woes—Syria, Libya, Turkey—before eventually concluding with syllogistic finality: "So all of this is part of a larger disease that exists in the United States."

"But that's been going on way before Obama," Meredith said.

"Oh, yeah," he said. "That's how we've been operating since this country's inception."

"Obama's a Leo," MeKenna said, "in case anybody's curious."

As the evening unraveled and the lake boiled with rain, our talk grew expansive, and the group became curious about the origins of my brother's mediumship. "I would hear stuff," Andy said. "And I would be like: *I'm going fucking insane. I'm losing my mind.*" A few years ago, when his wife's uncle died, freakish things started happening in the house. Furniture would move. They were lying in bed one night when a picture frame skated across the dresser. "Every time we fought, something would intervene. We would walk into a room screaming at each other—two Scorpios, right?—and the lights would start flickering, or the volume on the TV would go wildly up and down." One night, he woke up and saw the apparition of his wife's uncle loitering in the bedroom's corner.

"I didn't understand any of it, I didn't know what the fuck was going on," he said. "But eventually I got to a point where I was like: *I get it.* And I could start hearing the messages. I would pray and I would actually start hearing responses."

I had heard bits and pieces of this story before, but always in the elusive, half-joking manner in which Andy tended to relay them. To hear him speak so earnestly now was a little unnerving, and I glanced at the kids to see whether they might roll their eyes or snicker at him. But they never did.

He started transmitting dispatches from his wife's dead relatives, which was difficult, he said, because they were Dutch and only spoke broken English. (At this point in the story, my skepticism flared—*what, they can break through the space-time continuum but have no access to Google Translate?*) He started doing readings for his wife, predicting that certain events would happen within a given timeline, and to her astonishment, they consistently panned out. Soon she was dragging friends over on girls' nights "when they were all hammered at two o'clock in the morning," so he could do readings for them too. Sometimes he'd find himself wandering out of the house and driving to the grocery store for no apparent reason. It wasn't until he saw a particular shopper that he realized why he was there. "I'd be walking the aisles and find myself saying: 'Is your name Mandy?' And I'd be like, 'Uh, your mom's here.'"

"That's some *Long Island Medium* shit," MeKenna said.

Andy turned to me and, seeming to register my skepticism, remarked, "Barrett thinks I'm full of shit because he's never seen it before."

"Analytical Aquarius," Fargus said, rather wearily.

"All weekend, I think he's been googling 'How to test your psychic brother,'" Andy said.

I felt, for the first time, somewhat ashamed of my hidebound incredulity, perhaps because I was newly aware of how desperately my brother needed this story—one in which his injury wasn't some random misfortune, but a godsend that had endowed him with a spiritual purpose. Perhaps this was related to the wider cultural appeal of a worldview like astrology. After all, at least some of these millennials were professing to read our current turmoil by the stars, which offered the tantalizing prospect that if I could understand such celestial oscillations, then maybe I could rest assured in knowing that Saturn would soon be in retrograde, that Trump would be ousted, that words like "truth" and "facts" might one day mean something again. Given the grief we've endured at the hands of this administration, to say nothing of the head-swiveling instability caused by our most recent recession, one could be forgiven for pursuing such a totalizing narrative, with the reassuring plot twists of conflict, climax, and feel-good denouement. What united my brother and these kids was that they were looking for a benign, large-hearted way of being in the world, a story that could cleanly explain what was happening and why, and I couldn't help admiring the sheer blamelessness of that.

As the rain slowed to a drizzle, we headed back toward the encampment, where the air was flavored with bonfires and lights were still glowing in the

Maplewood Hotel. Perhaps a séance or two was yet underway? Our farewell was full of hugs and cute promises to hang out tomorrow. Maybe it was owing to the day's marathon of activities, but I found myself weirdly enamored of these Spiritualist kids, who were now somewhat adorably counseling my brother on finding a New Age community. MeKenna offered to put Andy in touch with her mom. Fargus and Meredith were confident that there were Spiritualist churches in California. But Andy confessed that he was scared to come out publicly as a medium. "The energy here is really safe," he said. "But back home I'm just a freak at 2:00 a.m. for drunk friends who want to talk to dead relatives."

—

The next morning I woke at dawn to tunnels of sunshine blaring through the window. Songbirds chirped metallically in the trees. My sleep had been scanty and thin, not only because of Andy's prodigious snoring, which resembled the flatulent-sounding horn of a sea freighter, but also because our accommodations were decidedly rustic. Our narrow room boasted two twin beds, each monastically appointed with scratchy blankets and crick-inducing pillows. Indeed, the bedding seemed to have been last updated during the Reagan administration.

Likely part of my sleeplessness derived from our upcoming class with Reverend Mychael Shane, a medium who offered an eight-hour (!) workshop on enhancing your mediumistic skills. If ever there were a test that could prove my brother's claims, this would be it, which was why I hurried us across campus, admonishing Andy, who was still dripping from a brisk shower, as we veered toward the Assembly Hall.

Warily we made our way toward the rostrum, over which a large stained-glass window read CHURCH OF THE LIVING SPIRIT. There sat Reverend Mychael Shane, a beefy heap of a man with wisps of silver hair and soft bearish eyes, wearing a lavender polo and ecru slacks. Sitting in a horseshoe of folding chairs around him were our fellow classmates. There was Mark and Allen, a couple from a Spiritualist church in South Florida; Karen, a local medium who served in the Healing Temple; Reverend Jane, an internationally renowned psychic with feathered bangs and disco-era makeup; and Margaret, a self-avowed "Mychael Shane groupie." Over the subsequent eight hours, we were offered a whirlwind tour of physical mediumship, including things like apportations and "trance channelings."

During introductions, Andy told the group the story about his brain injury, at which point Rev. Shane launched into a personalized sermon.

"You know there's nothing wrong with you," he said.

Andy laughed. "Can I get that in writing, please?"

"I'm really trying to be serious here, OK?" Shane said, noticeably peeved. "There's really nothing wrong with you. Who has a right to say even that there is? Who can say that you have a problem or something's not working right? Maybe you're thinking, *Why did these things happen to me?* Only you are gonna find out the answer. Luckily, you have the support of your family. I mean, your brother is sitting right there."

Andy looked at me. The rest of the group looked at me. I gave a sheepish little wave. Suddenly, I felt like some scurrilous gatecrasher, here only to poke fun at some downtrodden individuals, my own brother among them. Soon I had a memory of Andy splayed on his hospital cot, his forehead gashed and bleeding, a nest of IV tubes snarling up his arms.

Then, almost as an afterthought, Shane advised Andy to invest in PepsiCo and Aflac.

My brother turned to me, his eyes throttle-popped and spooked. Later he would tell me that he just closed deals with both of those companies.

"You're always going to appear off to others," Shane continued. "That's never going to change, but that's OK. Because you are a divine, beautiful entity that has purpose and is necessary and needed in this world."

The next segment of class involved billet readings. Shane explained that, one by one, each of us would come to the front and have silver dollars duct-taped over our eyes, which would then be covered by an eyemask and a bandana. Everyone else in the room would jot a question on a notecard, and on the other side, we'd scribble a number. "Could be 11, could be 10,043. Doesn't matter." Everyone's notecards would get placed in a wicker basket, which would then be handed to the blindfolded medium, who, in turn, would "read" both sides of the cards. Feats like these, Shane told us, can be "the worm on the hook to get people interested in this stuff."

The early results were pitiful. Reverend Jane went zero for six. Mark and Allen batted about .300. I got two of the numbers right and felt momentarily cocky—do psychic abilities perhaps run in the family?—but then flubbed every subsequent card.

"Can you see through there?" Shane asked Andy after I blindfolded him. There was something ceremonial, if not eerily religious, about this tableau, with Andy sitting before me, eyes closed, humble as a monk, waiting for me to test him.

"No," Andy said. "I wish I could. I actually have a fair amount of anxiety in claustrophobic spaces. Ever since my injury, I don't do well with tight spots."

I returned to my seat and watched as Andy began shrugging in a jerky, vaguely Tourettic way, and when he reached for the first card, his hand quavered noticeably, reminding me of the spasms he suffered from cerebral edema during those long, anguished nights in the ICU. For a moment, I wanted to call this whole thing off, but then he placed the first notecard against his forehead and inhaled deeply, audibly. "Nine," he said. "And uh, I'm not sure if it's my claustrophobia, or something I'm picking up, but the number nine and a question about space."

He handed the card to Reverend Shane. "The number is a nine. And the question is: 'What is a sacred space for me to go to?'"

"Good job," said Karen, the healer.

"Not bad," Shane said, "Well, my job is done. See you all later."

Everyone laughed.

Andy rummaged through the basket before extracting the next card. "I see a one and a seven, so maybe seventy-one, but I'm not getting the question." He passed the card to Shane. "Seventeen," the reverend said. "So that's what's called spiritual dyslexia. The question is: 'Where are my shoes from?'"

For the next card, my brother said, "I don't know if it's the answer to the question or the number, but there's only 'one.'"

"There is a circle with a one in it," Shane said. "Not bad. OK, a couple more."

Even with the blindfold, I could tell my brother was distressed. His cheeks were flushed, a paddled crimson, and his forehead was a geyser of sweat. Shane's assistant, Cynthia, noticed this, too. "You're almost there," she said. He bungled the next one, which was my card, but I didn't reveal this. Then, unbidden, he said, "Well, that was my brother's card."

I shook my head, happily perplexed, but before I could unleash a cynical rejoinder, he was plucking another card from the basket. "I see the number 2019. And I see my tattoo"—inked on his left arm was the symbol for infinity.

"Your tattoo is on there," Shane said. "And the question is: 'What will be the big news story for 2019?'"

At this point, people in the room were shaking their heads, their eyes mirthful and guileless, astonished in a childlike way. I turned around to gauge the reactions of two Lily Dale facilitators, who had been loitering in the back throughout the proceedings and who now gave Shane a covert thumbs-up, as if to certify that my brother was the real deal, the genuine article. The next afternoon, one of these women would suggest that Andy give readings at the 4:00 p.m. church service. Another would urge him to get certified by the Lily Dale Board. Even Reverend Shane would offer to be Andy's mentor at the end of the night.

Andy couldn't read the last card, but even with a couple of blunders, the room was still full of swift converts to his cause. Karen the Healer said, "Could you tell me your last name again, so that when you're rich and famous I can say I met you?"

"That made me *really* uncomfortable," Andy said.

"You got every number right," Mark said. (And most of the questions too, I think.)

"That's one for the records," Allen said.

—

By the time the workshop had ended, it was midnight, and a big moon loomed overhead, washing the campus lawns with a thin ethereal light. Somewhat predictably, our walk back to the hotel was punctuated by sprees of unmitigated fraternal boasting ("So, bro, how do you like *them* apples?"—that sort of thing), and I was worried that my brother's laughter, as it ricocheted across the courtyard, would rouse some angry spirits or perhaps a few pilgrims trying to catch some post-séance shut-eye. I asked Andy what he felt as he was blindfolded, how he was able to intuit so many cards.

"I could feel these different energies approaching me," he said. "To be honest, I was really uncomfortable, so I just asked them to make it go fast."

A silence fell between us as we shuffled under a vault of wind-hissed elm trees, and without really thinking it over, I found myself asking the question that had been grating at me all week and that, I realize now, was the whole reason we came.

"A year ago, Mom called me in the middle of the night and said you were worried about me. Do you remember that?"

"Yeah," he said.

"Do you remember why you were worried?" I asked. As soon as I posed the question, I regretted it. The truth was, I didn't know what to make of what I'd witnessed that night, and suddenly I was leery of what he might say.

"I kept seeing visions of you killing yourself."

I stopped and looked at my brother, who kept walking and peering around. Even in the twilight, I could see that his eyes were darkened with stress and little sleep, the oncoming erosion of middle age, and on the other side of the continent, there was a whole other life waiting for him. It was a minor cruelty to remember that this week wouldn't last, that somehow we had become men in our mid-thirties, duty-bound to jobs and the burdens of our own families. The next day, we'd drive back to Buffalo, and at some point that night, he'd vanish without a trace, taking an Uber to the airport, leaving me to wake alone in the pre-dawn stillness of a sullen July morning.

But right then, in the dark of the Spiritualist encampment, I was ready to believe my brother knew something that I simply could not fathom. If he intuited my past struggles—if he could somehow divine the place in my life where the narrative began to break down, where the plot took a swerve— then maybe he could also foresee the future, which had come to seem ever more uncertain, a monstrous void of flux and foreboding. Given what I'd just seen him do, I wanted to believe my brother knew the ending to this story. I wanted to believe that I would listen. But all I could manage was a blithering acknowledgment, a little brother's sheepish confession.

"That was a really lonely time for me," I said.

He was quiet for a moment. Then he shrugged. "Well, you weren't alone," he said.

—

The next morning, pilgrims were queuing up at the doors of the Healing Temple. There were elderly people inching toward the entrance with the help of metal walkers, plus a posse of young women with slovenly topknots, their tote bags emblazoned with FEMINIST WITCHES. A maroon-haired woman from Cleveland rapped with me about Lebron James's recent trade to the Lakers, then offered to balance my chakras with the swings of her pendulum necklace. The line moved slowly. And eventually, the early parishioners, who were already inside the temple, began to emerge from its heavy oaken doors—their faces radiant and changed.

Next to the temple's walkway was Lily Dale's gnarled and stunted prayer tree, whose crown of spired branches had been tessellated with thousands of ribbons in every possible shade of teal and magenta, orange and pink. On them, lonesome Americans had scribbled abridged prayers, hopeful bulletins, little valentines to the dead. "Mom, I miss you every day. Enjoy Heaven!" or "Love + Light to Those in Need" or "Unify My Family."

Back home, this effusion of wishful thinking would've struck me as saccharine and pathetic. But here, under gentle wind chimes and blue sky, I found myself shorn of cynicism, earnestly moved by these barefaced gestures of desolation and heartache. When future historians try to understand how we reckoned with our present disaster, they'll need only to comb through these variegated streamers to see how desperate and mournful we'd become. I thought of Susan, waiting for more Scrabble-letter dispatches from her mom. I thought of Ashley, back home in Connecticut, stocking product for Walgreens. And I thought of those bright-eyed millennials, our spirit guides—Erica and MeKenna, Kate and Fargus, Meredith and Bobby. Six of the colored tassels I affixed to the prayer tree were for them. Then my mind turned to my own mom and dad, to the rest of my family, all of whom were worried about me and Andy, hoping against hope that, despite everything, we'd be OK.

Inside the temple, nine healers stood at the altar. They wore bright white smocks, like special envoys from heaven. Seated before each of them, in a wooden chair, was a congregant with upturned palms and shuttered eyes. The healers waved their hands over each congregant's body, their movements mime-like and untouching, a silent legerdemain. A tall man with a gray ponytail stood at the back of the room and played a wooden flute whose soulful, dirgy tones were somehow both solacing and elegiac. Piquant incense perfumed the air, and eventually, the temple commandant pointed me toward the altar. I took a seat in front of a soft-voiced, bespectacled man who directed me to close my eyes. Put at the front of your mind, he told me, all your dead, all those who've passed into spirit. "We believe in everlasting life," he said, "so know that those people are with you right now."

You'll think I'm exaggerating, but something started happening to me. As the man performed his arcane ministrations, some trapdoor on the left side of my brow flew open, and ages of stratified blackness were leaking out. Soon there were tears running from my eyes.

Somehow I was transported to a moment from twenty years ago, when I was standing at the edge of a river in the midst of my first adult-grade depression. Twelve years old, with a dark, spinning brain, I had wandered away from my family's camp and was peering into the depths of a river, watching the brunette water froth and churn over a herd of jagged stones. I cannot tell you what came over me next, but in a moment I was there, disappearing into the violence of a brown crystalline burst. The tide was alive, a man's hands, and almost immediately I was regretting my decision. But when I managed to breach the river's surface, I could see my brother appear on shore, a blur of dark jeans and red t-shirt, entering the water just as soon as I went under. Somehow I was being tillered toward a raft of downed branches, where my brother had pulled us to refuge, where I had a moment to calm down and wipe the water from my eyes. I found that I was crying, still terrified, still boyishly confused about what I had done and what I still might do. How near that story of total obliteration had been, of following my dead to the other side of the river, of wanting so desperately a final and irrevocable exit.

My brother said nothing. His face was full of a terrible understanding. Always, even across time and distance, his face has been full of this terrible understanding. Then he was telling me it was time to go, and with our heads barely above the surface, he reached out to me, and I held on to him, and he ferried me back across the water.

DISASTER CITY

At the beginning of a pestilence and when it ends, there's always a propensity for rhetoric.

—ALBERT CAMUS

Nobody in their wildest dreams would have ever thought that we'd need tens of thousands of ventilators.

—45th President, DONALD J. TRUMP

"That's quite an armband you've got there. What does SIMUVAC mean? Sounds important."

"Short for simulated evacuation. A new state program they're still battling over funds for."

"But this evacuation isn't simulated. It's real."

"We know that. But we thought we could use it as a model."

"A form of practice? Are you saying you saw

a chance to use the real event in order to rehearse
the simulation?"

"We took it right into the streets."

"How's it going?" I said.

"The insertion curve isn't as smooth as we
would've liked . . . we don't have our victims laid
out where we'd want them if this was an actual
simulation. In other words, we're forced to take
our victims as we find them."

—DON DELILLO, *White Noise*

Part I: Simulacra and Simulation

It is late February, three weeks before the end of the world, and right now I
lie entombed beneath nearly sixteen tons of rubble. Three hours have passed
like this, with me semi-conscious and unable to speak, limb-tangled in the
remains of this charred and decimated building. All afternoon I have been
waiting for the movieland shouts of the heroic first responders. I have been
waiting for the inquisitive sniff of the search-and-rescue dogs. I've been waiting for someone to staunch my wounds, to call my loved ones, to tell me,
through the crack in the rubble, to hold on, that everything will be all right.
But instead there's only been this: the indifferent roar of a plane overhead,
plus the distant ebullience of birdsong.

Out of nowhere I hear the hard crunch of gravel, the footfalls of a heavy
person. "Hey, Barrett," the voice says. "This is one of the Observer Controllers. Real World: How you holding up? You doing OK?"

The real world. This weekend, I've begun scrutinizing that phrase with
a kind of stoner-ish intensity. After all, in the real world, it's a sundrenched
morning in late winter, and however many miles from where I'm lying,
there's a pandemic brewing in Wuhan, China, the scope of which none of

us understand. Not even those of us here in Disaster City, a fifty-two-acre training compound for search-and-rescue teams, one that's been designed to anticipate every last possible disaster. Based in College Station, Texas, the facility was founded in 1997 and is the brainchild of a Texas A&M professor named G. Kemble Bennett. After the World Trade Center bombing in 1993, Bennett wondered if his college could create a "mock community," one that would allow first responders to engage in more realistic, hands-on training. Ever since, the compound has served as a gauntlet of woe, a place where, as its website states, "tragedy and training meet [in a world] where anything is possible."

Most of FEMA's search-and-rescue workers now train at Disaster City, and since 1998 the property has been a member of the National Domestic Preparedness Consortium, a group of training centers overseen by the Department of Homeland Security. It is part of a system that is supposed to prepare us for all eventualities, from hurricanes to electrical fires, from nuclear strikes to global pandemics. Disaster City makes a difference, its website claims, by "recognizing and preparing for the unique challenges and opportunities the future holds."

This weekend's simulation is something they do every year, an Operational Readiness Exercise, this one involving a "CBRN" (read: *see-burn*) drill. Across the next two days, some two hundred first responders will participate, and I myself will serve as one of over a hundred "Living Victims"— people willing to get bedecked in prosthetic gore and bloody makeup, only to subject themselves to a whole catalog of misfortune. The coup de grâce of today's exercise is what I'm doing right now, the "Rubble Entombment," which has been going on for the last few hours and which, I must confess, has only just started to fuck with my head.

"Barrett! Real World: Talk to me. You in there?"

If this were the "Real World," there's no doubt that I'd be severely dehydrated. No doubt that I'd be mewling from shock. But instead I've been reading Baudrillard on my phone, and for the time being, anyway, haven't yet lost all sense of reason. This is why when the Observer Controller leans down and asks again if I'm all right, I clear my throat and, in a loud, bright voice, tell him that I'm fine.

Part II: My Childhood Did Not Take Place

Spending a weekend inside a disaster simulation might not be most people's idea of leisure, but I have to admit I've been drawn to such exercises for about as long as I can remember. During those bright summer days of my suburban childhood, I invariably attended my local police department's annual "Safety Town" seminars. Here, school-aged children would learn best practices for gun and motor vehicle safety, gas and electrical precautions, as well as strategies for how we could protect ourselves whenever our parents left the house. It was an event at which I served with great distinction as our town sheriff's "Deputy Volunteer Assistant." And I confess that during school, while the other kids played at recess, I would often stay inside and proceed to disturb my third grade teacher by doing elaborate schematic drawings of my home's and school's floor plans, using a color-coded system of arrows and asterisks to highlight, in the event of a tornado or fire, the most expeditious routes of egress. It was this recess activity in particular that had caused the school administration to call home and ask my mom whether everything was all right and to maybe get a better sense of just what exactly was bothering this kid.

In the contemporary imagination, obsessive-compulsive disorder exists as a quaint, neurotic condition, a quirk of hand-washing and drawer-organizing on the order of, say, Bill Murray in *What About Bob?* or Jack Nicholson in *As Good As It Gets*. As someone who suffered from this grim headstorm for twenty years, I cannot tell you how offended I get by these daffy caricatures and how far afield they are from the actual torments of this condition. Take for just one example a much-cited case study in the

OCD literature, about a fifteen-year-old Ethiopian girl named Bira who mitigated her obsessive worries by eating a mud-and-straw wall in her family's provincial hut, a case of pica that continued for several years and that resulted in the girl consuming some eight square meters of bricks. Or consider the incident of a poor Brazilian man who became so unduly fixated on the shape of his eye sockets that he constantly prodded and palpated their contours, doing this with such frequency and force that he eventually ended up blinding himself.

The average person has some four thousand thoughts a day, and for the obsessive-compulsive, most of these are given over to extremely irrational fears, which usually consist of a harebrained, "what if" variety. *What if I drive my car off the side of this bridge? What if I swan-dive off the ledge at this swanky rooftop party? What if this store-bought aspirin has been surreptitiously laced with cyanide?* Most of us experience these unhappy musings but can dismiss them as unreasonable and therefore impertinent. But the obsessive-compulsive gets inextricably snagged on them and will go to extreme lengths to mitigate their voltage.

For my part, I had developed a morbid fear of disasters, owing to a formative encounter with the 1996 movie *Twister*, starring Helen Hunt and Bill Paxton. Upon leaving the theater, I became a preadolescent scholar of wind patterns and cloud formations. On rainy days, my thoughts were downright actuarial, and most of my compulsions took the form of prayer. Kneeling on my bedroom's brown austere carpet, I whispered fearful apostrophes to God, dozens if not hundreds of times, their lengthy appeals and divine bargainings taking over twenty-five minutes to recite. I also washed my hands obsessively, using a bitter admixture of bar soap and Clorox bleach, which left my hands hurt and abraded, and turned the surface of my palms a weird, bad-candy pink. Bear in mind that I was only twelve years old at this point. And I'll admit that on particularly bad days weather-wise, I was not above covertly grabbing my parents' cordless landline phone and skulking inconspicuously into my bedroom, where I would proceed to call the National

Weather Service hotline and ask the operator, in worried tones, whether there were any tornadoes on the horizon for my hometown in southeastern Wisconsin. Actually, I began to call the hotline with such regularity and zeal that the otherwise genial operators began to recognize the prepubescent timbre of my voice, and would either ask to speak to my parents or assure me that Wisconsin was not at all at risk and please, honey, do not call us again.

The answer to why my parents didn't just escort me over to the nearest mental health care provider is that traditional therapy is actually woefully inefficacious in trying to treat this disorder. The Internet abounds with cases of patients who, in thrall to psychoanalysis, actually end up exacerbating their compulsions, as was the case for one Christian woman in the 1960s who suffered from incessant blasphemous thoughts about having sex with Jesus. After her Freudian therapist gave her a lesson on sexual symbolism and innuendo exegesis, she thereupon found it extremely difficult to close drawers or ride train cars, insert electrical plugs or, for obvious reasons, eat bananas.

When it comes to OCD, one of the more inimical responses that loved ones can have is something called the "Family Accommodation Method." This is where instead of ferrying the individual to the appropriate mental health care services, the parents and siblings of the obsessive-compulsive get conscripted into the person's rituals, no matter their frequency or ridiculousness. This can explain why on stormy days I would corral my entire family into our home's unfinished basement, carrying provisions of a flashlight and transistor radio, plus an assortment of snacks, and asking that everyone stay hunkered down there with me until eventually the storm would pass. Only my older brother opted out of this accommodation, instead adopting what the relevant literature calls "hostile noncompliance." He huffed petulantly anytime my parents forced him to join us in the basement and openly declaimed that this was "bullshit" and that I was being "ridiculous." And true though his psychological appraisals may have been, they weren't exactly therapeutically helpful at the time, nor were the cruel nicknames he'd given me, including "Tornado Boy" and "The Twister Kid."

Let's not spend any more time on this. Suffice to say that as time passed, my anxieties lessened, and as I entered adulthood, my obsessive thoughts took on a more political register. In some sense, this was to be expected. After all, history shows that expressions of OCD dovetail rather neatly with outflashings of social panic, as evidenced by "syphilis phobia" in the 1920s or "AIDS phobia" in the 1980s, when new facts about these phenomena were just coming into public consciousness. Shortly after Trump was elected, I found myself stocking dry goods and water jugs in the storage closet of my basement, along with a Go Bag, iodine tablets, and more than a couple first-aid kits. Things reached some sort of high point with the early reports of the coronavirus, when I began exercising such extreme measures of cleanliness and sterility that my university students could do nothing but furrow their brows and tap their temples anytime I entered the lecture hall, since my pre-class routine was to immediately start Cloroxing surfaces. (Throughout those months, I'm afraid my reputation among the student body changed dramatically, going from something along the lines of Robin Williams in *Dead Poets Society* to, like, some sort of loathsome paranoid nudnik, a person who insisted that kids with even the slightest sniffle "please refrain from attending classes.")

Around this time, Disaster City posted on their website a request for "Victim Volunteers," people willing to don "moulage" and lie in rubble in order to give the nation's first responders some vivid, lifelike training. Their social media accounts showed images of grinning volunteers, their faces speckled with gore, with captions like "Family Fun Under a Few Tons of Rubble" or "I haven't enjoyed myself this much in years!" Soon I was on the phone with Ms. Merribeth Kahlich, the head of communications for Texas A&M Task Force 1, the state's FEMA response team and one of Disaster City's institutional affiliates. "So," she said, "I understand you want to embed and get a sense of what it's like to be in a 'Compromised Victim Situation'?"

And even though this phrase sent a bolt of hot dread through me, I said that I wanted the full treatment, to help out "in any way I can." "Now, sweetie," she said, "let me ask you a question: Do you have your own hard hat?" Perhaps you'll balk at the blasé way that Ms. Kalich just assumes the average American might have this. But it turns out that I *do* have my own hard hat. (Most emergency preparedness guides advise individuals to procure protective headwear, particularly if they live in disaster-prone areas.) Yet the reason I didn't tell Ms. Kalich this is that I was worried that any overeagerness on my part might have revealed me to be a neurotic halfwit (which in fact I am) and underscored the extent to which my trip to Disaster City wasn't entirely journalistic. "Well," Merribeth said. "You should be all set." Then, when I asked about the rubble entombment, she offered me a grim warning. "Honey, sometimes there's just enough room for you in there. So if you're the least bit claustrophobic, I suggest that you start getting that mind of yours right."

Part III: Enchanted Kingdoms

I arrive at Disaster City at dawn under vast Lone-Star skies. All Victim Volunteers have been asked to report to Building 119 for orientation and check-in, and during my walk from the parking lot, the campus lies in unrevealing darkness, so I can't quite see what the day will have in store.

After several minutes of compulsive tapping and self-exhortation, I finally summon the courage to enter the building, which is bustling with activity, like a midcentury newsroom before a big story will break. The two Victim Volunteer Coordinators—Nyssa and LaNell—are busy in-taking new arrivals, who are required to fill out a lengthy liability waiver, and those volunteers who've already signed away their rights have lined up beside long foldout tables, where there are plastic tubs of provisions—hardhats and leather gloves, flashlights and protective glasses. Because I quickly discern that both Nyssa and LaNell control my placement in the rubble pile, I'm already conjuring ways of asking them to position me in one of its less harrowing sectors. But any hope of a cozy arrangement is swiftly upended, because it turns out that Merribeth has already signed me up for the "full entombment." Or as one of the other coordinators puts it, "Yeah, I believe he's doing all the nasty stuff on our list. He's *that guy*." (Incidentally, a camera crew for the BBC was also present that weekend, and whenever I saw them around campus, we seemed to regard each other with open animus, like coaches from opposing teams. Later, however, I found out these Brits weren't actually participating in the exercise—the cowards—and I confess to feeling a weird but thoroughgoing American pride about this.)

Soon all the volunteers are welcomed and thanked, since our presence is necessary for "the realism of today's simulation." This introduction is offered by one of the "Observer Controllers," members of the task force who will be patrolling the grounds throughout the exercise and assessing their colleagues' efficiency in executing their deployments. Because FEMA teams can only deploy as federal task forces during out-of-state disasters, we are now invited to briskly imagine that we're all residents of something called "Disaster City, Louisiana," a small town in Brayton Parish with a daytime population of thirty-five hundred. Apparently, our largest employer, ChemCo, has experienced a massive pipeline explosion, the seismic force of which has decimated our manufacturing plant and has compromised the structural integrity of several nearby residences.

In order to faithfully reenact the typical chronology of this sort of event, local EMTs and first responders will start by conducting what's called a "Hasty Search," during which they will look to corral and decontaminate any of the exposed area's "Walking Wounded." Sometime later this morning, Texas A&M Task Force 1 (Texas's FEMA response team) and Texas A&M Task Force 2 (their state-based equivalent) will assist local authorities in rescue operations and will be given rear-echelon support from an auxiliary unit of the Texas National Guard, who would likely be deployed by the governor for an event of this magnitude. They will be bringing with them something called a "Wet Decontamination Trailer," which sounds to me like some sort of medieval torture implement. Once the "Hot Zones" are cleared of the Walking Wounded, the task force will perform live rescues in the collapsed buildings, so the three-act structure of today's simulation will be: Walking Wounded, Decon Bath, and then Rubble Entombment. "We will be rescuing throughout the day and night," he says, "and we'll probably stop sometime around ten o'clock."

Up until now, I'd been regarding my involvement in today's simulation as roughly equivalent to LARPing—you get dressed up and play the part, but the psychic burden pretty much ends there. But LaNell explains that many of us will be placed in very deep, very dark spaces and that our cellphones probably won't have service, so we should get "prepared for that."

"Don't think 'I'm gonna be fine,'" LaNell says, "because it's very cold under the concrete, so take the sleeping bags and take the mats. We don't want you to become a true victim."

"Because we did have some of those last year," Nyssa adds.

This prompts some of the Victim Volunteers who attended last year's event to tell us newbies about someone who'd been left in the rubble pile for seven hours and another person who, after she'd been exhumed, pale and in need of fluids (I'm guessing), was thereupon discovered to have a mild case of hypothermia, which meant that the task force had to call an ambulance.

This litany of today's expected woes raises a question about my fellow Victim Volunteers, which is, what would possess a person to willingly endure rubble piles and coffin-like enclosures, without any kind of assurance that they'll actually be found or, as the liability waiver makes clear, even that they'll be safe? Some light journalistic probing reveals a pretty narrow window of possible answers, everything from "for school credit" (this from a gently pimpled adolescent in a Texas A&M sweatshirt) to "I wanted to help out with the national cause" (a gravel-voiced man named Alex, who works as a police officer in Dallas). What becomes immediately clear to me is that I am the lone person among the other Victim Volunteers who actually worries about any of this stuff happening. Anytime I casually query the others about their heart rates or cortisol levels, given today's planned events, they sort of laugh me off and say, no, they don't much worry about collapsed buildings or hazmat situations. Mostly they're here because they were looking for a kooky novelty with which they could pass a Saturday. Even when I mention the WHO's provisos about pandemic flus or the risks of biochemical attacks, my fellow Victims either assume that I am engaging in some ironic, deadpan humor or they treat me like a little kid whose worries are downright Chicken-Littlish. Two older women make an aw-phooey gesture with their hands, and say, "Oh, bless your heart, sweetie."

We have now loosely congregated outside, under the building's low portico, where Nyssa and LaNell are waiting for us with buckets of flour and ash. This will be our "moulage" for the Walking Wounded exercise, as we're supposed to have been confected with all manner of hazardous chemicals. The idea is that we will all stand on a rhomboid of grass and proceed to outstretch our arms as if for crucifixion, letting the VVCs chuck handfuls of this stuff onto our bodies and faces, until all of us resemble beignets.

Powdered and primped, we are soon released by Nyssa and LaNell into the streets of Disaster City, and I hang back and take it all in, since this is my first good look at the campus. From the top of the hill, what I'm afforded is a vista of gloom, a true panorama of death and destruction. To my immediate right is a full-size reenactment of a train derailment, with Amtrak passenger cars lying toppled on top of one another and spavined mid-sized sedans pancaked between them. Further into town, there are two large hummocks of rubble, at least sixty feet high, which look like nothing so much as collapsed Jenga towers. Beneath these piles is a warren of tunnels where we Victims will later be placed, the darkened crevices of which, I'm told, are often tenanted by rats and scorpions, bobcats and snakes.

It turns out that almost all of these woeful tableaux have been modeled after the landscapes of actual disasters. For instance, a parking garage where two crushed and glittering cars dangle from its second story, their hoods pinned by a collapsed cement ceiling, was inspired by the World Trade Center bombing in 1993. But if bombings aren't your thing, you can slip into another darkening building where a full-scale replica of a suburban cinema sits ghoulishly uninhabited. So vividly does it recall the interior of the Aurora movie theater shooting, you can't help but skedaddle out of there and hightail it down the street. For obvious, childhood-related reasons, I steer way clear of the tornado rubble exhibit, where a cyclone has churned a two-story motel into an alp of chipper-shredded bits.

Theatrically speaking, I haven't been much impressed by my fellow Victim Volunteers. After all, throughout the Walking Wounded Exercise, most of them have splintered off into little cliques of twos and threes, each of them strolling laughingly down the debris-laden boulevards. One dramatic outlier is a stoic fellow named John Jahnke, whose grizzled jawline and Promethean cheekbones pretty much make him a dead ringer for Woody Harrelson. I sit down next to him on the collapsed roof of a fictional pancake house, and for a while, we rest together in the accretive silence, with him gazing pensively into the middle distance, like a sea captain recalling a particularly traumatic voyage. Like most older eccentrics, he begins speaking without social nicety or contextualizing preface: "One of the things you learn right away is to get yourself to the high ground," he says. "Because a lot of times if you're not a victim in drastic need, they'll leave you, so you want to be able to watch the action. Because if you get yourself into a place where you can't see anything, well then it's really a boring situation."

Within the Disaster City community, John is considered to be something of a gray eminence. He's been volunteering as a victim for the last ten years and has participated in as many as "thirty or forty" exercises. "I've been in that building there," he says, pointing, "collapsed by a bomb. I've been in two of those cars there" (directing my attention to the cantilevered sedans on the far side of campus). "And I've been in this store here, where my bomb blew up prematurely" (no clue what he means by this). He then gestures to the Stonehenge of Amtrak trains to our left, explaining that one time, after the first responders strapped him into a gurney, he kind of lost it psychologically. It was the first time in his tenure as a Victim Volunteer that he realized that, in terms of realism, everyone has their limits.

In nearly all of my interviews with the task force members, they kept referring to Disaster City as "a Disneyland for first responders." Doubtless they were referring to the fact that Disaster City furnishes a whole Epcot of high-octane simulations, on which these guys get to practice assorted acts of heroism. But I'm inclined to think that the comparison between Disneyland and Disaster City is apt in ways I doubt they could've intended. After all, for nearly fifty years, critical theorists have been suggesting that Disneyland functions in the popular imagination as a locus of gauzy-edged nostalgia, what with its enchanted kingdoms and picturesque Main Streets, all harkening back to some simpler, quainter time in American history that never actually existed. A similar nostalgia is underway here too, though, but of a more morbid and distressing kind. Because as you traipse down Disaster City's own heavily themed "Main Street," you are given to see life-sized re-creations of retail storefronts whose quaint names are doubtlessly meant to evoke the mom-and-pop stores of some mythical hometown—"Parker's Hardware," "Breaches Clothing Co.," and "Bennett's Barbeque" (whose tagline reads: *Saw 'Em Off and We'll Do the Rest*).

What thinkers like Baudrillard and Umberto Eco have been positing for years is that the intense theming at Disney is, on some level, meant to convince Americans that the country outside the theme park's turnstiles is still real and authentic, when of course we all know that Walmart and McDonald's are just as flimsy and artificial as anything inside Disney—that American life itself depends upon similar narratives of enchantment. After a while I begin to think that beyond whatever preparatory education it hopes to impart, Disaster City's true purpose, at least for me, is to concentrate every permutation of woe into one place, thereby allowing its inhabitants to believe that the world outside Disaster City's confines is, comparatively, safe. But what any obsessive-compulsive knows—and what the COVID-19 pandemic will later make clear—is that the real world possesses far more threats and potentialities than are dreamt of in College Station's philosophy.

Part IV: This Is Not a Test

All afternoon on Saturday, the simulation starts to break down, and it seems impossible to enumerate all the many slippages between reality and re-creation. Perhaps the most obvious example is my incredibly convoluted relationship with my on-campus press liaison, a person named Vita Vaughn. Anytime I'm not engaged in hair-raising simulations, Vita sort of hovers in my vicinity, just in case I need anything. This is extremely weird in and of itself, but the plot thickens and eventually turns almost DeLillo-ish and postmodern, because it turns out that Vita is training to be a communications officer with Texas A&M Task Force 1 the next time they deploy. So even though I'm here as a credentialed representative of *Harper's Magazine*, there's a sense in which our interactions are serving as a dress rehearsal for Vita's eventual conversations with *real* journalists. Vita tells me that eventually she will do mock press briefings, during which her colleagues in Communications and Marketing will sit in an ersatz media gallery and pummel her with questions, while she herself stands at a chestnut-colored lectern. Apparently, they will try to stump her with facetious but heart-rending ones, stuff like, "But what about the babies, Vita? What about *the babies?*"

This blurriness between reality and its simulation gets intensified later, when Vita ferries me to the Texas Task Force's Base of Operations (also called "The Boo"), a little grotto of tents and temporary huts that, from a distance, looks rather like a carnies' outpost or a Roman bivouac. Every now and then, Vita and I, wearing protective eyewear and requisite hardhats, will slip into the tents and casually observe the guys in their navy-blue task force uniforms, all standing brawnily around and talking animatedly about casualty counts or "breaching and shoring." At one point, Vita introduces me to

Steve Lopez, a squat, shorn muscular man who serves as Texas Task Force 2's diminutive and roundly admired team leader. But before I can even extend an introductory hand—a gesture that in three weeks' time will strike me as unsafe—Steve squints in confusion, and he looks to Vita for clarification, saying, "Wait, like, is this real, or is this part of the simulation thing?"

Throughout these interactions, Vita keeps misidentifying me as a writer from "*Harper's Bazaar* magazine," which prompts me to waste a bunch of time wondering how a fashion organ might cover the events at Disaster City: "Containment Couture: How Hazmats Will Overrun Athleisure as Your Work-from-Home Daily Wear" or "You Down with PPE? Yeah, You Know Me: How Gloves, Masks, and Protective Eyewear Will Soon Become the New Urban Chic." Even so, most of the first responders seem terrified to get interviewed by me—one of them actually ducks behind a fellow task force member and says, jocularly, "Ask him, not me!" For a while, I'm puzzled by this caginess, until I realize that apart from their more immediate role of locating victims and extracting them, the task force members also bear the responsibility of controlling the disaster-response narrative, not only issuing germane info about victim data and how the public can stay safe, but also exuding an attitude of superior competence and total control in situations that are themselves manifestly unsafe.

Later, Vita introduces me to a task force member named Casey England, a trim, ginger-haired person with a wholesome, farm-boy complexion. When I ask him whether these simulations ever wear on him, he says, "Yeah, man. I think they can." He grew up just north of Oklahoma City, and when he was a sophomore in high school, he felt the OKC bombing in his feet. His parents still live there, he tells me, and they've been to the memorial a few times, but whenever his mom asks if he wants to go, he says he doesn't want to see it. "And she's like, 'Why? But this is what you do. You respond to things like that.' And I told her, 'Yeah, but when I do it, it's not real.'" Even when he deploys for a genuine emergency, he tells me, he pretends it's just training. He has to tell himself: "These aren't real people. Those aren't real lives. That's not really their house. They didn't just really lose their loves ones. It's all a training exercise, and when I leave, it's all gonna be OK."

And yet it isn't until the Wet Decontamination Bath that the simulation starts to really mess with my head. Because at around 2:00 p.m., I and the only other two Victim Volunteers who are brave enough to endure this part of the exercise are soon couriered over to the Wet Decon Trailer, where men in dun-colored hazmats and rubber boots the color of traffic cones proceed to "cut away" our clothes until we're summarily reduced to our nethers. These men in Mylex breathe through long, dark, anteater-ish snouts, and they take us by the elbow and lead us up the ramp. The Decon Trailer itself looks like a compact car wash, with long translucent noodles of plastic that you have to part like a stage curtain in order to get inside, and once there, I'm surrounded by a whole botany of pendant rubber hoses, each of which has a different liquid function—wash, rinse, disinfect—and once again, I'm made to stand in a little cylindrical wash bin while another guy in a hazmat tells me to lift my arms and outstretch my hands. When I do, he proceeds to blast me with a stream of gelid water. "Is it cold?" he asks. "Yeah, man," I say. "It's fucking cold." This makes him laugh.

Once I'm done with this humiliating ablution, I'm sort of birthed out of the plastic noodles on the Decon Trailer's other end, and here I stand dripping in College Station's unseasonable 40 degree temperatures while two other guys in hazmat suits scan my body with some sort of toxicity detector that looks straight out of *Inspector Gadget*. And this is when I really start to lose it. Because even though several dozen first responders and National Guardsmen begin to congregate in a three-deep semicircle to watch me undergo this procedure—their expressions looking far more amused and spectatorial than they do educational or curious—I am nevertheless deeply distressed to realize that this whole ordeal is chillingly reminiscent of the sanitary protocols that Chinese doctors have been following in light of the recent COVID-19 epidemic, and for the first time all weekend, I feel like I'm inhabiting some future eventuality, that the simulation is grimly anticipating, to a breathtaking degree, what in a few weeks' time will become rote and commonplace, what many people will experience all over this country. And this premonition of fear and trepidation won't leave me even after the toxicity scan ends, because even though this is supposed to be the country's mecca of disaster preparedness, I find that no one—not the task force, nor the National Guard, nor the police and fire fighters from the nearby city of Bryan—will have thought to bring to this exercise *towels* (!) for the Victim Volunteers to dry off with. And so at this point, I'm shivering visibly, like a cartoon of an electrocuted person, until one of the Victim Volunteer Coordinators soon arrives on a four wheeler to "rescue" me, and soon we are cruising at ten miles per hour to the shower barracks on the opposite end of campus, where I am made to stand under a very hot faucet (presumably to decrease the hypothermia risk) and where I stay for what turns out to be like thirty minutes, because even this Victim Volunteer Coordinator still can't find a towel for me or my compatriots. Eventually, when he does return, he immediately apologizes, because apparently he could only find "this," he says. And when I poke my head out of the shower curtain, he's handing me a pilled swatch of blue cloth that LaNell uses as a dog towel (readily identifiable by the tufts of German shepherd fur still matted to its fabric), along with three urine-colored Disaster City t-shirts, which have the word VICTIM emblazoned in bold black letters across the chest.

By now, my stress levels are so high that I don't join the others in returning to Building 119, but instead abscond to the privacy of my car, where I proceed to become a veritable zoo of neurotic worries. Here I spend the next half hour trying to regroup and calm down, calling both my wife and mom, each of whom offer commiserative familial noises and keep saying, again and again, in assuasive tones, that there's nothing to worry about, Barrett, that all of this is fake.

Part V: Acts of God

While the simulations at Disaster City are for training and preparedness, some of the earliest disaster mockups were actually designed for entertainment. At the crack of the twentieth century, visitors strolling down Surf Avenue in Coney Island could gawk at a reenactment of the Mount Pelée volcano eruption, which had occurred in 1902 on the French island of Martinique. Elsewhere they could clutch their hearts at a simulation of the Galveston flood of 1900, a gruesome inundation that claimed the lives of over eight thousand Texans. It isn't hard to see how these amusements served as a kind of masochistic death wish, that the wolfish interest in faux calamity was an attempt on the part of fin-de-siècle Americans to reconcile themselves to the horrific events that had become, by the end of the Industrial Age, all too routine and expected. As the historian Ted Steinberg puts it, "there existed no better way to come to grips with the anxiety spawned by the spate of turn-of-the-century disasters than to schedule a trial run with apocalypse."

Obviously, this tracks pretty neatly with my own motivations for coming to Disaster City, but Steinberg contends that these simulations ended up having a more insidious social function, working to normalize disasters and thus sap them of any moral or political dimension. Up until the early twentieth century, government officials were apt to characterize natural disasters as nothing more than "acts of God," a convenient rhetorical maneuver that pitted any calamity on the fickle whims of heaven and sought to keep the engine of urban, industrial capital chugging toward productivity and profit. Such brass-tacks logic, of course, came at the expense of citizen safety and perpetuated the very circumstances (irresponsible land development, slipshod fire codes, shoddy masonry) that would often cause these disasters in the first place.

One of history's more glaring examples of this tendency, as Steinberg notes in his book *Acts of God*, involves the railroad magnate Henry Flagler.

In 1905, after constructing a rail line from Jacksonville to Miami, Flagler proposed building an even more ambitious track to extend from Homestead to Key West, wanting to exploit the surge of maritime commerce that was funneling in from the West Indies. The subsequent construction project came with a price tag of two million dollars and necessitated forty thousand workers, some seven hundred of whom would eventually drown during that decade's frequent hurricanes. In response to each storm, Flagler apparently responded with only a two-word telegram: "Keep going." Later analysis of the construction project revealed that by building twenty miles of causeways along the keys, the rail line's support mechanism inhibited tide waters from receding, which thereby amplified water levels during intense storms and put residents at an even greater risk of drowning. This is precisely what happened during the 1935 hurricane in Islamorada, Florida, where roughly 160 residents, out of a population of 250, were dragged from their homes and carried out to sea.

Up until this point, the state of Florida maintained a strict "see no hurricane" policy, so as to secure the interest of potential residents and attract the investment of land developers. But after the 1935 hurricane, the media shamed its government into acknowledging the state's outsized disaster risk. While this led to some meager reforms in insurance policies, the more lasting consequence was the countervailing effort to disassociate Florida from these tempests. Because these events were usually dubbed "the Florida Hurricanes," the U.S. Weather Bureau, in 1950, decided to give the storms female names, taking a page from the 1941 George Stewart novel, *Storm*, in which an intrepid meteorologist christens typhoons after women. Cheap misogyny aside, a more subtle machination was at work here, because by associating storms with women and thereby invoking braindead stereotypes about them (fickle, erratic, unpredictable), these municipal authorities were going a step further in naturalizing these events, suggesting that Mother Nature (and all her tempests) could not be foreseen or mitigated but must be countenanced instead as merely the cost of doing business.

Part VI: Code Purple

After the Decontamination Bath, I eventually return to Building 119, where LaNell soon gives us our dramatic roles for the upcoming "Rubble Entombment." On the top of mine, there are bold-faced letters reading "Tango 26," which are underscored by the following stage directions. For this scenario, I will be in a "large, survivable void," but I'll only be able to tap lightly on the walls around me ("skin or wood on concrete"). "If not found by 7:00 p.m. on Saturday," the instructions read, "begin lightly tapping with a rock on concrete ONLY when requested. If not found by 9:00 p.m., begin tapping loudly with a rock until found. You cannot talk, but you can follow searchers' commands." If I have an emergency or real-world problem, I'm supposed to yell "Real World," "For Real," or "Code Purple."

Now, the volunteers are leaning over and sharing their notecards, sort of jealously appraising each other's assignments like, "Hey, what did you get?" I turn to one woman named Denise—the person who fell asleep in the rubble pile last year and who had been forgotten about for seven hours—and I ask her, "Is this right? If I'm not found by nine o'clock, start banging on the wall with a rock?" And she goes, "Barrett, if you're not found by nine o'clock, I'd recommend you start screaming."

Tango 26 is located in Rubble Pile 2, which is in Hot Zone 1, a vector nestled between the strip mall and the half-collapsed parking garage. Wearing my motley assemblage of leather gloves and hardhat, I clumsily ascend an Everest of rebar and concrete, at the apex of which is a haphazard stack of wooden pallets, which Casey, the aforementioned first responder, begins chucking out of the way. In time he reveals a twelve-foot sheet of plywood, which will essentially function as the lid of my coffin. Lifting it up and resting it on his shoulder, in sort of the braced squat of a shot-putter, Casey says, "In you go." I lean over and peer into the catacomb, where my nostrils are assaulted by its moldering cologne of mud. Its floor is a shallow broth of mulch-colored water.

"Wait a minute," I say, "this is me?"

"This is you," he says.

I hop into my crypt, where I'm newly flooded with anxiety. But before they close the lid, I say, "Hey, Casey, this is all fake, right?" And he says, "Yessir, it's all training." Then I listen to the scrap and clatter of pallets getting piled on top of me and will myself into a kind of self-protective fugue state.

The first hour passes with a lot of controlled breathing. For a while, I make a game of training my gaze on the granular swirl of concrete, essentially treating it as one of those optical illusions posters. Dimensions-wise, my tomb is the size of a really large household appliance—think dishwasher or storage cooler—and with my back against one wall, I have to scrunch my knees up to a vinyasa squat in order to sit comfortably. The tomb's lone feature of hope is a tiny shard of daylight that squeaks through one corner of the ceiling and through which I can just barely perceive a blessed shred of sky. Basically, I will treat this shard of daylight the same way that Tom Hanks treats that one volleyball in *Cast Away*.

It doesn't take me long to realize that I'm surrounded by other victims. Actually, when I press my ear to the concrete wall, I can make out someone snoring, but I can't quite decide whether this suspends my disbelief or confirms it. And to my right is another Victim Volunteer named "Fred," who keeps caterwauling his own name and pleading for someone to help him. Fred is also clanging a stone against a piece of rebar, which produces a sound that recalls the brassy staccato of chain gangs or maybe an Old West prisoner dragging a tin cup across the bars of his cage. For a while I use a rock to tap out in Morse code, "Hey, Fred. Please shut the fuck up," but either Fred isn't listening or he's none the wiser when it comes to emergency communicational tactics. Eventually, I come to regard Fred as a weird kind of cellmate, with the psychodrama between us getting carried out almost exclusively through a makeshift system of taps and clanks. We do a call-and-response-type thing that I actually find quite solacing—its subtext is *you're not alone in this*—but then Fred is back to shrieking his own name, and I have the morbid wish that, in the simulation anyway, Fred would just die already.

For my stint in the rubble pile, I've brought with me two books—*An Actor Prepares* (a vade mecum for method acting) and *Everyday Mindfulness for OCD* (which has been helpful in curbing my anxieties)—but because he has been on my mind all weekend, I instead eschew both of these books and download Jean Baudrillard's *The Evil Demon of Images* onto my phone. In it, Baudrillard contends that the most nefarious aspect of any simulation is the degree to which it can predict reality even before it happens, thereby inuring us to calamities and thus preempting any meaningful response we civilians might have to them. It's a sentiment that makes me think of Hurricane Pam, a Category 3 storm that hit New Orleans in 2004 and left over a half a million buildings either flood-damaged or decimated. If you don't remember this incident, well, that's because it never happened. Instead, as Robert C. Bell and Robert M. Ficociello note in their book *America's Disaster Culture*, it was a simulation created by a FEMA contractor called IEM, a group that wanted to demonstrate how overwhelmed emergency response teams would be without better institutional planning. Imagining a storm of 120-mile-per-hour winds and rains in excess of twenty inches, Hurricane Pam predicted, with a kind of prophetic accuracy, the devastating aftereffects of Hurricane Katrina. But because the local and federal governments were unwilling to heed the contractor's advice and failed to address the underlying problems that would give rise to a crisis—poverty, crumbling levees, an unjust health care system—Hurricane Pam did little, in the end, but give our country a false sense of preparedness. Or as Bell and Ficociello put it, "the simulation precedes and actually creates the disaster."

It is with a morbid fascination that I find myself googling "simulation covid epidemic." Almost immediately I stumble across a YouTube video for something called "Event 201," an exercise in global pandemics. This was carried out in October 2019—i.e., *before* the actual outbreak—and was overseen by the World Economic Forum, the Bill and Melinda Gates Foundation, and the Johns Hopkins University Center for Health Security. The exercise went so far as to produce fake news clips from something called GNN, or Global News Network, whose anchors outline, in harried tones, the fictional virus's lethal consequences. "It began in healthy looking pigs," one clip says, "months, perhaps years, ago. A new coronavirus spread silently within herds. Gradually, farmers started getting sick. Infected people got a respiratory illness with symptoms ranging from mild, flu-like signs to severe pneumonia. The sickest required intensive care. Many died. Experts agree that unless it is quickly controlled it could lead to a severe worldwide pandemic, an outbreak that circles the globe and affects people everywhere."

The mission of Event 201's Pandemic Emergency Board was to provide recommendations to the global community for responding to the chain reaction of challenges that would be created by a worldwide pandemic. The panel included Adrian Thomas from Johnson & Johnson, Sofia Borges from the UN Foundation, Christopher Elias from the Bill and Melinda Gates Foundation, and even George Gao from China's CDC. So eerily and uncannily did this group anticipate deaths, travel bans, and economic ripple effects that over the next few months I will find myself returning to this simulation again and again, almost as if it were a compulsion.

I'm shaken out of these reveries by the sound of the rescuers' approach. What comes first is the wet respiration of their SCBAs, then the thump of their footfalls overhead—the papery scrape of gravel, the molar crack of stone. "Search and Rescue!" they yell. "Is anybody in there?" And even though I'm banging my fist so forcefully against the wall that my forearm is throbbing something awful, they of course don't find me but instead locate my deranged cellmate Fred. As it happens, Fred doesn't remember his stage directions, because when they ask him if he's hurt, Fred says, "Uh, I don't actually know if I can move. I guess I'll have to take my physical condition from you," which I've come to regard as the disaster-simulation equivalent of an untalented stage actor stopping in mid-dialogue and bellowing, "Line!"

Now Fred is trying to tell the first responder his name, which the hazmat guy keeps hearing as "Brett." Eventually, Fred gets so frustrated that he calls upon NATO's phonetic alphabet, yelling, "No, no, no—it's Foxtrot, Romeo, Echo, Delta!" And because I'm forbidden by thespian fiat from saying anything, I have to endure this miscommunication in silence, even though there's a herd of hazmatted guys standing directly above me. I feel a terrifying desperation about the search and rescue team being so close but being unable to call out to them, sort of the way Scrooge must have felt in those visions of Christmas past when trying to get the attention of his childhood phantoms.

Soon I can hear the low mutter of trucks, plus the weird staticky cadence of the EMTs' walkie-talkies retreating into the distance. And birds! How strange it is to hear the soft contralto of birds calling from the trees, their arpeggios somehow both indifferent and salubrious. It's difficult to describe the desolation I feel as my little sliver of sky darkens through my crack in the ceiling, going as it does from the milky glaucomic blue of late afternoon to the bruise-like indigo of early evening, a gradient change that pretty clearly indicates that I'll probably be staying here for the rest of the night. Later, when I reported this feeling to a fellow Victim Volunteer, a seasoned thespian on the disaster-simulation circuit, she said, "Oh, yeah, I know that feeling. I call that 'The Hour of Doom.'" (In fact, because the task force didn't find me, the Observer Controllers decide to bring me out after another two hours, and I have to climb unceremoniously out of the tomb myself.)

For the time being, though, crumpled in the rubble pile, compulsively tapping on my cement wall, I think I'm now in a position to understand what's been bugging me all weekend. Because the more time I spend at Disaster City, the more I get the sense that I'm playing a role in a palliative narrative, that I'm instantiating a myth that the country repeatedly tells itself—that there was nothing we could've done, that no one can be blamed. After all, the very existence of a place like this seems to sanction and sacralize the inevitability of such events, since in each case the simulation itself is not an effort of preemption or prevention, but a dress rehearsal for what we've blithely come to accept as the standard disaster response of containment and restoration. By now, it should go without saying that the warnings of Hurricane Pam and Event 201 were not heeded, since the cost of those preparations would have necessitated fundamental changes to the existing social system. Later, when I ask Stephen Bjune of Texas Task Force 1 whether FEMA teams ever get consulted by developers or municipalities, particularly when those bodies are legislating on fire codes or building regulations, he sighs and pauses for a moment, before saying, "No, unfortunately."

Part VII: After Action Report

Four weeks later, I'm once again in confinement, but this time as part of a real quarantine, the Great American Cloistering of 2020. As the real disaster unfolds, members of Texas Task Force 1 will deploy to help out with the early quarantines, and their hazmat practice in late February will turn out to have been fortuitous.

From my bunker of self-isolation, I will engage in such assiduous routines of decontamination that by late March my house will reek of Pine-Sol and disinfectant, and my hands will be scrubbed and pumiced, as clean as an infant's conscience. But by that point, it will no longer feel like neurosis: in fact, if it wasn't the case before now, the nation has since become roaringly obsessive-compulsive. How quickly the memes of sudsy hands start to proliferate, the YouTube clips of proper washing techniques. Celebrities will exhort their followers to rinse for at least twenty seconds, and even Google will get into the sanitation game, changing their homepage logo to a cartoon of Ignaz Semmelweis—the Hungarian physician and father of modern antiseptics (a person on whom I wrote a four-page biography when I was only eleven).

But beyond these eerie convergences with my childhood obsessions, what will strike me most is how quickly the virus gets placed inside the familiar disaster narratives. Once the disease hits American cities, a swift linguistic campaign will get underway, with talking heads casting COVID-19 as an unforeseen and unpredictable menace, one in which human institutions could not—and should not—be complicit. The examples of this tendency will be as legion as they are abhorrent. U.S. Treasury Secretary Steven Mnuchin: "No one expected this." U.S. Senator Mitt Romney: "This is an Act of Nature." *Prospect* magazine: "It is essentially an 'Act of God.'" Fox News contributor Stephen Moore: "[It's] an act of nature." Even the Old Gray Lady will participate in the naturalization, suggesting "this crisis is caused by an act of nature that has struck at least 113 countries rather than [it being caused by] irresponsible policies."

But perhaps the truest measure of our historical amnesia will be the scores of American companies who cite Acts of God clauses in order to avoid the EPA regulations in their government contracts. One corporate lawyer, Brian Israel of Arnold & Porter Kaye Scholer LLP, will say that, by early March, his firm had already fielded at least one request from a company that claimed it could not perform groundwater testing because its employees were unwilling to work during the worst throes of the pandemic. By all accounts, as of this writing, the EPA is likely to approve these requests, this despite the fact that the World Health Organization has suggested that climate change accelerates the spread of infectious diseases and that manmade environmental degradation—particularly in the form of deforestation—has been linked to 31 percent of new viral outbreaks.

Cloistered in my apartment, with empty Purell bottles and dry Clorox wipes scattered all around me, I will watch, with fear and loathing, as the familiar machinations of disaster capitalism begin to churn and accelerate: with Trump suggesting that we end the payroll tax or the pharmaceutical lobby securing profits for a vaccine. And with no small amount of dismay, I will watch as Americans willingly forfeit their civil liberties in the name of new surveillance measures, violating Ben Franklin's grievously forgotten saying, "Those who would give up essential Liberty, to purchase a little temporary Safety, deserve neither Liberty nor Safety." Or as disaster scholar Scott Gabriel Knowles puts it, "Countenancing lies about preparedness because they make us feel safe is a weak response to government... it makes it possible for policy makers to pursue actions that citizens may not approve or even be aware of, or if they are aware, may not fully understand due to 'wartime' security measures."

It's this lugubrious line of thinking that will haunt me all throughout the quarantine, watching from my apartment window as lights glow in other buildings, as all of us zone out to flickering screens. All of our interactions are now virtual—all of us now live in the simulation—a place where it is increasingly difficult to distinguish between what is real and what is imagined, between which fears are legitimate and which are obsessive-compulsive. Isolated in my own neuroses, I can't say for certain how we got here, though I increasingly sense that it has little to do with acts of God or even acts of nature. Disaster preparedness is not, in the end, the same as disaster prevention. The latter would require something that is, from our current vantage, inconceivable: the political will to abandon the pernicious practices that currently support our economy. It would require a reckoning with the larger role of human agency, an acknowledgment that no matter the scope of the disaster, no matter the exertions of essential workers, no matter how many times we bleach and scrub, rinse and disinfect, all of this is merely triage. We keep washing, but our hands are not clean.

CHURCH NOT MADE WITH HANDS

1. Exodus

Once, during a temperate summer, a Christian girl whom I was dating claimed to see "so much of God's light" within me. Though at the time I wondered what particular torsion of mind made divine valences legible to her—what, in other words, made her so special—I was nevertheless flattered to be counted among the elect, flattered in the way that secular folks are when confronted for the first time with fulsome Christian kindness.

In the end, the compliment failed as evangelism. The last time I perused the Bible with any kind of rigor was the eleventh grade, during a fling with Christianity that seems common among my contemporaries. But over the last few months, the Christian girl's statement has colonized my head, particularly whenever I spend time with my group of closest friends. Almost uniformly atheistic or agnostic, these academics and musicians, poets and doctors, have nevertheless begun to strike me as a weird kind of religious sect, a tribe banished from the city, in part because all of us had begun to seem, in uncountable ways, so irretrievably lost. Which is not to say we lacked ambition. Over the last eight years, we watched each other attend grad school and submit dissertations, sign book deals and get promotions, but while our workweek had been varnished with professionalism and achievement, our weekends had become imbued with an altogether more desperate form of longing. I suppose we had entered that period of adulthood in which one's youthful aspirations give way to the resigned weariness of middle age. Suddenly, pop culture like *Thirtysomething* and *The Big Chill* felt urgent and necessary to us. Desperately we approximated that generation's solutions, pillaging their fragments to shore against our ruins.

Of the many routes we took to soften the blow of this revelation, the most salient was the rather adolescent recourse to drugs. Arguably, this could be seen as making up for lost time, since many of us, in our youth, had been sanitized overachievers, millennial do-gooders who followed a stately procession from high school to top-tier college, and were thus woefully naive when it came to hallucinogenic indulgence. Our talk during this time was vacuous and sad. "Barrett," one of my friends (a public defender) asked me, with sheer earnestness, "have you ever tried smoking marijuana and then listening to the music of Bob Marley?" Another night two friends, both grad students in their late thirties, ate mushrooms for the first time. On the night of their experiment, they biked through long flaxen meadows and very quickly became as woozy and loquacious as Dorothy among the poppies. "What is that? Is that an elfin castle?" they squealed, pointing to a haggard building that sidled the train tracks. All night they giggled like children, and I wanted very badly for their trip to end.

Of course the quasi-religious tenor of these outings wasn't difficult to locate at a distance of years. It seemed we were trying to imbue the deadened landscape of reality with the qualia of divine significance, recovering the sacral mystery of a world long before science had exsanguinated everything. Even the teetotalers among us were touched by these transcendental longings, though they channeled them into more familiar pursuits: yoga, Tinder, the vague and seemingly futile devotion to "being present." And yet I don't mean to exempt myself from these accusations. If anything, I am the worst offender. Among friends, my quests are the subject of gentle mockery, and at dinner parties, they place bets on how long my fervor for vegetarianism will last. Will it be longer than my bout with "Effective Altruism," they wonder, or the months I spent practicing Shambhala? Remember the Keto diet and those three weeks of celibacy? Hey, Barrett, are you still reading David Graeber, or this week, is it Eckhart Tolle? We all laugh, but I can't help but hear an echo of the playground taunt, the epithet we had for such people when I was a boy. We called them poseurs—people who adopted certain modes of existence not as an authentic identity but as fad, as cursory fashion. Such unfortunates were roundly shunned and condemned to the mulch-softened periphery. But I'm beginning to see now that our derision was misplaced. The poseur doesn't rifle through credos with a frantic longing to please. Rather there's something darker and more urgent that propels his search, a nameless dread that makes his journey seem clumsy and errant.

For my own part, the crisis began shortly after I was hired as a tenure-track professor at a small Midwestern university. While such tidings should have been a happy affair, in the weeks after signing my contract I suddenly saw the course of my life radically foreshortened into a distressingly narrow road that pointed unswervingly toward death. This feeling was not at all helped by the barrage of emails I received from the human resources department at my new employer, who informed me about accidental death insurance ("a good idea for commuters like you"), as well as the protocol for retirement, for which I would be eligible after thirty years of service. *Thirty years of service?* Soon, visions of my dotage were freely available to me. In my mind's eye, I manifested as an wizened professor hunched over a disheveled desk, croaking to some apple-cheeked undergrad tired interpretations of *Beloved* and *White Noise*. Readily imaginable were scenes of geriatric-me standing behind a walnut lectern and suffering a bout of incontinence while shoals of unruffled students futzed with their VR headsets. What should have been a cause for celebration instead struck me as a mortal taunt: *death is near.*

If my spiritual restlessness didn't seem like an idiosyncratic dilemma, it was because I saw it faithfully represented in a spate of contemporary novels, the most recent of which was Michel Houellebecq's *Submission.* The book centers upon a misanthropic Huysmans scholar named Francois who teaches literature at the Sorbonne. Anhedonic, single, and alcoholic, Francois mourns his dwindling sexual prospects with a dose of Updikean fervor and regards the approval of his dissertation as a kind of death, the end of an intellectual quest that had given his life meaning. I confess to practically melting with commiseration upon confronting this sentiment in the novel's opening pages. "I spent the night of my defense alone and very drunk . . . I realized that part of my life, probably the best part, was behind me."

Francois solaces himself with visits to prostitutes, hoping these carnal gratifications will mitigate his despair. But their galvanizing effects are regrettably short-lived. One of the book's central questions is whether, like Huysmans, who converted to Catholicism after wavering darkly between "the muzzle of a pistol and the foot of the Cross," Francois can undergo a similar rebirth and resuscitate some semblance of feeling for the world he inhabits.

Yet this is a world growing stranger every day. The novel takes place in 2022, and an amiable Islamic moderate named Mohammed Ben Abbes has won the most recent election, running on a platform of regressive social reforms and igniting turmoil among the electorate. Soon after his inauguration, burka mandates go into effect and polygamy becomes voguish again. When Francois can be bothered to glance at these upheavals, he regards them through the cataracts of a solipsist—corpses in the street and the shuttering of his university are read as nothing more than harbingers of his own mortality.

If his spiritual journey ends in ambivalence, it is not for want of trying. Toward the middle of the novel, as Paris crumbles, Francois retreats to the countryside and visits the Black Madonna at Rocamadour, where he maintains the larkish hope that he can vault himself into piety. Sitting before the statue, Francois meditates on the history of Christian pilgrimages and feels his "individuality dissolving," but in a moment of droll bathos, he realizes that a couple days have passed since his last meal and dismisses his widening moral aperture as "an attack of mystical hypoglycemia." Eventually, he wolfs down a pile of duck legs, giving into the urges of his "damaged, perishable body."

In the end, a member of the Muslim Brotherhood offers Francois a chance to return to academic life, so long as he embraces Islam. Francois undertakes the conversion not as a Pascalian bet or a Kierkegaardian leap, but rather as a calculated career-driven maneuver. Just before the curtain goes down, Francois realizes that, despite Huysmans's lofty example of religious transfiguration, the novelist's "true subject had been bourgeois happiness." Such hearth-warmed comforts involved having "artist friends over for a pot-au-feu with horseradish sauce, accompanied by an 'honest' wine and followed by brandy and tobacco." It's this image of bonhomie that propels Francois to become a Muslim and join the Brotherhood, along with the promise that he'd get "three wives without too much trouble." The conversion, in other words, is nothing more than a pious shell game. While Francois has endorsed the Islamic faith, the gesture is perfunctory, and his perception of the world—as a banquet of sensual delights—remains bullishly unchanged.

Houellebecq was vilified in his native France, where the novel was condemned as an Islamophobic rant, its author a craven reactionary. This opinion seemed to disregard the flurry of interviews that Houellebecq gave during the book's promotional tour in which he professed a genuine interest in the succor of faith, particularly after losing his parents. Intentional fallacies notwithstanding, *Submission* does seem to earnestly wonder whether neoliberal hedonism can endure as a viable ideology, a sentiment that proved far more amenable in the U.S., where the book enjoyed a favorable showing.

Perhaps we Americans could sense that in a hedonistic vacuum a tyrant could more easily rear his head. Perhaps a hunger for spiritual solutions didn't seem so ridiculous.

In some sense, the history of American belles lettres was built upon the genre of spiritual quests. I suppose it's not surprising that a country founded by pilgrims would covet stories about motley seafarers hunting down white whales or New England scofflaws venturing into forests. But as much as these stories were billed as swashbuckling adventures against many-tentacled villains (whales for Melville, trains for Thoreau), their climaxes hardly ever pivoted on the lampooning of fish or the vanquishing of foes. Instead, what lent these stories their voltage was that their protagonists underwent an encompassing change of vision—they ended up seeing the world in a new way. The wayfarers aboard the *Pequod* recognize that "all visible objects, man, are but as pasteboard masks," and their voyage is as much a perceptual expedition as it is a nautical one. They want to stick their fingers through the holes of the mask and palpate the divine mysteries lurking beneath. The tenant of Walden Pond experiences a similar attunement of mind when his onerous regime of yardwork and moseying allows him to escape "the games and amusements" of the nineteenth century and reawaken to "what is sublime and noble."

To some contemporary readers, such characters will seem, at worst, like contemptible prigs, and at best, naive fools. We all know there's no quicker way to offend the modern sensibility than to suggest that the world has been endowed with sacral mystery, that certain aspects of nature will elude even the adept, grasping fingers of science. So what does this mean for an American readership weaned on tales of spiritual epiphany and God-haunted perception? After Nietzsche sounded the death knell for religion, after Lyotard dissolved the possibility of grand unifying narratives, it has been interesting to witness the reemergence of this foundational genre, with more and more contemporary novelists (like Houellebecq, Sheila Heti, and Karl Ove Knausgaard) fashioning what we might call "the post-religious quest."

2. Crop Rotation

If there is a persistent anxiety that undergirds this burgeoning genre, it is the way in which the trajectories of our personal narratives remain stubbornly infused with the motifs of Judeo-Christian parables, particularly those of wandering, persecution, and redemption. Nowhere in recent memory is this more apparent than in Sheila Heti's novel *How Should a Person Be?*—a book that was roundly mischaracterized as a bildungsroman about millennial friendship, when it could've been more accurately shelved next to the works of Kierkegaard or Rilke. Described by its author as "a novel from life," the book stands as a notable touchstone in the emerging landscape of autofiction. But unlike other practitioners of this school, who deliberately muddy the line between author and protagonist, Heti endows her text with a useful ironic distance, allowing the book to transcend the concave fixations of autobiography and enter, instead, the outward realm of representation. She does this by comparing the itinerancy of her friends to the aimlessness of the Israelites who "took what they had, which was nothing, and left their routines as slaves in Egypt to follow Moses into the desert in search of the promised land." The novel, in other words, is meant to be read as a contemporary update of Exodus, an allegory for millennials who see themselves as unshackled from religion, ideology, and history and are thus free to hunt down the riches of this ostensible "promised land."

What this nirvana might look like in a post-religious age is suggested on the second page of Heti's book. "How should a person be? I sometimes wonder about it, and I can't help answering like this: a celebrity... My hope is to live a simple life... By *a simple life*, I mean a life of undying fame that I don't have to participate in. I don't want anything to change, except to be as famous as one can be, but without that changing anything." The next three-hundred-some-odd pages follow the exploits of a group of Canadian friends who doggedly pursue this brand of stardom. In their late twenties or early thirties, they are fledgling artists, armchair intellectuals, and tepid writers who stand in cool judgment of the world around them, trading unleavened opinions about the culture, often with the bemused acedia of dorm-room stoners. Their preoccupations, such as they are, are fundamentally adolescent—they want community without sacrifice; celebrity without inconvenience.

For Sheila, the book's main character, the effort to garner recognition allows her to experience a special "kinship" with Paris Hilton, the fame-craving heiress whose sex tape Sheila watches with no small amount of commiseration—"She was just another white girl going through her life with her clothes off"—but Sheila locates more immediate examples of inhabiting the world in the deportments of her friends, an investigation that engines the book's conflict. What seems like innocuous adulation—a loose version of Stanley Cavell's perfectionism—soon degenerates into a creepy form of appropriation. Sheila begins cannibalizing the personality of her friend Margaux, going so far as to record their conversations and use them as fodder for a play she's struggling to write, a form of imitation that reaches a zenith during a trip to Miami. There, Sheila buys the same yellow dress as Margaux, a twinning that practically disembowels their friendship.

Like so many others of her generation who were fed a steady diet of the-world-is-your-oyster bromides, Sheila crumbles and second-guesses whenever she attempts to commit herself to larger causes. How else are we to understand a moment toward the outset of the book when Sheila decodes an upsetting dream with her therapist? During the course of the nightmare, Sheila finds herself at an airport, "trying to get somewhere, to someplace higher and better"—a Freud-for-Dummies metaphor for personal ambition—but when she finally chooses a route and purchases a ticket, she ends up leaping from the jet during takeoff and landing safely on a knoll of trash bags. Soon she comes upon the smoldering ruins of a wrecked plane, which she presumes to be her flight, and with a spritz of elation, she congratulates herself on wisely absconding from the doomed voyage. But during the dream's coda, she learns that the ruins belong to a different flight, that her plane is still soaring uneventfully through the air, and it's impossible for her to catch up with it.

The dream, as her analyst soon explains, vivifies the extent to which Sheila has been stultified by the broad pastures of freedom and choice, like the shopper in a checkout line clutching his head about which knickknack to purchase. "You remember the *puer aeternus*—the eternal child—Peter Pan—the boy who never grows up, who never becomes a man?" the analyst says. "Such people will suddenly tell you they have another plan, and they always do it the moment things start getting difficult. But it's their everlasting switching that's the dangerous thing, not what they choose." Such an affliction reminds me of the aesthete from Kierkegaard's *Either/Or*—a book that Heti has cited as an influence—who mentions "crop rotation" as one possible elixir for boredom and despair.

> One is tired of living in the country, one moves to the city; one is tired of one's native land, one travels abroad; one is *europamude*, one goes to America, and so on; finally, one indulges in a dream of endless travel from star to star. Or the movement is different but still an extension. One is tired of dining off porcelain, one dines off silver; one tires of that, one dines off gold; one burns half of Rome to get an idea of the conflagration at Troy. This method defeats itself; it is the bad infinite.

For a while, this system of flux can flatter your taste for novelty, and the glinting carousel of modern hedonism takes a long time to complete its circle before the rider realizes his horse lacks a true destination. Through the prism of religious thought, these crop rotations often took the form of toggling between graven images and false idols, as experienced by the Israelites during their jaunt through the wilderness, embracing by turns ersatz lords and molten calves.

It is with a shudder of embarrassment that I return to this passage from

Heti's novel. It condemns so thunderously my own revolving door of sur-rogate beliefs, from CrossFit to Transcendental Meditation, from Effective Altruism to a bout of YOLO-inspired travel, almost none of which has re-quired from me any of the sacrifice and service we might otherwise expect from true communal engagement.

Like Francois of *Submission*, Sheila's inability to make choices stems from an impairment of vision, one so endemic to contemporary culture that readers could be forgiven for missing it. Starved for recognition, preoccu-pied with the hygiene of her reputation, she remains blind to the ways in which her actions have corroded her most intimate personal relationships. But in the end, Heti refrains from offering her readers a nostrum for our desolation in the world. Instead, the book closes with a thinly veiled meta-phor for the irritation of ethical questing: Sheila watches her friends bound across a handball court, playing a game whose rules are alien to them, their bodies flailing gorgeously in the attempt.

3. Neverland

While Heti diagnoses the modern existential problem as a childlike inability to make choices—what we might call the "Peter Pan syndrome"—the Nor-wegian writer Karl Ove Knausgaard believes our fundamental error is not one of moral temporizing, but of grossly impaired perception. The urgent spiritual problem, for Knausgaard, is that we are not enough like children. Contemporary adults, as a result of our long tenure on earth, have become inured to the dazzling wonders of the natural world, unable to perceive ho-liness in the sargassum of everyday life. As a tonic to these ossified habits of mind, Knausgaard suggests, in his novel *Autumn*, that we perform CPR on our inner child and aim to resurrect a fascination with humdrum objects, such as apples, wasps, and plastic bags or buttons, piss, and ambulances (a few of the subjects to which the book's chapters are devoted). Borrowing the epistolary conceit of Marilynne Robinson's *Gilead*, the novel is written as a valentine to his unborn daughter and labors to capture "these astounding things, which . . . are easy to lose sight of."

The book is a compilation of essayistic squibs, and because its writer assumes the reader has grown callous to the world, its vocal register veers, with dismaying regularity, into the condescending enthusiasm of an elementary school teacher. Take, for example, a chapter called "Teeth" in which the author ruminates on the apparent similarities between mountains and molars. "When the first teeth appear, these little stones slowly pushed up through the child's red gums, appearing at first like sharp little points, then standing there like miniature white towers in the mouth, it is hard not to be astonished, for where do they come from?" The daffy wonderment of this last clause kills me, for it suggests that the reader has nothing better to do than meditate upon the quiddity of something so biologically straightforward as the arrival of new teeth. More concerning is that these cerebrations are hardly ever fastened to a life of politics or culture, nor do they purport to be pragmatically instructive. Nowhere does the book announce itself more plainly as an enemy to actionable meaning than in the chapter "Plastic Bags"—three inert pages that recall the noisome poetics of that one scene from *American Beauty*. After rhapsodizing about a plastic bag floating on the sea near the west coast of Norway, Knausgaard concludes, "This moment was not the beginning of anything, not even of an insight, nor was it the conclusion of anything . . . I was still in the middle of something and always would be."

Despite his solemn pledge to offer his daughter a new way of apprehending the world, it is difficult to see how the book constitutes a meaningful corrective to the habits of perception encouraged by contemporary culture—particularly, those of the Internet. For me, the book called to mind nothing so much as the catwalk of Instagram, where even the most banal and comparatively trivial aspects of our lives—what we had for breakfast, say, or the creamsicle hue of a sunset—get enshrined as extraordinary simply because we experienced them. These habits of aestheticization rely upon a logic of undifferentiation. Knausgaard reveals this logic when describing a splash of petrol, with its whorl of incandescent color, as "beautiful as conches or galaxies." Because all the world has been slathered with beauty, brimming with divinity if only we look for it, as Knausgaard seems to suggest, there is no reason to believe that any single object contains more value or warrants more attention than any other—petrol, conches, or galaxies, all sublime and beauteous.

Perhaps this approach is only natural for an author whose work has come to define the genre of autofiction, an aesthetic that has bred novelists who are erroneously fascinated by the wormholes of their own consciousness and who remain fundamentally doubtful about our ability to connect with other people.* As readers we are meant to see confessions about trips to sperm banks or first experiences with masturbation as courageous and vulnerable. Candor and exhibitionism are this genre's twin virtues. But hardly does this rhetorical striptease strike me as particularly brave at a moment of peak transparency, when all of us subject ourselves to the great Sauron's eye of social media. The confessional mode in this context doesn't seem like a daring act of a literary mutineer, but the mimesis of a culture which prizes individualism and champions every passing iteration of the self. Such a vantage doesn't subvert the powers that be, but accords with a brand of capitalism where vast amounts of personal data are harvested for profit. After all, data miners, with a kind of Knausgaardian omnivorousness, make no distinction between the flotsam of our lives—everything is relevant, everything has value.

---

* One signal example is Tao Lin's *Taipei*, whose last paragraph dramatizes the extent to which other people manifest to his protagonist as nothing more than figurants or figments, marionettes without souls: "He was startled, entering his room, to see Erin already moving, *as if independent of his perception.* He briefly discerned her movements as incremental—not continuous, but in frames per second—and, like with insects or large predators, unpredictable and dangerous. He wanted to move backward and close the door and be alone again, in the bathroom" (italics mine).

Because *Autumn* fixates without discrimination on the minutiae of random objects and rarely makes a gesture of connection toward the reader, it's hard not to feel lonely within these pages. The epiphanies Knausgaard describes are so narrowly subjective, so onanistically disposed, that as I made my way through the book I couldn't help but feel the way I did when watching my friends take drugs, geeking out over the timbre of birdsong or the scrollwork of ripples on wind-blown water. Their sense of wonder—a gosh-wow appreciation for the world—was a private and inaccessible form of ecstasy, a walled garden, for them alone.

Certainly these novels are not without merit, but the extent to which they might supply an earnest reader with a tenable way of apprehending the world at a moment that has rejected grand narratives and collective meaning is grievously limited. I suspect Knausgaard's books have garnered a sizable audience in America because they celebrate a kind of perception in which we are so thoroughly well-practiced—to see the saga of the world as co-terminous with the story of ourselves. It is chilling to me that in a novel that purports to be a record of "the things that make life worth living" the author has devoted not a single chapter to a friend or a member of his family. If they enter into the novel at all, these intimates are merely supernumeraries in the far more compelling drama of dusk falling over his countryside home or the moment when a brood of porpoises surfaces near his boat in an expanse of oil-dark water. Autofiction, in the end, leaves both the writer and the reader to themselves. Or as Knausgaard admits to his daughter at the end of the first chapter, "it is primarily for my own sake that I'm doing this."

4. The Walking Dead

Despite their shortcomings, these books are nevertheless important because they underscore the idée fixe of the post-religious quest: the problem of vision. By this token, these characters are the distant offspring of Binx Bolling from Walker Percy's *The Moviegoer*, the caddish New Orleans stock broker who undertook a "search" for meaning on the occasion of his thirtieth birthday. Like the characters of Heti's, Knausgaard's, and Houellebecq's novels, Binx becomes concerned about his misanthropic view of other people, which thwarts any chance of a democratic community. "For some time now the impression has been growing upon me that everyone is dead," he says.

> It happens when I speak to people. In the middle of a sentence it will come over me: yes, beyond a doubt this is death. There is little to do but groan and make an excuse as quickly as one can. At such times it seems that the conversation is spoken by automatons who have no choice in what they say. I hear myself or someone else saying things like: "In my opinion the Russian people are a great people, but—" or "Yes, what you say about the hypocrisy of the North is questionably true. However—" and I think to myself: this is death.

Part of the reason I have chased down these post-religious quests is that I increasingly suffer from this kind of jaundiced perception. Particularly in the wake of the 2016 election, I have found myself subjecting other people to vulgar taxonomies, watching them shed any nuance of history and become corpses whenever glimpsed through the begrimed looking glass of political identity. When one of my uncles revealed a profane gratitude for Trump's xenophobic immigration policies, it was difficult to remember the afternoon when my older brother, a toddler at the time, plunged neck-deep into a sinkhole in the Mississippi River and this uncle risked his life to save him. Or when a close friend, a fervent champion of identity politics, blithely condemned the Christianity of my wife's family, it was equally hard to remember that this was a person who volunteered at a women's shelter and called her grandmother once a week. No longer manifestations of sublime mystery, gifted with the fluke of consciousness, born of a thousand minute experiences, they had become, through the defects of my perception, dead mouthpieces for dead opinions, always victims of false consciousness, already agents of bad faith. All around me were dead Republicans and dead Democrats, dead snowflakes and dead working-class voters, dead virtue signalers and dead trolls, dead boomers and dead millennials, dead beta-males and dead deplorables. Very quickly the world became a zone of corpses, feeding off the carrion of pundits and demagogues, and I began to see everyone univocally, as though they were only what they betrayed. It was in such moments that I had forgotten my obligations as a writer, which is to eschew generalization for particularity—I had forgotten that in the jurisdiction of my perceptions I always have a choice.

"The kind of vision the fiction writer needs to have, or to develop, in order to increase the meaning of his story," Flannery O'Connor writes in her essay, "The Nature and Aim of Fiction," "is called anagogical vision, and that is the kind of vision able to see different levels of reality in one image or situation." O'Connor has taken her salient term from medieval commentators of the Bible who perceived in the dense brambles of scripture three types of meaning. "Allegorical" saw one line referring to another; "tropological" dealt with prescriptions and solutions—"what should be done"; but "anagogical meaning" concerned "the Divine life and our participation in it." O'Connor puts it like this:

> Although this was a method applied to biblical exegesis, it was also an attitude toward all of creation, and a way of reading nature which included most possibilities, and I think it is this enlarged view of the human scene that the fiction writer has to cultivate if he is ever going to write stories that have any chance of becoming a permanent part of our literature. It seems to be a paradox that the larger and more complex the personal view, the easier it is to compress it into fiction.

A longtime skeptic of O'Connor, I have often wondered why her stories are reliably peopled by goons and outcasts, misfits and desperadoes, and why these contemptible figures, in one way or other, are almost always afforded some fleeting moment of redemption, an iota of grace. Though she can hardly be said to have succeeded in every effort—a few of her tales depend too heavily on the careful bonsai of themes—I suspect that, for her, writing stories was, in some sense, a religious practice, a way of training her gaze complexly on unwholesome figures and trying to see them as more than what they were, trying to see them holographically, as both depraved and divine—as, to borrow a phrase from David Foster Wallace, both flesh and not.

No other character from O'Connor's oeuvre enacts this ambition more tellingly than Hazel Motes from her novel *Wise Blood*. A twenty-two-year-old grandson of an itinerant preacher, Motes loses his faith while fighting in World War II and returns home to become an evangelist of non-faith, instituting with no apparent irony something called "the Church Without Christ." With the self-unawareness of Gertrude, he protests the dangers of believing in the world of God and sin, and spews atheistic brimstone on street corners, attracting the attention of outcasts and conmen. Eventually, Hazel realizes the sinfulness of his blasphemous campaign and buys a satchel of quicklime with which he blinds himself, a form of self-mutilation that inaugurates his new regime of penance. Soon he straps barbed wire around his torso and pours a glitter of broken glass into his shoes. Baffled by this gruesome atonement, Mrs. Flood, his landlady, ends up becoming strangely obsessed with him. "What possible reason could a person have for wanting to destroy their sight?" she wonders. "What possible reason could a sane person have for wanting to not enjoy himself anymore?"

A modern reader will, as I do, bristle at the fanatical nature of O'Connor's parable. Yet I find myself eerily moved by a character who, at the end of his rope, struggles to the point of self-blindness in order to see the world from an other-directed vantage. So backward-seeming and retrograde does this desire seem that it rarely shows up in contemporary fiction. But now and then these practitioners of anagogic vision—these heroes of perception— still return to the present realm. You can find one such character in David Foster Wallace's story "Church Not Made with Hands," in which an art therapist named Day fails to rescue his step-daughter, Esther, after their backyard pool malfunctions and its subaquatic drain pulls her under. Unable to swim, Day is forced to watch the girl wriggle helplessly beneath the Windex-blue water, a trauma from which she ultimately survives but not without significant brain injury.

Much of the story is told through Day's "dreampaintings"— impressionistic hybrids of memory and delusion, flashback and fantasy, demonstrating the extent to which guilt has marooned Day upon the island of his own subjectivity. Wallace dramatizes this isolation in one dreampainting where Day sits in a field, miming the movements of his old art history professor, who's teaching him how to swim. "The dry field is an island. The blue water all around is peppered with dry islands. Esther lies on a thin clean steel bed on the next island. Water moves in the channel between them."

In between hospital visits and these oneiric visions, Day works for the county's mental health department and helps victims of trauma process their grief. One client is a mother whose son was murdered in a gang-related dispute and who refuses to clean up the blood that remains splattered on her kitchen tile. Another client turns out to be Day's old art professor, a Jesuit who has been cited for disturbing the peace by kneeling in a public field and praying to a painting that depicts an image of himself praying. Like Day, these characters are grievously sequestered on their own islands, pre- occupied by fixations that foreclose the possibility of connecting with other people. Day's boss, Dr. Ndiawar, "likes to make a steeple with his hands and to look at it while he speaks." His coworker, Eric Yang, has a "special talent" where he can mentally rotate three-dimensional objects, assessing every an- gle of banal items, such as a phone bill, which distracts him from noticing the suffering of other people. But there's a curious moment toward the end of the story when Day remembers a moment from college, when the old art history professor gave a lecture on Vermeer's *View of Delft*. The painting, he suggests, offers a stark rebuke to the myopia of these individual subjectivities, for it has been rendered with such infallible clarity that it provides a "window onto interiors in which all conflicts have been resolved," so that "the viewer sees as God sees."

It is precisely this perception—the image of how God would see us, if God were to exist—to which the old art history professor prays in the public field and which strikes me as the artistic vantage that Wallace hoped to achieve in the story, one beyond the nearsighted imperatives of his own subjectivity. He can't have it, of course, but the story, even in its ineluctable failure, testifies to the curative powers of art, serving as a prism through which we might see ourselves and other people from a more merciful, god-like vantage, one whose perceptive aperture allows for the entrance of "the most possibilities." (It's telling that the art history professor is the one who teaches Day how to swim in the crucial dreampainting—he's teaching Day how we might swim across the water and make it to Esther's island.) The alternative, of course, is to view the world exclusively as a diary, through a self-made frame, a steeple constructed with our own two hands. But for those of us whose lives have been marred by tragedy and disaster, who find ourselves wandering and lost, it is precisely this monochromatic narrative of self that we are trying to escape. Or as Dr. Ndiawar reminds us—even our "one best church leaves no hand free to open the door." Only by relinquishing our own constructions, only by aiming our gaze toward something larger than ourselves, can we enter into a communion with other people.

5. *Ménage à God*

At the end of the summer, two of my close friends got married in the mountains of Salt Lake City, and our group traveled there for the long weekend.

While we mocked the most immediate connection—Mormonism, with its chastity belts, decaffeinated beverages, and golden spectacles in the sand—the more preoccupying thought was that traveling to a holy land with this group of friends was so metaphorically apposite that it seemed to confirm the existence of fate. In our rented sedan, we traversed through the barren landscape, snapping photos of the mountains on our smartphones and promptly updating our social media. Soon we arrived at our Airbnb, a basement apartment outfitted with the slender gadget Alexa—Amazon's talking bot—whom we gradually anthropomorphized as we asked her more and more questions. Almost uniformly existential in nature, the queries began to strike me as moving and sad. "Alexa, do you think there's an oversoul?" "Alexa, do you think this marriage will last?" "Alexa, when will I die?" I was reminded of that one scene from *2001: A Space Odyssey*, when the black obelisk appears on a craggy mountainside and a cluster of bewildered apes start screeching and thumping the ground in an attempt to decipher its meaning. I was reminded, too, of the end of Heti's novel, when her friends amuse themselves by playing a game whose rules they do not understand.

All this cynicism and doubt left me only when we were sitting on the deck of a ski lodge, waiting for the wedding to start. The deck jutted out over a splay of mountains, which were smothered verdantly with sumac and pine, their peaks dolloped with old snow, but down here, it was still sunny and warm, with everyone sipping champagne and my friends picking lint from each other's blazers or pushing behind an ear a rogue strand of hair. A concerto played over unseen speakers, lending everything a regal tinge, and soon I was swept up by a Knausgaard-type feeling, where everything from the configuration of the clouds to the ostinato of the mountain birds seemed inflected with divine meaning. But deep down I knew the goodwill brought on by aestheticism was merely an isolating sensation and, for me anyway, simply would not last.

Soon everyone took their seats. As the nervous flower girl, no older than three, tottered down the center aisle, I remembered a moment from my own wedding, when my wife's grandfather, a devout Christian, offered a tender homily, suggesting that marriage was a triangle with God at its apex, that as you drew closer to God, you drew closer to each other. After the ceremony, during the wee hours of the reception, my wife and I kicked off our shoes and wandered down to the beach with our friends, where they lampooned her grandfather's suggestion. "You guys need to have a ménage à trois with God," they said. "A ménage à God." In that moment we squealed with laughter, but I'm beginning to see now that, even though I can't sign up to his particular religion, the marrow of his advice nevertheless remains. What else is marriage, after all, but a public renunciation of self, a wholesale shift in vision? Though faith has always been a light under a door I could not open, to crib a phrase from Eudora Welty, I suppose my own spiritual quest has found its destination in marriage, in a commitment that requires a daily abandonment of the self, not a diary but a dialogue, one of several ways we might go about constructing a church not made with hands.

Night was falling. A soft wind tussled the trees in the mountains, and under a modest altar, my friends made their pledge. The two women, with hands threaded at the fingers, were vowing to see the world not through the myopia of I, but the panorama of us. Of course, the extraordinary heroism of this oath has been cheapened by the tropes of matrimony—the pictures, the cake, the Cupid Shuffle—not to mention the ozone of cynicism and the oft-repeated statistics about separation and divorce. But at this moment of history, our persistent coupling seems like an act of defiance, the only semi-divine commitment most of us will ever make. It is in the context of these thoughts that I'm watching as my two friends smile radiantly in the mountains and lean in to kiss. How easily we forget that it's only when they both close their eyes that they choose to connect.

Acknowledgments

I am truly grateful to Dan Smetanka for his dedication to this book and for his wisdom and encouragement throughout the process. And I cannot thank Samantha Shea enough for her tireless advocacy of my work and for her help in finding it a home. I am also deeply indebted to all the editors who improved, published, and anthologized these essays, including Carolyn Kuebler, Cheryl Strayed, Christopher Beha, S. P. MacIntyre, Joshua Wolf Shenk, Daniel Levin Becker, Daniel Gumbiner, Scott Gast, Nicholas Jackson, Ted Scheinman, Andrew Malan Milward, Hannah Dow, Nadja Spiegelman, Eryn Loeb, Jon Baskin, Rachel Wong, Rachel Wiseman, Robert Macfarlane, Robert Boyers, and Jason Wilson. I am particularly grateful to Seyward Darby, who helped me find my way through Summerland, and to Rachel Poser, who reached out at a crucial moment and whose guidance and friendship has made me a better writer and a more dexterous thinker.

Further thanks is owed to the University of Wisconsin–Madison MFA Program and to the Wisconsin Institute for Creative Writing. Without their generous support, this book would not exist. In particular, I want to thank Lorrie Moore, Judith Claire Mitchell, Jesse Lee Kercheval, Amaud Jamaul

Johnson, Ron Kuka, Danielle Evans, Ron Wallace, and Amy Quan Barry. David Michael Kaplan and Laura Krughoff were early champions of my writing, and I cannot thank them enough for their stewardship and advice.

I am fortunate to have friends, mentors, and fellow writers who were the first readers of these essays or who offered guidance and commiseration that have proven to be invaluable: Michael Sheehan, Krista Eastman, Lydia Conklin, Zac Fulton, Alyssa Knickerbocker, Christopher Mohar, Kerry Kretchmar, Hannah Oberman-Breindal, Marian Palaia, Yuko Sakata, Andrew Burtless, Angela Woodward, Josh Kalscheur, Katie Childs, Andrew Kay, Nicholas Gulig, Derrick Austin, Natalie Eilbert, Sarah Fuchs, Marcela Fuentes, Jamel Brinkley, Nate Brown, Thea Brown, Brandon Taylor, Ryan Walsh, Alexander Lumans, Rachel Swearingen, Kevin Gonzalez, Lauren Shapiro, Will Blythe, Amanda Rea, Jordan Cohen, Sarah Polenska, David Henzie-Skogen, Teresa Curtis, Rita Mae Reese, Adam Fell, Kerri Mack, Kate Knudson, Robert Thomas, Aaron Fai, Kristen Muir, William Parke-Sutherland, Stephanie Budge, Megan McDonald, Norbert Tavares, Sabra Katz-Wise, Robert Kehoe, Geoff Krombach, and Daniel Dineen. Special thanks to Steve Acheson, a friend and a winter soldier. And it would be difficult to overstate my gratitude to my family for their love and generosity; and especially to Mom and Dad, Taylor and Andy, for their unwavering support; and, above all, to Meghan, for sharing this life with me.

BARRETT SWANSON's essays have appeared in *Harper's Magazine, The New Yorker, The Paris Review, The Believer,* and *The New York Times Magazine,* among other publications. He is the recipient of a Pushcart Prize and has been anthologized in two editions of *The Best American Travel Writing.* He was the Halls Emerging Artist Fellow at the Wisconsin Institute for Creative Writing. He lives in Madison, Wisconsin. Find out more at barrettswanson.com.